THE BO

M E R I D I A N

Crossing Aesthetics

Werner Hamacher

Editor

Translated by
Charlotte Mandell

Stanford
University
Press

———

Stanford
California
2003

THE BOOK TO COME

Maurice Blanchot

Stanford University Press
Stanford, California

Originally published in French in 1959 under the title
Le livre à venir, © 1959, Editions Gallimard

Assistance for the translation was provided by
the French Ministry of Culture

Printed in the United States of America
on acid-free, archival-quality paper

Library of Congress Cataloging-in-Publication Data
Blanchot, Maurice.
 [Livre à venir. English]
 The book to come / Maurice Blanchot ; translated by
Charlotte Mandell.
  p. cm. — (Meridian)
 ISBN 0-8047-4223-5 (cloth : alk. paper) —
 ISBN 0-8047-4224-3 (pbk. : alk. paper)
  1. Literature, Modern—20th century—History and
criticism. 2. Literature—Philosophy. I. Mandell, Charlotte.
II. Title. III. Meridian (Stanford, Calif.)
 PN773 .B513 2002
 809'.04—dc21   2002009244

Original Printing 2003

Last figure below indicates year of this printing:
12   11   10   09   08   07   06   05   04   03

Typeset by Noyes Composition in 10.9 / 13 Adobe Garamond

Contents

IV. WHERE IS LITERATURE GOING?

Maurice Blanchot, novelist and critic, was born in 1907.
His life is wholly devoted to literature and to the silence unique to it.

Translator's Note

Through the ever-subtle (and never more so than when, as here, dealing with the subtlest verbal registers of Mallarmé, Proust, Beckett) syntactic music of Maurice Blanchot, there flourish two much-beloved groups of words, whose ambiguities in fact pervade ordinary French usage, but which are here frequently and trenchantly put into play.

First is the simple-seeming word *expérience*. A good deal of the time it serves the same purposes and covers the same terrain as the word it looks so much like in English. The word however also means, in ordinary French, "experiment" in the scientific sense—but also (and here the reader is warned to be wary) in the literary or artistic sense, as when one speaks of an experimental novel. There are more than a few sentences in this book in which the translator has candidly had to guess which hand of the word was gesturing in the text. "The Experience of Proust" is also "Proust's Experiment." And a sentence that plausibly reads "The experience of literature is a total experience" might suddenly seem far richer a statement if read as "The literary experiment is a total experience," or "The experience of literature is utterly an experiment." To rescue my author from my own opinions (which seems decent chivalry for a translator), I have usually chosen the simplest, if perhaps least imaginative, way of handling this issue, that is, construing what seems most obvious at the moment, and alerting the reader, herewith, to the problem of the word's surprising range of meaning.

The second group of words is that built around the Latin verb *errare* and its reflexes and various French descendants. *Errare* meant to wander around, as lost travelers did. When this wandering was intellectual as well as ineffectual, one was said to be in *error*, not knowing one's location, or just being wrong. So *err, error, erroneous* (in English as in French) all stem from this root, which means wandering about. Only *errant* saves this sense in English, and then mostly metaphorically. But French preserves consciously much of the radical meaning, so the words, when Blanchot uses them, work curiously to make error almost a good thing (since wandering, the nomadic, are after all forms of research, discovery, mental process, learning), while at the same time calling this very research into question at times, since it is by nature *erreur*, and getting it wrong seems inextricably interwoven with the experimental path.

The translator wants to express heartfelt thanks to a number of friends and colleagues who have helped her over some of the rockiest steeps of Blanchot's wonderful and at times bewildering style(s). As often before, Professors Odile Chilton and Marina Van Zuylen of Bard College have been immensely generous with their time, vast learning and formidable wit. My friends Lydia Davis, Pierre Joris, Nicole Peyrafitte, Dorota Czerner, and Russell Richardson have helped with idiom and scholarly reference, and my husband, Robert Kelly, who was especially helpful with the chapter on Mallarmé, has spent many midnight hours (happily, he tells me) ransacking French websites.

CHARLOTTE MANDELL
Annandale-on-Hudson
August 2001

THE BOOK TO COME

PART I

The Song of the Sirens

§ 1 Encountering the Imaginary

The Sirens: it seems they did indeed sing, but in an unfulfilling way, one that only gave a sign of where the real sources and real happiness of song opened. Still, by means of their imperfect songs that were only a song still to come, they did lead the sailor toward that space where singing might truly begin. They did not deceive him, in fact: they actually led him to his goal. But what happened once the place was reached? What was this place? One where there was nothing left but to disappear, because music, in this region of source and origin, had itself disappeared more completely than in any other place in the world: sea where, ears blocked, the living sank, and where the Sirens, as proof of their good will, had also, one day, to disappear.

What was the nature of the Sirens' song? Where did its fault lie? Why did this fault make it so powerful? Some have always answered: It was an inhuman song—a natural noise no doubt (are there any other kinds?), but on the fringes of nature, foreign in every possible way to man, very low, and awakening in him that extreme delight in falling that he cannot satisfy in the normal conditions of life. But, say others, the enchantment was stranger than that: it did nothing but reproduce the habitual song of men, and because the Sirens, who were only animals, quite beautiful because of the reflection of feminine beauty, could sing as men sing, they made the song so strange that they gave birth in anyone who heard it to a suspicion of the inhumanity of every human song. Is it through despair, then, that men passionate for their own song came to perish? Through a despair very close to rapture. There was something wonderful in this real song, this common, secret song, simple and everyday, that they had to recognize right away, sung in an unreal way by foreign, even imaginary powers, song of the abyss that, once heard, would open an abyss in each word and would beckon those who heard it to vanish into it.

This song, we must remember, was aimed at sailors, men who take risks and feel bold impulses, and it was also a means of navigation: it was a distance, and it revealed the possibility of traveling this distance, of making the song into the movement toward the song, and of making this movement the expression of the greatest desire. Strange navigation, but toward what end? It has always been possible to think that those who approached it did nothing but come near to it, and died because of impatience, because they prematurely asserted: here it is; here, here I will cast anchor. According to others, it was on the contrary too late: the goal had already been passed; the enchantment, by an enigmatic promise, exposed men to being unfaithful to themselves, to their human song and even to the essence of the song, by awakening the hope and desire for a wonderful beyond, and this beyond represented only a desert, as if the motherland of music were the only place completely deprived of music, a place of aridity and dryness where silence, like noise, burned, in one who once had the disposition for it, all passageways to song. Was there, then, an evil principle in this invitation to the depths? Were the Sirens, as tradition has sought to persuade us, only the false voices that must not be listened to, the trickery of seduction that only disloyal and deceitful beings could resist?

There has always been a rather ignoble effort among men to discredit the Sirens by flatly accusing them of lying: liars when they sang, deceivers when they sighed, fictive when they were touched; in every respect nonexistent, with a childish nonexistence that the good sense of Ulysses was enough to exterminate.

It is true, Ulysses conquered them, but in what way? Ulysses, with his stubbornness and prudence, his treachery, which led him to enjoy the entertainment of the Sirens, without risks and without accepting the consequences; his was a cowardly, moderate, and calm enjoyment, as befits a Greek of the decadent era who will never deserve to be the hero of the *Iliad*. His is a fortunate and secure cowardliness, based on privilege, which places him outside of the common condition—others having no right to the happiness of the elite, but only a right to the pleasure of watching their leader writhe ridiculously, with grimaces of ecstasy in the void, a right also to the satisfaction of mastering their master (that is no doubt the lesson they understood, the true song of the Sirens for them). Ulysses' attitude, that surprising deafness of one who is deaf because he is listening, is enough to communicate to the Sirens a despair reserved till now for humans and to turn them, through this despair, into actual beautiful girls, real this one time only and worthy of their promise, thus capable of disappearing into the truth and profundity of their song.

After the Sirens had been conquered by the power of the technique that always tries to play safely with unreal (inspired) powers, Ulysses was still not done with them. They reached him where he did not want to fall and, hidden in the heart of *The Odyssey*, which has become their tomb, they engaged him, him and many others, in this fortunate, unfortunate navigation, which is that of the tale, the song that is not immediate, but narrated, hence made apparently inoffensive: ode becomes episode.

THE SECRET LAW OF THE NARRATIVE

That is not an allegory. There is an obscure struggle underway between any narrative and the encounter with the Sirens, that enigmatic song that is powerful because of its defect. It is a struggle in which Ulysses' prudence, whatever human truth there is in him—mystification, stubborn aptitude not to play the game of the gods—was always used and perfected. What we call the novel was born from this struggle. With the novel, the preliminary voyage is foregrounded, that which carries Ulysses to the point of encounter. This voyage is an entirely human story; it concerns the time of men, it is linked to the passions of men, it actually takes place, and it is rich enough and varied enough to absorb all the strength and all the attention of the narrators. Now that the tale has become a novel, far from seeming to be impoverished, it assumes the richness and amplitude of an exploration that sometimes embraces the immensity sailed, sometimes limits itself to a small square of space on the deck, sometimes descends into the bowels of the ship where one never knew the hope of the sea. The watchword that is imposed on the sailors is this: any allusion to a goal or a destination must be excluded. With good reason, certainly. No one can begin a journey with the deliberate intention of reaching the Isle of Capraea, no one can head for this island, and whoever decided to would still go there only by chance, a chance to which he is linked by a connection that is difficult to penetrate. The watchword is thus silence, discretion, oblivion.

We must acknowledge that predestined modesty, the wish to aim at nothing and to lead to nothing, would be enough to make many novels praiseworthy books and the novelistic genre the most agreeable of genres, the one that has given itself the task of forgetting, by dint of discretion and joyous nullity, what others degrade by calling essential. Diversion is its profound song. To keep changing direction, to set off as if by chance and shun any goal, by a movement of anxiety that is transformed into pleasant distraction—that was its original and surest justification. To make a game of human time, and of the game a free occupation, stripped of any immediate interest and usefulness, essentially superficial and able, by this surface movement, nonetheless to absorb the entire being—that is not a negligible thing. But it is clear that if the novel today lacks this role, it is because technique has transformed the time of men and their ways of being diverted from it.

The narrative begins where the novel does not go but still leads us by its refusals and its rich negligence. The narrative is heroically and pretentiously the narrative of one single episode, that of Ulysses' meeting and the insufficient and magnetic song of the Sirens. Apparently, outside of this great and naïve claim, nothing has changed, and the narrative seems, by its form, to continue to answer to ordinary narrative calling. Thus, Nerval's *Aurélia* presents itself as the simple relation of an encounter, as does Rimbaud's *Une saison en enfer* [A season in hell], and Breton's *Nadja*. Something has taken place, something one has lived through and then tells about, just as Ulysses needed to live through the event and survive it to become Homer, who tells about him. It is true that the narrative, in general, is the narrative of an exceptional event that escapes the forms of daily time and the world of ordinary truth, perhaps of all truth. That is why, with so much insistence, it rejects all that could link it to the frivolity of a fiction (the novel, on the contrary, which says nothing but what is credible and familiar, wants very much to pass as fiction). In the *Gorgias*, Plato says: "Listen to a good story. You will think it's a fable, but according to me it's a story. I will tell you as a truth what I am about to tell you." What he recounts, however, is the story of the Last Judgment.

Yet the nature of narrative is in no way foretold, when one sees in it the true account of an exceptional event, which took place and which one could try to report. Narrative is not the relating of an event but this event itself, the approach of this event, the place where it is called on to unfold, an event still to come, by the magnetic power of which the narrative itself can hope to come true.

That is a very delicate relationship, no doubt a kind of extravagance, but it is the secret law of narrative. Narrative is the movement toward a point—one that is not only unknown, ignored, and foreign, but such that it seems, even before and outside of this movement, to have no kind of reality; yet one that is so imperious that it is from that point alone that the narrative draws its attraction, in such a way that it cannot even "begin" before having reached it; but it is only the narrative and the unforeseeable movement of the narrative that provide the space where the point becomes real, powerful, and alluring.

WHEN ULYSSES BECOMES HOMER

What would happen if, instead of being two distinct people conveniently sharing their roles, Ulysses and Homer were one and the same person? If Homer's narrative were nothing other than the movement completed by Ulysses in the heart of the space that the Song of the Sirens opens to him? If Homer could narrate only when, under the name of Ulysses, a Ulysses free of shackles but settled, he goes toward that place where the ability to speak and narrate seems promised to him, just as long as he disappears into it?

That is one of the strange qualities, or should we say one of the aims, of narration. It "relates" only itself, and at the same time as this relation occurs, it produces what it recounts, what is possible as an account only if it actualizes what happens in this account, for then it possesses the point or the framework where the reality that the narrative "describes" can endlessly join with its reality as narrative, can guarantee it and find in it its guarantee.

But isn't this naïve folly? In one sense. That is why there is no narrative, that is why there is no lack of narrative.

To hear the Song of the Sirens, he had to stop being Ulysses and become Homer, but it is only in Homer's narrative that the actual meeting occurs in which Ulysses becomes the one who enters into that relationship with the power of the elements and the voice of the abyss.

That seems obscure; it evokes the predicament of the primal man as if, in order to be created, he himself needed to utter, in an entirely human way, the divine *Fiat lux* [Let there be light] that can open his own eyes.

This way of presenting things, in fact, simplifies them very much: hence the kind of artificial or theoretical complication that emerges from it. It is indeed true that it is only in Melville's book that Ahab encounters

Moby Dick; but it is also true that this encounter alone allows Melville to write the book, such an overwhelming, immoderate, and unique encounter that it goes beyond all the levels in which it occurs, all the moments one wants to place it in; it seems to take place well before the book begins, but it is such that it also can take place only once, in the future of the work, in the sea that the work will have become, a limitless ocean.

Between Ahab and the whale there plays out a drama that could be called metaphysical in a vague sense of the word, the same struggle that is played out between the Sirens and Ulysses. Each of these pairs wants to be everything, wants to be the absolute world, which makes coexistence with the other absolute world impossible; and yet each one has no greater desire than this very coexistence, this encounter. To unite in the same space Ahab and the whale, the Sirens and Ulysses—that is the secret wish that makes Ulysses Homer, makes Ahab Melville, and the world that results from this union the greatest, most terrible, and most beautiful of possible worlds, alas a book, nothing but a book.

Between Ahab and Ulysses, the one who has the greatest wish for power is not the most out of control. There is, in Ulysses, that premeditated tenacity that leads to universal empire: his ruse is to seem to limit his ability, to seek coldly and with calculation what he can still do, faced with the other power. He will be everything, if he keeps a limit, a gap between the real and the imaginary, precisely the gap that the Song of the Sirens invites him to cross. The result is a sort of victory for him, somber disaster for Ahab. We cannot deny that Ulysses heard a little of what Ahab saw, but he held firm in the midst of hearing, while Ahab lost himself in the image. One denied himself the metamorphosis into which the other penetrated and disappeared. After the ordeal, Ulysses finds himself as he was, and the world is found to be perhaps poorer, but firmer and surer. Ahab does not find himself again and, for Melville himself, the world endlessly threatens to sink into this worldless space toward which the fascination of one single image draws him.

THE METAMORPHOSIS

The narrative is linked to this metamorphosis to which Ulysses and Ahab allude. The action it makes present is that of metamorphosis on all the levels it can attain. If, for the sake of convenience—for this assertion is not exact—we say that what moves the novel forward is day-to-day, collective, or personal time, or more precisely, the wish to give a voice to time, then, in order to advance, the narrative has that *other* time, that other voyage, which is the passage from the actual song to the imaginary song, the movement that causes the real song, little by little although right away (and this "little by little although right away" is the very time of metamorphosis), to become imaginary, enigmatic song, which is always far away, and which designates this distance as a space to travel, and the place to which it leads as the point where singing can stop being a lure.

The narrative can travel this space, and what moves it is transformation, which the empty fullness of this space demands, a transformation that, acting in every direction, of course powerfully transforms the one who writes, but transforms the narrative itself no less, and all that is in play in the narrative, where in one sense nothing happens except this very transition. And yet, for Melville, what is there more important than the encounter with Moby Dick, an encounter that takes place now, and is "at the same time" always yet to come, so that he never stops going toward it by a relentless and disorderly pursuit, but since it seems to have no less a relationship with the origin, it also seems to send him back to the profundity of the past: an experience under the fascination of which Proust lived and in part succeeded in writing.

Some will object: but it is to the "life" of Melville, of Nerval, of Proust that this event of which they speak first belongs. That is because they have already encountered Aurélia, because they have stumbled on the uneven pavement, seen the three steeples that first set them to write about it. They use much art to communicate their actual impressions to us, and they are artists in that they find an equivalent—of form, image, story, or words— to make us participate in a vision close to their own. Things are unfortunately not so simple. All the ambiguity stems from the ambiguity of time, which enters into play here, and which allows us to say and feel that the fascinating image of the experience is, at a certain moment, present, while this presence does not belong to any present, and even destroys the present into which it seems to introduce itself. It is true, Ulysses actually sailed and, one day, on a certain date, he encountered the enigmatic song. He can thus say: now, this is happening now. But what has happened now? The presence of a song only still to come. And what has he touched in the present? Not the event of the encounter become present, but the opening of this infinite movement that is the encounter itself, an encounter that is always apart from the place and the moment in which it is spoken, for it is this very apartness, this imaginary distance, in which absence is realized and only at the end of which the event begins to take place, a point where the real truth of the encounter occurs, from which, in any case, the language that utters it wants to take birth.

Always still to come, always already past, always present in a beginning so abrupt that it cuts off your breath, and still unfurling as the return and the eternal new beginning—"Ah," said Goethe, "in times lived before, you were my sister or my wife"—such is the event for which narrative is the approach. This event turns the concordances of time upside down, but still asserts time, a particular way for time to be accomplished, time unique to the narrative that is introduced into the lived life of the narrator in a way that transforms it, time of metamorphoses in which, in an imaginary simultaneity and under the form of the space that art seeks to realize, the different temporal ecstasies coincide.

§ 2 The Experience of Proust

1. The Secret of Writing

Can there be a pure narrative? Every narrative seeks to hide itself in novelistic density, even if only out of discretion. Proust is one of the masters of this dissimulation. While the imaginary journey of narrative leads other writers into the unreality of a scintillating space, for Marcel Proust everything happens as if it were fortunately superimposed onto the journey of his actual life, the life that has brought him, through the world's hazards and the work of destructive time, to the fabulous point where he encounters the event that makes every narrative possible. Moreover, this encounter, far from exposing him to the void of the chasm, seems to provide him with the only space where the movement of his existence can be, not only understood, but also restored, actually experienced, actually accomplished. It is only when, like Ulysses, he is within sight of the island of Sirens, where he hears their enigmatic song, that his whole long, sad wandering is fulfilled in the form of the true instants that make it, although past, present. This is a fortunate, surprising coincidence. But how, then, can he ever "get to that point," if he must be there already in order for the sterile previous migration to become the real, true movement capable of leading him there?

By a fascinating confusion, Proust draws peculiarities from the time proper to the narrative, singularities that penetrate his life, resources that allow him, too, to save actual time. There is in his work a perhaps deceptive but wonderful interweaving of all the forms of time. We never know—and very quickly he himself can no longer tell—to what time the event he recalls belongs, if it is happening only in the world of narrative or if it actually happens so that the moment of the narrative can happen, from which point forward whatever has occurred becomes reality and truth. Similarly, Proust, speaking of time and living what he speaks, and able to speak only through this other time that is his language, in a blend that is sometimes deliberate, sometimes ideal, mixes all possibilities, all contradictions, all the ways in which time becomes time. Thus he ends up living in the mode of the time of the narrative, and finds in his life the magical simultaneities that allow him to tell about his life or at least to recognize in it the movement of transformation by which it moves toward the work and toward the time of the work, in which it will be fulfilled.

THE FOUR TIMES

Time: a unique word in which are collected the most varied experiences, which Proust distinguishes, certainly, with his attentive probity, but which, overlapping, are transformed to make up a new and almost sacred reality. Let us recall only a few of its forms. First real, destructive time, the terrifying Moloch that produces death and the death of forgetfulness. (How can one trust such a time? How could it lead us to anything but a nowhere, without reality?) Time, and this is still the same, that, by this destructive action, also gives us what it takes away from us, and infinitely more, since it gives us things, events, and beings in an unreal presence that raises them to the point where they move us. But that is still nothing but the chance of spontaneous memories.

Time is capable of a stranger turn. Some insignificant incident, which took place at a certain moment, now long ago, forgotten, and not only forgotten, unperceived—the course of time brings it back, and not as a memory, but as an actual event,[1] which occurs anew, at a new moment in time. Thus the footstep that stumbles on the irregular cobblestones of the Guermantes courtyard is suddenly—nothing is more sudden—the same footstep that stumbled over the uneven flagstones of the Baptistery of San Marco: the same footstep, not "a double, an echo of a past sensation . . . but this very sensation itself," a minute incident, but deeply moving, one that tears apart the fabric of time and by this rending introduces us to another world: outside of time, says Proust hurriedly. Yes, he asserts, time is abolished, since, at once, in a real act of capturing—fugitive but irrefutable—I hold the Venice instant and the Guermantes instant, not a past and a present, but one single presence that causes incompatible moments, separated by the entire course of lived life, to coincide in a palpable simultaneity. Here, then, time is erased by time itself; here death, the death that is the work of time, is suspended, neutralized, made vain and inoffensive. What an instant! A moment that is "freed from the order of time" and that recreates in me "a man freed from the order of time."

But right away, by a contradiction he scarcely notices, so necessary and fertile is it, Proust, as if inadvertently, says of this minute outside of time that it allowed him "to obtain, to isolate, to immobilize—for the length of time of a flash of lightning—what he never apprehends: a little time in its pure state." Why this reversal? Why does what is outside of time manage to contain pure time? It is because, by this simultaneity that made the Venice footstep and the Guermantes footstep actually coincide, the then of the past and the here of the present, like two "nows" summoned to superimpose themselves, by this conjunction of these two presents that abolish time, Proust also experienced the incomparable, unique ecstasy of time. To live the abolition of time, to live this movement, rapid as "lightning," by which two instants, infinitely separated, come (*little by little although immediately*) to encounter each other, joining together like two presences that, through the metamorphosis of desire, could identify each other, is to travel the entire extent of the reality of time, and by traveling it, to experience time as space and empty place, that is to say, free of the events that always ordinarily fill it. Pure time, without events, moving vacancy, agitated distance, interior space in the process of becoming, where the ecstasies of time spread out in fascinating simultaneity—what is all that, then? It is the very time of narrative, the time that is not *outside* [*hors*] time, but that is experienced as actually *outside* [*dehors*], in space, that imaginary space where art finds and arranges its resources.

THE TIME OF WRITING

The experience of Proust has always seemed mysterious because of the importance he assigns to it, based on phenomena to which psychologists do not lend any exceptional value, although these phenomena may perhaps already have dangerously transported Nietzsche. But whatever the "sensations" are, they serve as a code for the experience he describes. What makes this experience essential is that it is, for him, the experience of an original structure of time, which (at a certain point, he is strongly aware of this) is related to the possibility of writing, as if this opening had suddenly introduced him to that time unique to narrative without which he can indeed write—he doesn't fail to do that—but he has still not yet begun to

write. It is a decisive experience, the great discovery of *Le temps retrouvé*
[Time regained], his encounter with the song of the Sirens, from which
he draws, in a seemingly absurd way, the certainty that now he is a writer,
for why should these phenomena of reminiscence, even extremely happy
or troubling ones, why should this taste of past and present that he suddenly has in his mouth, as he asserts, take away from him the doubts
about his literary gifts that until now had tormented him? Isn't it absurd,
as absurd as the feeling might seem that one day, in the street, transports
the unknown Roussel and suddenly gives him fame and the certainty of
fame? "Just like the time I tasted the madeleine, all anxiety about the future, all intellectual doubt, were cleared away. Those doubts that had as-
sailed me earlier about the reality of my literary gifts, and even the reality
of literature, were miraculously dispelled."

   We see that what is given to him at that instant is not only the assurance of his calling, the affirmation of his gifts, but also the very essence of
literature—he has touched it, experienced it in its pure state, by experiencing the transformation of time into an imaginary space (the space
unique to images), in that moving absence, without events to hide it,
without presence to obstruct it, in this emptiness always in the process of
becoming: that remoteness and distance that make up the milieu and the
principle of metamorphoses and of what Proust calls metaphors. But it is
no longer a matter of applying psychology; on the contrary, there is no
more interiority, for everything that is interior is deployed outwardly,
takes the form of an image. Yes, at this time, everything becomes image,
and the essence of the image is to be entirely outside, without intimacy,
and yet more inaccessible and more mysterious than the innermost
thought; without signification, but summoning the profundity of every
possible meaning; unrevealed and yet manifest, having that presence-
absence that constitutes the attraction and the fascination of the Sirens.

   That Proust is aware of having discovered—and, he says, before writing—the secret of writing; that he thinks, by a movement of distraction
that turned him away from the course of things, that he has been placed
in that time of writing when it seems that it is time itself that, instead of
being lost in events, will take up writing—all this Proust shows again by
trying to rediscover in other writers that he admires (Chateaubriand,
Nerval, Baudelaire) similar experiences. But a doubt comes to him when,
during the Guermantes reception, he thinks he is having a sort of reverse
experience (since he will see time "exteriorized" in faces on which aging

has placed the disguise of a comedy mask). The painful thought comes to him that if he owes his ability to enter into a decisive contact with the essence of literature to a transformed inwardness of time, then he owes to destructive time, whose formidable power of mutability he contemplates, the much more constant threat of seeing himself, moment by moment, losing the "time" to write.

This is a pathetic doubt, a doubt that he does not go into, for he avoids asking himself if this death—in which he suddenly perceives the main obstacle to the completion of his book, and about which he knows that it is not only the end of his life, but is also at work in all the intermittencies of his being—is not perhaps also the center of this imagination that he calls divine. And we ourselves arrive at another doubt, at another questioning, which touches on the conditions in which such an important experience, to which his entire oeuvre is linked, has just occurred. Where is this experience produced? In what "time"? In what world? And who is the person who has experienced it? Is it Proust, the actual Proust, the son of Adrien Proust? Is it Proust already become a writer and telling in the fifteen volumes of his grandiose work about how his calling was formed, progressively, thanks to that maturation that made the anguished child, will-less and over-sensitive, into the strange, energetically concentrated man, gathered into that pen to which all the life that still remains to him, and all the preserved childhood, is communicated? Not at all, as we know. None of these Prousts is at issue. The dates, if they were necessary, would prove it, since this revelation to which *Le temps retrouvé* alludes as to the decisive event that will set in motion the work that is not yet written, takes place—in the book—during the war, at a time when *Swann* is already published and when a large part of the work is composed. Is Proust not telling the truth, then? But he does not owe us this truth, and he would certainly be unable to tell it to us. He could only express it, make it real, concrete, and true, by projecting it into the very time of which it is the implementation, whence the work draws its necessity: the time of the narrative, when, although he says "I," it is no longer the real Proust or the writer Proust who has the ability to speak, but their metamorphosis into that shadow that is the narrator turned into a "character" of the book, the one who in the story writes a story that is the work itself, and produces in his turn other metamorphoses of himself that are the different "I's" whose experiences he recounts. Proust has become elusive, because he has become inseparable from the quadruple metamorphosis that is only the movement of the book toward the work. Similarly, the event he describes is not only an event that occurs in the world of the story, this Guermantes society whose truth lies only in fiction, but is also event and advent of the story itself and the realization, in the story, of that original time of the narrative whose fascinating structure he only crystallizes, the ability that makes coincide, in one single fantastic point, the present, the past, and even the future, although Proust seems to neglect it (since at this point the entire future of the work is present, given as the completed text).

IMMEDIATELY, ALTHOUGH LITTLE BY LITTLE

We must add that Proust's work is quite different from the *Bildungsroman* with which it is tempting to confuse it. No doubt the fifteen volumes of *Le temps retrouvé* do nothing but retrace how the one who is writing these fifteen volumes was formed, and they describe the eventful moments of this calling. "Thus my whole life up to that day could have, and could not have, been summed up under this title: A calling. It could not have been in the sense that literature had not played any role in my life. It could have been in that this life, the memories of its sorrows and its joys, formed a reserve like the albumen found in the ovule of plants and in which it draws its nourishment to transform itself into a seed . . . " But if one holds strictly to this interpretation, one neglects what is for Proust the essential point: this revelation by which, just like that, immediately although little by little, in this seizure of another time, he is introduced into the transformed intimacy of time, where he arranges pure time as the principle of metamorphosis, and where he can arrange the imaginary as a space already made synonymous with the ability to write.

All the time of Proust's life must indeed be necessary, all the time of the actual voyage, for him to arrive at this single moment with which the imaginary journey of the work begins and which, in the work, marking the summit where it culminates and comes to an end, also marks the very low point where the one who is supposed to write it must now undertake it, faced with the nothingness that calls him and with the death that is already ravaging his mind and his memory. All the real time is necessary to arrive at this unreal movement, but, although there may be a perhaps ungraspable relationship—which in any case Proust refuses to grasp—between the two forms of becoming, what he also affirms is that this revelation is in no way the necessary effect of a progressive development: it has the irregularity of chance, the gracious strength of an unmerited gift, which does not in the least recompense a long and skilful labor of development. *Le temps retrouvé* is the story of a calling that owes every-thing to time experienced [*la durée*], but owes it everything only so that it could escape it suddenly, by an unforeseeable leap, and find the point where the pure inwardness of time, having become imaginary space, of-fers all things that "transparent unity" in which, "losing their first aspect of things," they can come "to line up next to each other in a kind of order, penetrated by the same light, . . . converted into one single substance, with the vast surfaces of a monotone shimmering. No impurity has re-mained. The surfaces have become reflective. All things are portrayed there, but by reflection, without altering their homogeneous substance. All that was different has been converted and absorbed."[2]

The experience of imaginary time that Proust had can take place only in an imaginary time, and only by making the one exposed to it an imag-inary being, a wandering image, always there, always absent, fixed and convulsive, like the beauty of which André Breton has spoken. Metamor-phosis of time, it first transforms the present in which it seems to be pro-duced, drawing it into the undefined profundity where the "present" starts the "past" anew, but where the past opens up onto the future that it re-peats, so that what comes always comes again, and again, and again. In-deed, the revelation takes place now, here, for the first time, but the im-age that is present to us here and for the first time is the presence of an "already other time," and what it reveals to us is that "now" is "before," and "here" is somewhere else, a place always other, where he who believes that he can calmly witness this transformation from outside can only transform it into potency if he lets himself be drawn out of himself by it, and compelled into that movement where a part of himself, beginning with the hand that is writing, becomes imaginary.

This is a shift that Proust, through his energetic decision, tried to make into a movement of resurrection of the past. But what did he reconstitute? What did he save? The imaginary past of an already entirely imaginary be-ing, separated from himself by a whole vacillating and fugitive series of "I's," who little by little stripped him of a self, freed him from the past, and by this heroic sacrifice, placed him at the service of the imagination, which he could then make serve him.

THE CALL OF THE UNKNOWN

Proust, however, did not seem to realize that he permitted neither pause nor rest in this vertiginous movement, and that when he seems to fix on some instant of the actual past by uniting it, through a relationship of

sparkling identity, with some present instant, it is just as much to draw
the present outside of the present, and the past outside of its determined
reality—leading us, by this open relationship, always farther, in every direction, handing us over to the distant and giving us this distance where
everything is always given, everything is taken away, incessantly. However,
once at least, Proust found himself before this call of the unknown, when
in front of the three trees that he observes and does not manage to connect with the impression or the memory he feels is ready to be awakened,
he accedes to the strangeness of what he will never be able to grasp again,
which is nonetheless there, in him, around him, but which he can welcome only by an infinite movement of ignorance. Here, communication
remains unfinished, it is still open, disappointing and agonizing for him,
but perhaps it is then less deceptive than any other and closer to the demand of all communication.

2. Surprising Patience

We have noted that the appearance of the book published under the
title *Jean Santeuil* contained a narrative comparable to the narrative of the
final experience of *Le temps retrouvé*. We even came to the conclusion that
in it we had the prototype of the event as it was actually lived by Proust,
son of Adrien Proust: so great is the need to locate that which cannot be
located. Thus it was not far from the Geneva lake that, in the course of a
boring walk, Jean Santeuil has a sudden glimpse at the end of some fields,
and where he recognizes, with a thrill of happiness, the sea at Bergmeil,
near which he used to vacation and which for him was then nothing but
an ordinary spectacle. Jean Santeuil wonders at this new happiness. He
does not see in it the simple pleasure of a spontaneous memory, since it is
not a question of a memory, but of "the transmutation of the memory
into a directly felt reality." He concludes that he is faced with something
very important, a communication that is not of the present, or of the past,
but the outpouring of the imagination in which a field is established between the two, and he resolves henceforth to write only in order to make
such moments come to life again, or to respond to the inspiration that
this transport of joy gives him.

This is, in fact, impressive. Almost all the experience of *Le temps perdu*
[Lost time] can be found here: the phenomenon of reminiscence, the
metamorphosis it presages (transmutation of the past into the present),

the feeling that there is here a door open onto the domain unique to the imagination, and finally the resolution to write in light of such moments and to bring them back to light.

One could naïvely wonder, then: how is it that Proust, who from that moment on holds the key to his art, writes only *Jean Santeuil* and not his actual work—and, in this sense, continues not to write? The answer can only be naïve. It lies in this draft of a work that Proust, so desirous of making books and of being thought of as a writer, does not hesitate to reject, even to forget, as if it had never existed, just as he has the feeling that the experience of which he speaks has not yet taken place so long as it has not drawn him into the infinity of movement that is this experience. *Jean Santeuil* is perhaps closer to the actual Proust, when he writes it, than the narrator of *Le temps perdu* is, but this proximity is only the sign that he remains on the surface of the sphere and that he has not truly engaged himself in the new time, which causes him to glimpse the shimmering of a changing sensation. That is why he writes, yet it is really Saint-Simon, La Bruyère, Flaubert who write in his place, or at least Proust the man of culture, the one who relies, as is necessary, on the art of previous writers, instead of entrusting himself, with all its risks and dangers, to that transformation that the imagination demands and that must first reach his language.

THE FAILURE OF PURE NARRATIVE

Still, this page of *Jean Santeuil*, and this book, teach us something else. It seems that Proust has conceived of a purer art, concentrated on moments alone, without padding, without summoning voluntary memories or general truths formed or grasped again by intelligence, to which later on he will think he has accorded a large place in his work: in sum, a "pure" narrative made only of those points from which it is formed, like the sky, where apart from the stars there is only emptiness. The page of *Jean Santeuil* that we have analyzed asserts this, more or less: "For the pleasure that it [the imagination] gives us is a sign of the superiority, which I trust enough to write nothing of what I saw, of what I thought, of what I reasoned, of what I remembered, to write only when a past instant was suddenly brought to life again in a smell, in a sight that it caused to burst forth and above which palpitated the imagination, and only when this joy gave me inspiration." Proust wants to write only to respond to inspiration. This inspiration is given to him by the joy that the phenomena of reminiscence cause in him. This joy that inspires him is, according to him, a sign as well of the importance of these phenomena, of their essential value, a sign that in them the imagination makes itself known and grasps the essence of our life. The joy that gives him the power to write thus does not authorize him to write anything at all, but only to communicate these instants of joy and truth that "palpitate" behind these instants.

The art he is aiming for here can only be made of brief moments: joy is instantaneous, and the instants it highlights are only instants. Faithfulness to pure impressions—that is what Proust demands of the novel; not that he keep to the certainties of habitual impressions, since he wants to give himself over only to certain privileged impressions, the ones in which, by the return of past sensation, the imagination is set in motion. But it is still the case that impressionism, which he admires in the other arts, offered him a model. Above all, the fact remains that he wants to write a book from which all nonessential moments would be excluded (which confirms, in part, Feuillerat's thesis, for whom the initial version of the work included fewer developments and "psychological dissertations" and was the expression of an art that sought its resources only in the momentary enchantment of involuntary memories). Proust certainly had the hope of writing such a book in *Jean Santeuil*. That is, at least, what a sentence drawn from the manuscript reminds us, one that was used as an epigraph: "Can I call this book a novel? It is less, perhaps, and much more, the unadulterated essence of my gathered life, pouring out of those wrenching hours. The book was never made, it was harvested." Each of these expressions fits the concept offered us by the page from *Jean Santeuil*. Pure narrative, since it is "without mixture," without any other matter than the essential, the essence that is communicated to writing in those privileged instants in which the conventional surface of being is ruptured, and Proust, by a taste for spontaneity that recalls automatic writing, claims to exclude all that would make his book the result of labor: the book will not be a cunningly fabricated work, but a work received by gift, come from him, not produced by him.

But does *Jean Santeuil* live up to this ideal? Not at all, and perhaps all the less so since it strives to do so. On the one hand, he continues to allow the largest space for ordinary novelistic material, for the scenes, figures, and general observations that the art of the memorialist (Saint-Simon) and the art of the moralist (La Bruyère) invite him to draw from his existence, the things that led him to school, into the *salons*, and made him a witness in the Dreyfus affair, etc. On the other hand, though, he consciously seeks to avoid the exterior and "ready-made" unity of a story; in that respect, he thinks he is faithful to his concept. The disjointed nature of the book stems not just from our having to deal with a book in rags: these fragments in which characters appear and disappear, in which scenes do not try to connect with other scenes, all this aims at avoiding impure novelistic discourse. Here and there, too, are a few "poetic" pages, reflections of those enchanted instants to which he wants at least fleetingly to bring us closer.

What is striking in the failure of this book is that, having sought to make us sensitive to "instants," he has portrayed them as scenes and, instead of surprising beings as they appear, he made something quite the opposite, formal portraits. But this stands out above all: if one wished to characterize this preliminary sketch in a few words from the work that followed it, one might say that while *Jean Santeuil*, to give us the feeling that life is made of separate hours, kept to a piecemeal concept, in which the void is not represented but remains void, *La recherche du temps perdu*, on the contrary, a massive, uninterrupted work, succeeded in adding the void as a fullness to the starry points and, this time, made the stars sparkle wonderfully, because they no longer lacked the immensity of the emptiness of space. This occurs in such a way that it is by the densest and most substantial continuity that the work succeeds in representing the most discontinuous things, the intermittence of those instants of light from which the possibility of writing comes to him.

THE SPACE OF THE WORK, THE SPHERE

Why does that occur? To what is this success due? This too can be said in a few words: it is because Proust—and this was, it seems, his progressive penetration of experience—felt that these instants in which, for him, the timeless shines, nonetheless expressed, by the assertion of a return, the movements closest to the metamorphosis of time, and these instants were "pure time." He discovered something about the space of the work that had to carry all the powers of duration at once, that had also to be nothing but the movement of the work toward itself and the authentic search for its origin, that had, finally, to be the place of the imagination; Proust felt little by little that the space of such a work had to come close, if one can settle here for a symbol, to the essence of the *sphere*; and in fact his entire book, his language, this style of slow curves, of fluid heaviness, of transparent density, always in movement, wonderfully made to express the infinitely varied rhythm of voluminous gyration, symbolizes the mystery and thickness of the sphere, its movement of rotation, with the high and the low, its celestial hemisphere (paradise of childhood, paradise of essential instants) and its infernal hemisphere (Sodom and Gomorrah, the destructive time, the laying bare of all illusions and all false human consolations), but a double hemisphere that, at a certain time, reverses itself, so that what was high becomes low and so that hell, and even the nihilism of time, can in turn become beneficial and exalt in pure, joyful flashes of lightning.

Proust discovers, then, that these privileged instants are not immobile points, real only once and to be represented as one unique and fleeting evanescence; rather, from the surface of the sphere to its center, they pass and pass again, going, incessantly although intermittently, toward the intimacy of their actual realization, going from their unreality to their hidden depth, which they reach when the imaginary and secret center of the sphere is attained, starting from which the sphere seems to be born again when it has been perfected. Proust has discovered his work's law of growth, that demand for deepening, for spherical enlarging, that overabundance and, as he says, overnourishment that it requires and that allows him to introduce the most "impure" materials, those "truths relative to passions, to characters, to customs," but which in reality he does not introduce as "truths," stable and immobile assertions, but as that which never stops developing, progressing by a slow movement of envelopment. It is a song of possibilities turning untiringly in ever tighter circles around the central point, which must surpass all possibility, since it is the one and only, the supremely real, the instant (but the instant that is in turn the condensation of every sphere).

In this sense, Feuillerat, who thinks that the progressive additions ("psychological dissertations," intellectual commentaries) have seriously altered the original aim, which was to write a novel of poetic instants, thinks just what Jean Santeuil naïvely thought, and thus does not recognize the secret of Proust's maturity, the maturity of that experience for which the space of novelistic imagination is a sphere, engendered, thanks to an infinitely slowed movement, by essential instants, themselves always in the process of becoming, and whose essence is not to be points of time but that imaginary duration that Proust, at the end of his work, discovers to be the very substance of those mysterious phenomena of scintillation.

Time in *Jean Santeuil* is almost absence (even if the book ends with an evocation of the aging that the young man observes in the face of his father; at the very most, as in Flaubert's *L'éducation sentimentale* [Sentimental education], the white spaces left between the chapters could remind us that behind what is happening, something else is happening), but it is above all absent from those shining instants that the narrative represents in a static way, without making us feel that the narrative itself can only be realized by going toward such instants as toward its origin and by drawing from them the movement that alone causes the narration to advance. Undoubtedly Proust never renounced interpreting those instants as signs of the timeless too; he always saw in them a presence freed from the order of time. The wonderful shock he experiences when he feels them, the certainty of finding himself after having been lost, this recognition is his mystical truth, which he does not want to call into question. It is his faith and his religion, just as he tends to believe that there is a world of timeless essences that art can help to represent.

From these ideas there could have resulted a novelistic conception quite different from his own, in which preoccupation with the eternal could (as sometimes with Joyce) have given place to a conflict between an order of hierarchical concepts and the disintegration of perceptible realities. None of this occurred, because Proust, even against himself, remained obedient to the truth of his experience, which not only disengages him from ordinary time but also engages him in an *other* time, that "pure" time in which duration can never be linear and cannot be reduced to events. That is why the narrative excludes the simple unfolding of a story, just as it has trouble contenting itself with "scenes" too clearly delimited and represented. Proust has a certain taste for classical scenes that he does not always abandon. Even the grandiose final scene has an exaggerated emphasis that seems scarcely appropriate to the dissolution of time of which it is trying to persuade us. But precisely what *Jean Santeuil*, as well as the different versions preserved for us in the *Carnets* [Notebooks], teaches us is the extraordinary labor of transformation that Proust kept pursuing in order to temper the overly sharp features of his portrayals and to bring to life those scenes that little by little, instead of remaining fixed and static views, stretch out into time, embed themselves, and sink into the whole, compelled by a slow, tireless movement—not a surface movement, but rather a deep, dense, voluminous one, in which the most diverse times are superimposed, as the contradictory powers and forms of time are inscribed in it. Thus, certain episodes—the games on the Champs-Elysées—seem lived, at once, at very different ages, lived and relived in the intermittent simultaneity of an entire life, not as pure moments, but in the moving density of spherical time.

POSTPONEMENT

Proust's work is a complete-incomplete work. When one reads *Jean Santeuil* and the innumerable intermediate versions in which he tried out the themes to which he wanted to give form, one is amazed by the help he received from destructive time, which, in him and against him, was the accomplice of his work. This work was above all threatened by an over-hasty completion. The longer it takes, the closer it gets to itself. In the movement of the book, we discern this postponement that withholds it, as if, foretelling the death that is at its end, it were trying, in order to avoid death, to run back on its own course. First laziness fights all the facile ambitions in Proust; then laziness turns into patience, and patience becomes tireless labor, feverish impatience that struggles with time, when time is measured. In 1914, the work is very close to its completion. But 1914 is war, it is the beginning of a strange time that, delivering Proust from the complacent author he carries in himself, gives him the chance to write without end and to make of his book, by a labor endlessly undertaken, that place of return that it must represent (so that whatever is most destructive in time—war—collaborates in the most intimate way with his work by lending him, as an aid, the universal death against which it wants to be constructed).

Jean Santeuil is the first result of this surprising patience. How does Proust, who hastens to publish *Les plaisirs et les jours* [Pleasures and days], a much less important book, manage to break off this preliminary sketch (which already includes three volumes), forgetting and burying it? Here the profundity of his inspiration, and his decision to follow it by supporting it in its infinite movement, are revealed. If *Jean Santeuil* had been completed and published, Proust would have been lost, his work made impossible, and Time itself definitively wasted. There is, then, something indescribably wonderful in this piece of writing, which has been brought back to daylight and which shows us how the greatest writers are threatened and how much energy, inertia, inactivity, attention, and distraction are needed to go to the end of what proposes itself to them. That is how *Jean Santeuil* truly speaks to us of Proust, of the experience of Proust, of that intimate, secret patience by which he gave himself time.

PART 11

The Literary Question

§ 3 "There could be no question of ending well"

"For me," thought the young Goethe, "there could be no question of ending well." But, after *Werther*, the opposite certainty came to him: he was not destined go under; either because he came to an agreement with what he called the demoniacal powers, or for more secret reasons, he stopped having faith in his ruin. That is singular enough, but here is something stranger: as soon as he had the certainty of escaping ruin, he changed his attitude about his poetic and intellectual forces; until then unreservedly extravagant, he became economical, prudent, careful not to waste any of his genius, and determined to stop risking this fortunate existence that the intimacy of fate still guaranteed him.

We can surely find explanations for this anomaly. We might say that the feeling of being saved was linked to the memory of the ruin that had threatened him at the time of *Werther*. We might say that before *Werther* he did not have to report to his own inner law, given an impetuosity that asks for no justification. Everything was given to him at once: the collapse where he met with utter ruin; in this ordeal the certainty of his blessed genius, incapable of failing; and the respect for this incapacity, for which he felt responsible ever after. This was the pact. The demon for Goethe was this limit: the inability to perish, and this negation: refusal to let him fail. From these came the certainty of a success he had to pay for with another failure.

THE OBSCURE DEMAND

The essential, however, remains obscure. Obscurity here engages us in a region where rules abandon us, where morality is silent, where there is no longer law or duty, where a good or bad conscience brings neither consolation nor remorse. In every age there has been implicitly recognized by those who have something to do with the strangeness of literary language an ambiguous status, a certain playfulness with regard to common laws, as if to leave space, by this game, for other, more difficult and more uncertain laws. That does not mean that those who write have the right to escape the consequences. Whoever has killed out of passion cannot alter the passion by invoking it as an excuse. Whoever comes up against, when writing, a truth that writing could not address is perhaps irresponsible, but must answer all the more for this irresponsibility; he must answer for it without calling it into question, without betraying it—that is the very secret about himself: the innocence that saves him is not his own; it is that of the place that he occupies, and occupies by mistake, and with which he does not coincide.

It is not enough to reduce the artist's life to many irreducible parts. And it is not his conduct that matters, his way of protecting himself by his problems or, on the contrary, of covering them up by his existence. Each person answers as he can and as he wishes. One person's answer will not suit anyone else; it is unsuitable; it answers to what we necessarily do not know, in this indecipherable, never exemplary sense: art offers us enigmas, but fortunately no hero.

What does it matter, then? What can the work of art that enlightens us on human relationships in general teach us? What kind of demand is asserted, which cannot be captured by any of the current moral forms, does not render guilty the one who fails it or innocent the one who thinks he accomplishes it, delivers us from all the injunctions of "I must," from all the claims of "I want," and from all the resources of "I can": to leave us free? But not free, or deprived of freedom, as if it drew us into one point where, the air of the possible having been exhausted, the bare relationship offers itself, which is not an ability, which even precedes all possibility of relationship.

How can this demand—a word introduced here because it is uncertain and because "demand" is here without demand—be taken hold of? It is certainly easier to demonstrate that the poetic work cannot accept law under any form, whether it be political, moral, human or not, temporal or eternal, a decision that limits it or places restrictions on its time or place. The work of art fears nothing from the law. What the law attains or proscribes or perverts is culture; it is what we think of art, historical customs, the course of the world, books and museums, sometimes artists, but why should they escape violence? Whatever difficulty a regime has with art can make us fear for this regime, but not for art. Art is also the hardest thing there is—indifference and neglect—because of its own historical vicissitudes.

When André Breton reminds us of the manifesto that he drafted with Trotsky, which gives expression to the "deliberate wish to keep to the slogan 'In art, everything is permitted,'" that is naturally essential, and the meeting of these two men, their writing joined on the same page on which this slogan is asserted, remains an exalting sign after so many years.[1] But "in art, everything is permitted" is still just the first necessity. That means that all language [*toutes les paroles*]—whether of a human order to be realized, of a truth to be maintained, or of a transcendence to preserve—can do nothing for the always more original language of art, can do nothing but let it be, simply because words never meet it, defining as they do, at least in present history, an order of relationships that enters into play only when the more primal relationship, manifest in art, has already been erased or covered over. The word *freedom* is not yet free enough to make us feel this relationship. Freedom is linked to the possible, it bears the extreme of human ability. But it is a question here of a relationship that is not an ability, of communication or language that is not accomplished as ability.

Rilke wanted the young poet to be able to ask himself: "Am I really forced to write?" in order to hear the answer: "Yes, I must." "So," he concluded, "build your life according to necessity." That is a detour to elevate the impulse to write even more, to the point of morality. Unfortunately, if writing is an enigma, this enigma gives no oracle, and no one is in the position to ask it questions. "Am I really forced to write?" How could he ask himself such a thing, he who lacks any initial language to give form to this question, and who can meet it only by an infinite movement that tests him, transforms him, dislodges him from his confident "I," his starting point, from which he thinks he can question sincerely? "Go into yourself, look for the need that makes you write." But the question can only make him come out of himself, leading him to where the need would be rather to escape that which is without law, without justice, and without measure. The answer "I must" can indeed, in fact, be heard; it is even constantly heard, but what "I must" does not include is the answer to a question that is not discovered, the approach to which suspends the answer and removes its necessity.

"It is a summons. I can do nothing, according to my nature, but assume a summons that no one has given to me. It is within this contradiction, always only within a contradiction, that I can live."[2] The contradiction that awaits the writer is even stronger. It is not a summons, he cannot assume it, no one has given it to him: he must become no one in order to welcome it. It is a contradiction in which he cannot live. That is why no writer, not even Goethe, could claim to save the freedom of his life for a work foretold; no one, without ridicule, can decide to devote himself to his work, even less to safeguard himself for it. The work demands much more: that one not worry about it, that one not seek it out as a goal, that one have with it the most profound relationship of carelessness and neglect. Whoever flees Friederike does not flee her in order to remain free; he is never less free than at that instant, for what frees him from bonds hands him over to flight, an impulse more dangerous than suicide pacts.[3] It's too simple to attribute creative fidelity to infidelity to one's vows. And, similarly when, seeing a little girl playing in front of the cathedral, Lawrence wonders whom he would like to save in the event of some catastrophe and is surprised at having chosen the child, this surprise reveals all the confusion that recourse to values introduces into art. As if it were not in the nature of the reality of the monument—and of all monuments and all books joined together—always to weigh less, in the scales, than the little girl playing; as if, in this lightness, in this absence of value, the infinite weight of the work were not concentrated.

RATHER THAN TO HIMSELF

From the Renaissance to Romanticism, there has been an impressive and often sublime effort to reduce art to genius, poetry to the subjective, and to have us think that what the poet expresses is himself, his most singular inwardness, the hidden profundity of his being, his distant "I," unexpressed, unable to be formulated. The painter realizes himself by painting, as the novelist embodies in his characters a vision in which he is revealed. The demand of the work is then the demand of this inwardness to be expressed: the poet has his song to make heard, the writer his message to deliver. "I have something to say"—that finally is the lowest level of the relationship the artist has with the demand of the work, of which the highest seems to be the torment of creative impetuosity in which the rational cannot be found.

This idea that in the poem it is Mallarmé who is expressing himself, that in "The Sunflowers" Van Gogh is revealing himself (though not the Van Gogh of biography) seems to explain to us the absolute quality the demand of the work has and yet the private character, irreducible to any general obligation, of such a demand. It occurs between the artist and himself; no one from outside can intervene; it is secret, like a passion that no outer authority can judge or understand.

But is it that way? Can we content ourselves with thinking that the taciturn, obstinate and repetitive passion that commands Cézanne to die with the brush in his hand and not to waste a single day, even to bury his mother, has no other source than the need to express himself? Rather than to himself, it is to the painting that the secret he seeks is linked, and this painting, from all obvious appearances, would have no interest for Cézanne if it spoke to him only of Cézanne, and not of painting, of the essence of painting, the approach to which is inaccessible to him. Let us call this demand painting, then, let us call it the work, or art, but calling it thus does not reveal to us whence it draws its authority, nor why this "authority" asks nothing of the one who bears it, draws him wholly to it and abandons him wholly, demands of him more than can be demanded, by any morality, of any man, and at the same time does not force him in the least, holds nothing either for or against him, maintains no relation with him, while at the same time summoning him to support this relation—and thus torments him and agitates him with a boundless joy.

It is one of the duties of our time to expose the writer to a sort of preliminary shame. He has to have a bad conscience, he has to feel at fault before he does anything. As soon as he starts to write, he hears himself joyfully exclaim: "Well, now you are lost. Should I stop, then? No, if you stop, you are lost." Thus speaks the devil, who also spoke to Goethe and made him that impersonal being, as soon as his life beyond himself began, powerless to fail because this supreme power had been taken from him. The force of the devil is that very different instances speak in his voice, so that one never knows what "You are lost" means. Sometimes it is the world, the world of daily life, the necessity of action, the law of work, the anxiety of people, the search for necessities. To speak when the world is perishing can awaken in the speaker only the suspicion of his own frivolity, the desire, at least, to bring himself closer, by his words, to the gravity of the moment by uttering useless, true, and simple words. "You are lost" means: "You speak without necessity, to distract you from necessity; vain speech, fatuous and guilty; speech of luxury and indigence." "So I should stop!" "No, if you stop, you are lost."

That is another demon, then, a more hidden one: never familiar, but never absent, close, so close it seems like a mistake; one that nonetheless does not impose itself, lets itself be easily forgotten (but this forgetting is the most serious of all); without authority, it does not order, does not condemn, does not absolve. In appearance, in relation to the voice of the law of the world, it is a quiet voice, of a gentle intimacy, and the "You are lost" itself has its gentleness: it is a promise as much as anything else, an invitation to glide on an imperceptible slope—to climb? to descend?— we do not know. "You are lost" is light, gay language addressed to no one, beside which the one addressed, escaping the solitude of what one calls oneself, enters into the other solitude, where all personal solitude is lacking, every place of one's own and every goal. There, indeed, there is no more fault, but also no innocence, nothing that can tie me or untie me, nothing to which "I" must answer, for what can be asked of one who has cast aside the possible? Nothing—except this, which is the strangest demand: that through it speak that which is without power, that starting from that point speech show itself as the absence of power, this naked-ness, powerlessness, but also impossibility, which is the first impulse of communication.

SPEECH OF THE POET AND NOT THE MASTER

What can a man do? asked Monsieur Teste.[4] That is a question about modern man. Language, in the world, above all is power. Whoever speaks is powerful and violent. To name is that violence that distances what is named in order to possess it in the useful form of a name. To name is enough to make man into this troublesome and shocking strangeness that has to trouble other living beings, even up to those solitary gods who are said to be mute. To name has been given only to a being capable of not being, capable of making this nothingness a power and this power the de-cisive violence that opens nature, dominates it and compels it. That is how language projects us into the dialectics of the master and the slave with which we are obsessed. The master has acquired the right of speech because he has gone so far as to risk death: alone, the master speaks, and his speech is commandment. The slave can do nothing but listen. To speak is what is important; he who can only listen depends on speech and only stands in second place. But hearing, this disinherited, subordinate, and secondary side, finally is revealed to be the place of power and the principle of true mastery.

We are tempted to think that the language of the poet is that of the master: when the poet speaks, it is a sovereign speech, the speech of one who has thrown himself into risk, says what has never yet been said, names what he does not understand, does nothing but speak, so that he no longer knows what he says. When Nietzsche asserts: "But art is terribly serious! . . . We surround ourselves with images that will make you tremble. We have the power to do it! Block your ears: your eyes will see our myths, our curses will reach you!" it is the speech of a poet that is the speech of a master, and perhaps this is inevitable, perhaps the madness that overtakes Nietzsche is there to make masterly language into a language without master, a sovereignty without contract. Thus Hölderlin's song, after the over-violent outburst of the hymns, becomes again, in madness, that of the innocence of the seasons.

But to interpret the speech of art and of literature in that way is to betray it. It is to mistake the demand that is within it. It is to seek it not at its source but, drawn into the dialectics of the master and the slave, after it has already become an instrument of power. We must, then, try to grasp again in the literary work the place where language is still a relationship without power, a language of naked relation, foreign to all mastery and all servitude, a language that speaks only to whoever does not speak in order to possess and have power, to know and have, to become master and to master oneself—that is, to a man who is scarcely a man. That is assuredly a difficult quest, although we may be, through poetry and the poetic experience, being fashionable by attempting it. It may even be that we, men of need, of labor and power, do not have the means to earn a position that would let us feel its approach. Perhaps it is really a question of something very simple. Perhaps this simplicity is always present to us, or at least an equal simplicity.

§ 4 Artaud

When Artaud was twenty-seven years old, he sent some poems to a magazine. The director of this journal politely rejected them. Artaud then tries to explain why he is partial to these defective poems: it is because he suffers from such a desolation of thought that he cannot abandon the forms, however insufficient, wrested from this central nonexistence. What are the poems thus obtained worth? An exchange of letters follows, and Jacques Rivière, the director of the journal, suddenly offers to publish the letters written about these nonpublishable poems (but this time accepted in part to appear as examples and evidence). Artaud accepts, on the condition that the truth isn't altered. The result is the famous correspondence with Jacques Rivière, an event of great significance.

Was Jacques Rivière aware of this anomaly? Poems that he judges insufficient and unworthy of being published stop being so when they are completed by a narrative of the experience of their insufficiency. As if what was lacking in them, their defect, became fullness and completion by the open expression of this lack and the grounding of its necessity. Rather than the work itself, it is assuredly the experience of the work, the movement that leads to it, that interests Jacques Rivière, and the anonymous, obscure trace that it clumsily represents. Even more, the failure that still does not attract him as much as it will later attract those who write and those who read becomes the perceptible sign of a central event of the mind on which Artaud's explanations throw a surprising light. We are, then, at the borders of a phenomenon to which literature and even art seem linked: as if it were not a poem unless it had as its tacit or overt "subject" its own coming into being as poem, and the impulse from which the work comes is one through which the work is sometimes realized, sometimes sacrificed.

Let us recall Rilke's letter here, written fifteen years or so earlier:

> The further, and the more personal, one goes, the more unique life becomes. The work of art is the necessary, irrefutable, forever definitive expression of this unique reality. . . . Therein dwells the prodigious help that it brings to the one who is forced to produce it. . . . It explains to us in no uncertain terms that we should give ourselves up to the most extreme ordeals, yet, it seems, not breathe a word of them, before burying ourselves in our work, not lessen them by speaking of them: for the unique, that which no one else could understand or has the right to understand, this sort of wandering that is unique to us, can become valid only by insinuating itself into our work in order there to reveal its law, the original design that only the transparency of art makes visible.

Rilke means, then, never to communicate directly the experience from which the work might come to us: this extreme ordeal has worth and truth only if it is buried in the work in which it appears, visible-invisible, under the distant daylight of art. But did Rilke himself always maintain this reserve? And did he not formulate it precisely to break it while still safeguarding it, knowing moreover that neither he nor anyone had the power to break this reserve, but only to maintain a relationship with it? This sort of wandering that is unique to us....

THE IMPOSSIBILITY OF THINKING THAT IS THOUGHT

The understanding, attention, and sensibility of Jacques Rivière are perfect. But in the dialogue, the role of misunderstanding remains obvious, although difficult to pin down. Artaud, at the time still very patient, constantly watches over this misunderstanding. He sees that his correspondent seeks to reassure him by promising him in the future the coherence that he lacks, or by showing him that the fragility of the mind is necessary to the mind. But Artaud does not want to be reassured. He is in contact with something so grave that he cannot suffer its reduction. He also feels the extraordinary, and for him almost unbelievable, rapport between the collapse of his thought and the poems that he succeeds in writing despite this "actual loss." On one hand, Jacques Rivière misunderstands the exceptional nature of the event, and on the other hand he misunderstands the extreme quality within these works of the mind, produced from the absence of mind.

When he writes to Rivière with a calm penetration that surprises his correspondent, Artaud is not surprised at being here the master of what he wants to say. Only poems expose him to the central loss of thought from which he suffers: it is an anguish that he recalls later with pungent expressions, saying, for instance: "I am speaking of the absence like a gap, of a kind of cold, imageless suffering, without feeling, like an indescribable clash of abortions." Why does he write poems, then? Why doesn't he content himself with being a man who uses his tongue for ordinary purposes? Everything indicates that poetry, linked for him "to that kind of erosion, at once essential and fleeting, of thought," and thus essentially involved in this central loss, also gives him the certainty of being the only thing capable of expressing that loss, and promises him, to a certain extent, to rescue this loss itself, to save his thought insofar as it is lost. Thus he will say with impatience and haughtiness: "I am the one who has best felt the stupefying disarray of his language in its relationships with thought. . . . I actually lose myself in my thought as one does when one dreams, or as one suddenly plunges back into one's thought. I am the one who knows the hiding places of loss."

It is not important for him "to think aright, to see aright," or to have thoughts that are well connected, well chosen and well expressed—all abilities he knows he possesses. And he is irritated when his friends say to him: but you think very well, it is a common problem to lack words. ("I am sometimes seen as over-brilliant in expressing my insufficiencies, my profound deficiency, and in revealing an incapacity for believing it is not imaginary and made up from start to finish.") He knows, with the profundity that the experience of pain gives him, that to think is not to have thoughts, and that the thoughts that he has only make him feel that he has not "yet *begun* to think." That is the grave torment into which he returns. It is as if he has touched, despite himself and by a pathetic mistake, whence his cries come, the point at which thinking is always unable to think: it "uncan" [*impouvoir*], to use his word, which is like the essential part of his thinking, but which makes it an extremely painful lack, a failing that immediately shines from this center and, consuming the physical substance of what he thinks, divides itself on all levels into a number of particular impossibilities.

That poetry is linked to this impossibility of thinking which is thought—that is the truth that cannot be revealed, for it always turns away and forces one to experience it beneath the level where one could truly experience it. This is not only a metaphysical difficulty, it is a rapture of pain, and poetry is this perpetual pain, it is "shadow" and "the night of the soul," "the absence of voice to cry out."

In a letter written twenty or so years later, when he has gone through ordeals that have made him a difficult and blazing being, he says with the greatest simplicity: "I began in literature by writing books to say that I could not write anything at all. My thought when I had something to write was what was the most denied to me." And again: "I have never written except to say that I had never done anything, could do nothing, and that doing something, I was actually doing nothing. My entire work was built, and can only be built, on nothingness." Common sense will immediately wonder: but why, if he has nothing to say, doesn't he in fact say nothing? It is because one can content oneself with saying nothing only when nothing is almost nothing; here, though it seems that it is a question of a nullity so radical that, by the excess it represents, the danger to which it is the approach, and the tension it provokes, it demands, as if to be delivered from it, the formation of an initial speech whereby words that say something will be distanced. Who has nothing to say? How could one not force oneself to begin to speak and to express oneself? "Ah well! It is my own weakness and my *absurdity* to want to write no matter what the cost and to express myself. I am a man who has suffered much in mind and because of this I have the *right* to speak."

DESCRIPTIONS OF A BATTLE

To this void that his work—naturally, it is not a work[1]—will exalt and denounce, traverse and preserve, that it will fill and that will fill it, Artaud will come close with an impulse of which he is a master. In the beginning, before this void, he still seeks to grasp some fullness he thinks is certain, which would place him in relation to its spontaneous richness, the integrity of his feeling, and such a perfect adhesion to the continuity of things that it is already crystallizing in him into poetry. He has this "profound faculty," he believes he has it, as well as the wealth of forms and words able to express it. But "at the instant the soul readies itself to organize its richness, its discoveries, this revelation, at that unconscious minute when the thing is on the point of emanating, a superior and evil will attacks the soul like vitriol, attacks the word-and-image mass, attacks the mass of feeling, and leaves me, *me*, panting as if at the very door to my life."

That Artaud is here the victim of the illusion of the immediate is easy enough to say; that is easy; but everything begins with the way in which he is distanced from this immediacy that he calls "life": not by a nostalgic fainting away or the imperceptible abandonment of a dream; quite the contrary, by such an obvious rupture that it introduces into the center of himself the assertion of a perpetual turning-away that becomes part of his innermost self, like the atrocious surprise of his actual nature.

Thus, by a sure and painful development, he comes to reverse the polarity of the impulse and to place dispossession first, not the "immediate totality" of which this dispossession seemed at first the simple lack. What is prime is not the fullness of being; what is prime is the crack and the fissure, erosion and destruction, intermittence and gnawing privation: being is not being, it is the lack of being, a living lack that makes life incomplete, fugitive, and inexpressible, except by the cry of a fierce abstinence.

Perhaps Artaud, when he thought he had the fullness of "inseparable reality," never did anything but descry the density of shadow projected behind him by this void, for the only thing that testifies in him to total fullness is the formidable power that denies it, an excessive negation that is always at work and capable of an infinite proliferation of emptiness. It is a pressure that is so terrible that it expresses him, while at the same time demanding that he devote himself completely to producing it and maintaining its expression.

Yet at the time of the correspondence with Jacques Rivière, and when he is still writing poems, he manifestly maintains the hope of making himself equal to himself, an equality that poems are destined to restore the instant they ruin it. He says then that "he is thinking at a lower rate"; "I am below myself, I know it, I suffer from it." Later, he will write: "It is this antinomy between my profound faculty and my outer difficulty that creates the torment I am dying from." At this instant, if he feels anxiety and guilt, it is for thinking below his thought, which he thus guards behind him in the certainty of its ideal integrity, so that in expressing it, even if by one single word, it would be revealed in its true greatness, absolute witness of himself. The torment stems from the fact that he cannot discharge his thought, and poetry remains inside him as the hope of canceling this debt, which it nevertheless can only stretch well beyond the limits of his existence. One sometimes has the impression in the correspondence with

Jacques Rivière that the little interest Rivière has in the poems, and his interest in the central trouble that Artaud is only too ready to describe, displaces the center of the writing. Artaud wrote against the void, to get out of it. In the correspondence with Rivière, though, he writes by exposing himself to it and by trying to express it and draw expression from it.

This displacement of the center of gravity (that *L'ombilic des limbes* [Limbo navel] and *Le pèse-nerfs* [Nerve-scale] represent) is the painful demand that forces him, abandoning all illusion, to be attentive to one single point. "Point of absence and the inane," around which he wanders with a kind of sarcastic lucidity, with good sense that is crafty at first, then pushed by movements of suffering in which we hear misery cry out, as formerly only Sade could cry out, and yet, also like Sade, without ever consenting, and with a fighting strength that never stops being equal to this void that it embraces.

> I want to surpass this point of absence, of futility. This shuffling in place that makes me crippled, inferior to everything and everyone. I have no life, I have no life! My internal effervescence is dead. . . . I can't manage to *think*. Do you understand this hollow, this intense and lasting nothingness. . . . I can neither go forward nor draw back. I am fixed in place, localized around a point always the same, which all my books translate.

We must not make the mistake of reading as analyses of a psychological state the precise, sure and detailed descriptions that he offers us. They are descriptions, but descriptions of a battle. The fight is in part imposed on him. The "void" is an "active void." The "I cannot think, I can't manage to think" is a summons to a more profound thought, a constant pressure, an oblivion that, never allowing itself to be forgotten, always demands a more perfect oblivion. Henceforth thinking is this step always to take backwards. The battle in which he is always conquered is always resumed at a lower level. Powerlessness is never powerless enough, the impossible is not the impossible. But at the same time, the fight is also one that Artaud wants to pursue, for in this struggle he does not renounce what he calls "life" (this outpouring, this dazzling vivacity), whose loss he cannot tolerate, which he wants to marry with his thought, which, by a grandiose and frightful obstinacy, he absolutely refuses to distinguish from thought, while this "life" is nothing other than "the erosion" of this life, "the emaciation" of this life, the intimacy of rupture and loss in which there is neither life nor thought, but only the torture of a fundamental lack through which the demand of a more decisive negation already asserts itself. And everything begins again. For Artaud will never accept the scandal of a thought separated from life, even when he is given over to the most direct and savage experience that ever made the essence of thought understood as separation, of that impossibility that it asserts against itself as the limit of its infinite power.

TO SUFFER, TO THINK

It would be tempting to compare what Artaud tells us to what Hölderlin or Mallarmé tells us: that inspiration is first that pure point where it is lacking. But we must resist this temptation of over-general assertions. Each poet says the same thing, but it is not the same thing; it is unique, we feel it. Artaud's point of view is his own. What he says is of an intensity that we could not bear. Here speaks a pain that refuses all profundity, all illusion, and all hope, but that, in this refusal, offers to thought "the ether of a new space." When we read these pages, we learn what we do not manage to know: the act of thinking can only be deeply shocking; what is to be thought about is in thought that which turns away from it and inexhaustibly exhausts itself in it; suffering and thinking are secretly linked, for if suffering, when it becomes extreme, is such that it destroys the capacity to suffer, always destroying ahead of itself, in time, the time when suffering could be grasped again and ended, it is perhaps the same with thought. Strange connections. Might it be that extreme thought and extreme suffering open onto the same horizon? Might suffering be, finally, thinking?

§ 5 Rousseau

I do not know if during his life Rousseau was persecuted, as he thought he was. But since he evidently did not stop being persecuted after his death, attracting hostile passions and, until his final years, the hatred, the deforming fury, and the abuse of seemingly reasonable men, we must think that there was some truth to this conjuration of hostility, of which he inexplicably felt himself the victim. Rousseau's enemies are so with an excess that justifies Rousseau. Maurras, judging him, abandons himself to the same impure distortion with which he reproaches Rousseau. As to those who wish Rousseau only well and feel themselves his companions from the start, we see, for instance with Jean Guéhenno, how far from easy it is for them to do him justice. One could say that there is in Rousseau something mysteriously warped that enrages those who do not like him and annoys those who do not wish to do him wrong, without their being able to be sure of this fault, and precisely because they cannot be sure of it.

I have always suspected this profound and elusive vice of this man to whom we owe literature. Rousseau, the man of the primal, of nature and truth, is the one who can fulfill these relationships only by writing; writing, all he can do is make them deviate from the certainty he has of them; in this deviation from which he suffers, to which he spiritedly, despairingly objects, he helps literature to become aware of itself by disengaging itself from old conventions and forming, through argumentation and contradiction, a new rectitude.

Of course, Rousseau's whole career is not thus explained. But his desire to be true and the difficulty of being so, the passion for origin, the happiness of the immediate present and the unhappiness that ensues, the need for

communication changed into solitude, the search for exile, then the condemnation to wander, and finally the obsession with strangeness, all form
part of the essence of the literary experience and, through this experience,
seem to us more readable, more important, more secretly justified.

Jean Starobinski's remarkable essay seems to me to confirm this point
of view and to emphasize it with a richness of reflections that enlighten us
not only about Rousseau, but also about the singularities of the literature
born with him.[1] This is already clear: in a century in which there is almost
no one who is not a great writer and who doesn't write with an easy and
skillful mastery, Rousseau is the first to write with displeasure [*ennui*],[2]
and with the feeling of a fault that he must continually aggravate to try to
escape it. "And from that instant I was lost." The excess of this statement
does not surprise us. At the same time, if his whole unhappy life seems to
him to emerge from the instant of wandering when he had the idea of
competing for the Academy, the entire richness of his renewed life has its
origin in that moment of change when he "saw another universe and became another man." The illumination of Vincennes, the "truly heavenly
fire" with which he feels himself enflamed, evokes the sacred nature of the
literary calling. On one hand, to write is evil, for it is to enter into the lie
of literature and the vanity of literary customs; on the other hand, it is to
make oneself capable of a ravishing change and to enter into a new, en-
thusiastic relationship "with truth, freedom, and virtue": isn't that extremely precious? No doubt it is, but it is to lose oneself again, since, having become other than what he was—another man in another
universe—now he is henceforth unfaithful to his true nature (this laziness,
this lack of concern, this unstable diversity that he prefers) and obliged to
let himself be carried away into a quest that still has no other aim than itself. Rousseau is surprisingly aware of the alienation that the act of writing
entrains, an evil alienation, even if it is an alienation in hopes of the
Good, and very unfortunate indeed for the one who undergoes it, as all
the Prophets before him did not fail to complain to the God who imposed
it on them.

Starobinski notes perfectly that Rousseau inaugurates the sort of writer
that we have all more or less become, desperate to write against writing,
"man of letters making a plea against letters," then burying himself in literature with the hope of getting out of it, then no longer refraining from
writing because he no longer has the possibility of communicating
anything.

THE NOMAD PASSION

What is striking is that this decision, in the beginning very clear and deliberate, reveals itself as linked with a power of strangeness under the threat of which he will little by little lose all stable rapport with a self. In the wandering passion that is his, he passes through several characteristic stages. After being the innocent walker of his youth, he is the glorious itinerant who goes from château to château and cannot stay fixed in the success that hunts and pursues him. This vagabondage of celebrity—like that of Valéry, going from salon to salon—is so contrary to the revelation that led him to write that he wants to withdraw by an exemplary and spectacular flight: the daily flight outside of the world, the public retreat to the life of the Forest. It is an attempt at "personal reform" in which it is easy to find motives that make it seem suspicious—and in fact why this rupture and this apparent solitude? To write more, to make new works, to establish new ties with society. "The work that I undertook could be carried out only in an absolute retreat."

To make use of the literary lie in order to denounce the social lie is, it is true, a very old privilege inherited from the Skeptics and the Cynics. But Rousseau, while still borrowing from the Ancients a tradition that he knows, nonetheless feels that with it, and through the solitary defiance it entails, literature will involve him in a new adventure and will reveal strange powers. In the exile he advocates with methodical and almost pedagogical decisiveness, he is already under the constraint of that infinite force of absence, of that communication by rupture that is literary presence: he who wants to be transparency itself can do nothing but hide himself and make himself obscure, a foreigner not only to others to protest against their foreignness, but soon to himself. "The decision I have made to write and to hide myself. . . ." If, due to this, this advocacy of rupture becomes a separation, evilly imposed on him, if the world from which he has a little arbitrarily made himself absent comes back to him as the rigged world of absence and distancing, if finally, having played at speaking to make his silent singularity heard, he hurls himself at the "profound, universal silence," "frightening and terrible silence," which hides from him the mystery he has become, then we are permitted to see in this episode, abnormal as it is, the extreme truth of the impulse he had to pursue, and that sense of vagrant necessity that he was the first to make inseparable from literary experience.

Who better than he has ever represented the succession of rash acts and the ever-increasing responsibilities that result from the irresponsible light-ness of writing? Nothing begins more easily: one writes in order to teach the world while winning agreeable fame from it. Then one gets hooked, one renounces the world a little, for one must write and one can only write by hiding oneself and distancing oneself. In the end, "nothing more is possible": the wish for asceticism is changed into an unwilling dispos-session, proud exile turned into the misfortune of infinite migration, soli-tary walks become the incomprehensible necessity to come and go with-out ever stopping. In this "immense labyrinth where one can only glimpse in the shadows false roads that lead one farther and farther away," what is the last wish of this man so tempted to be free? "I dared to desire and pro-pose that they should dispose of me in perpetual captivity rather than make me wander incessantly over the earth by expelling me successively from all the refuges that I might have chosen." This is a confession that is rich with meaning: a man once enchanted with the greatest freedom, imaginarily making free with everything by a realization without labor, now begs that someone stop him and hem him in, even if only to fix him in an eternal prison that seems to him less unbearable than the excess of his freedom. Or he will have to turn to and fro in the space of his solitude, which can no longer be anything but the indefinitely repeated echo of solitary speech: "Given over to myself alone, without friend, without ad-vice, without experience, in a foreign country. . . . " "Alone, foreign, iso-lated, without support, without family. . . . " "Alone, without support, friendless, defenseless. . . . " "Foreign, without relatives, without support, alone. . . . "[3]

"TO INVENT A NEW LANGUAGE"

It is when he undertakes, by an initiative whose quality of freshness proudly exalts him, to speak truthfully about the self that Rousseau will discover the insufficiency of traditional literature and the need to invent another kind, as fresh as his intention.[4] What is unique about this aim, then? It is that he does not intend to make a narrative or portrayal of his life. He wants, by means of a nonetheless historical narration, entering into immediate contact with himself, to reveal this immediate presence that he has so incomparably sensed, to place himself wholly in the light of day, to pass into the day and into the transparency of day, which is his in-timate origin. Neither Saint Augustine nor Montaigne nor all the rest ever attempted such a thing. Saint Augustine confesses in relation to God and to the church; he has Truth as mediator, and would not commit the fault of wanting to speak immediately about himself. Montaigne is no more certain of the outer truth than he is sure of his actual private life; the immediate is probably nowhere; uncertainty alone is what can reveal us to ourselves. But Rousseau never doubted the felicity of the immediate, or the original light that is its presence in himself, which his only task is to unveil in order to bear witness to himself and, even more, to that transparency in him. Thence the thought that what he is undertaking is without precedent and perhaps without hope. How can one speak of oneself, how can one speak with truth of oneself, and how, when speaking, can one confine oneself to the immediate and make literature the realm of original experience? Failure is inevitable, but the byways of failure are revelatory, for these contradictions are the reality of the literary task.

In his *Confessions*, Rousseau necessarily wants to say everything. "Everything" is first of all his entire story, his whole life, that which accuses him (and which alone can excuse him), the ignoble, the base, the perverse, but also the insignificant, the uncertain, the null. It is a phenomenal task, which he scarcely begins, even though this beginning already creates a scandal; he feels strongly that for this task he will have to break with all the rules of classical discourse. At the same time, he is aware that to say everything is not to exhaust his story, or his character, in an impossible integral narrative, but just as well to seek in his being or in language the moment of the first simplicity, where everything is already given, ahead of time, where all is possible. If he does not stop writing about himself, tirelessly beginning his autobiography over and over at a certain moment that is always interrupted, it is because he is incessantly and feverishly in search of this beginning, which always eludes him when he expresses it, while he had, before trying to express it, the calm, happy certainty of it. "Who am I?" Thus begins *The Confessions*, in which he wants not only to show himself "completely to the public," but to keep himself "incessantly before his own eyes," which will force him never to stop writing, in order to make impossible "the least gap," "the least void." Then come the *Dialogues*, in which he who has "said everything," as if he had said nothing, begins again to say everything, under this constraint: "If I silence anything, you will know nothing of me." Then come the *Reveries*: "What am I myself? That is what remains for me to seek out." If writing is indeed the strange passion for the incessant, who reveals it to us better than this man weary of writing, persecuted by speech and, refusing to keep silent, still throwing "in haste onto paper a few interrupted words" that he has scarcely "had time to reread, let alone correct"?

What matters is thus not the whole as it unfurls and develops in the story, if it be that of the heart; it is the entirety of the immediate, and the truth of that entirety. Here, Rousseau makes a discovery that helps him dangerously. The truth of origin is not confused with the truth of deeds: at the level on which it should be grasped and expressed, it is that which is not yet true, that which at least has no guarantee in the conformity with the firm outer reality. We will thus never be sure of having said this sort of truth, sure on the contrary of always having to say it anew, but in no way convicted of falsity if it occurs to us to express it by altering it and inventing it, for it is more real in the unreal than in the appearance of exactitude where in fixity it loses its own clarity. Rousseau discovers the legitimacy of an art without resemblance, he recognizes the truth of literature which is in its very mistake, and its power, which is not to represent, but to make present by the force of creative absence. "I am persuaded that one is always very well portrayed when one has portrayed oneself, even when the portrayal turns out to bear not the least resemblance." We are no longer in the domain of truth, notes Starobinski, we are from now on in the domain of authenticity. And here is his remarkable commentary: "Authentic speech is a speech that no longer forces itself to imitate a preexistent given: it is free to deform and invent, on condition that it remain faithful to its own law. Yet this inner law eludes all control and all discussion. The law of authenticity forbids nothing, but is never satisfied. It does not demand that speech *reproduce* a prior reality, but that it *produce* its truth in a free and uninterrupted development."

But what literature, sheltering such language, would be able to preserve its creative spontaneity? Writing well, with care, in a constant, well-balanced, and ruled form, according to the classical ideal on which books are based, no longer matters.

> Here it is my portrayal that is at stake, and not a book. I want to work, so to speak, in the *camera obscura*. . . . I take . . . my own side when it comes to style as well as to details. I will in no way try to make it uniform; I will always have the style that comes to me, I will change it according to my humor without scruple, I will say each thing as I feel it, as I see it, without research, without bother, without being embarrassed by the motley [*la bigarrure*]. . . . My uneven and natural style, sometimes quick and sometimes diffused, now wise and now mad, now serious and now gay, will itself form part of my story.

This last indication is striking. Rousseau sees perfectly that literature is that manner of speaking that speaks by its manner, as he sees that there is meaning, truth, and a sort of content of form, in which is communicated, despite words, all that their deceptive signification dissimulates.

To write without care, without bother, and without research is not so easy, as Rousseau shows us by his example. He must wait till, according to the law of reduplication of the story, the tragic Jean-Jacques is followed by the comic Jean-Jacques, so that the carelessness, the freedom from effort, and ordinary chatter finally take their place alongside Restif de la Bretonne in literature, and the result will not be very convincing. What impeded Rousseau in his aim of handing over the coarse material of his life by leaving it up to the reader to form a work himself with these elements—an essentially modern aim[5]—is that, despite him, in this incomprehensible process that he feels his existence becoming, under threat of an unacceptable condemnation, he cannot keep from pleading and appealing to the oratorical values of classical literature. (When one is before a judge who must be convinced, one must use the language of the judge, which is fine rhetoric.) Unless, in the case of Rousseau, so gifted with eloquence, he must reverse the situation and say that—to a certain extent, of course—this idea of being put on trial, of a judgment to which he is delivered and of a tribunal before which he must incessantly justify himself by endlessly telling about himself, is imposed on him by the literary form at which he excels and where his thought is obsessed with the demands of litigation. In this sense, it is indeed the duality, the discord between literary speech, still classical and Ciceronian, justifying, careful to be precise, and proud of speaking the mot juste—and primal speech, immediate, not at all "just," but not coming under any rules of justice, thus fundamentally innocent, this duality of language exposes the writer to feeling himself to be first Rousseau and then Jean-Jacques, then both at the same time, in a dichotomy that he embodies with admirable passion.

THE FASCINATION WITH EXTREMES

One of the most reliable books recently devoted to Rousseau's thought is by Pierre Burgelin.[6] The difficulty experienced by all the commentators—some rejoice in it, others remedy it—in giving coherence to an ensemble of works that only gives the appearance of being systematic can be explained, as we see in this book, in many ways. I think that one of the explanations is this: Rousseau's thoughts are not yet thoughts; their profundity, their inexhaustible richness, and the air of sophism that Diderot found in them all stem from the fact that on the level of literature at which they assert themselves they designate that more original moment, linked to literary reality, that demand for anteriority that forbids them from developing into concepts, that refuses them ideal clarity, and that, each time they seek to organize into a happy synthesis, stops them and delivers them to the fascination of extremes. Constantly we feel that a dialectical interpretation of Rousseau's ideas is possible: in the *Social Contract*, in *Emile*, and even in *Julie*; but constantly we intuit that the revelation of the unmediated and the denaturation of a pondered life make sense only by the opposition, where they are defined in a conflict without outcome. One might say that it is disease that fixes Jean-Jacques's thinking in an immobile antithesis. I will say that this disease is also literature, all of whose contradictory claims—absurd if one wants to think about them, unbearable if one welcomes them—Rousseau discerned, with firm clairvoyance and strong courage. What could be more unreasonable than wanting to make language the resting place of the immediate and the realm of a mediation, the grasping of origin and the movement of alienation or of strangeness, the certainty of what does nothing but begin and the uncertainty of what does nothing but begin again, the absolute truth of that which, nonetheless, is not yet true? We can begin to understand and set in order this unreason, we can accomplish it in fine works, we can live it in a bizarre passion. Most often, these three roles are distinct. Rousseau, who is the first to conceive of them, is one of the few to combine them; he will henceforth seem suspect, both to the thinker and to the writer, for having wanted imprudently *to be* one through the other.

§ 6 Joubert and Space

1. Author Without a Book, Writer Without Writing

That we think of [Joseph] Joubert as a writer who is close to us, closer than the great literary names with whom he was contemporary, is not only because of the (nonetheless distinguished) obscurity in which he lived, died, and then lived on. It is not enough during one's lifetime to be a name feebly illumined in order to shine, as Stendhal hoped, one or two centuries later. It is not even enough for a great work to be great and to stand apart, so that posterity, one day finally grateful, might set it anew in the brilliance of broad daylight. It is possible that humanity may one day know everything—beings, truths, and worlds—but there will always be some work of art—perhaps all of art—that will fall outside this universal knowledge. That is the privilege of artistic activity: what it produces often must remain unknown even by a god.

It remains true that many works are prematurely exhausted by being over-admired. This great torch of glory in which writers and artists, as they age, rejoice, and which throws its last glimmers on their death, burns a substance in them that will ever after be lacking from their work. The young Valéry used to seek in every well-known book the mistake that made it famous—an aristocrat's judgment. But we often have the impression that death will finally bring silence and calm to the work left to itself. During his life, even the most detached and negligent writer fights for his books. He lives, that is enough; he stands behind them, through this life that remains to him and with which he makes them present. But his death, even though unnoticed, reestablishes the secret and closes thought. Will this thought, now alone, spread or be checked, fail or succeed, find

49

or lose itself? And will it ever be alone? Even oblivion does not always re-ward those who seem to have earned it by the gift of great restraint that was in them.

Joubert had this gift. He never wrote a book. He only prepared himself to write one, resolutely seeking the right conditions that would allow him to write. Then he forgot even this aim. More precisely, what he sought, this source of writing, this space in which to write, this light to define in space, demanded of him and asserted in him characteristics that made him unfit for any ordinary literary work, or made him turn away from it. He was thus one of the first entirely modern writers, preferring the center over the sphere, sacrificing results for the discovery of their conditions, not writing in order to add one book to another, but to make himself master of the point whence all books seemed to come, which, once found, would exempt him from writing them.

One would wrong him, however, in attributing to him, as a clear and singly pursued intention, such a thought, which he discovers only little by little, which he often loses and obscures, and which he can later maintain only by transforming it into wisdom. That is why it is so easy to confuse him with one of those makers of maxims for which Nietzsche loved French literature. Almost all his editors, sometimes even today, in pre-senting us the reflections of his *Carnets* [Notebooks] grouped under sen-tentious captions and under general titles borrowed from the emptiest and vaguest philosophy—"family and society"; "wisdom and virtue"; "truth and errors"; "life and death"; "literary judgments"—favored this misread-ing, and failed to see the essentially new and even futuristic aspect of his research: the development of a thought that does not yet think, or of a po-etic language that tries to go back up toward itself.

Joubert is neither Chamfort nor Vauvenargues, nor is he La Rochefou-cauld. He does not make bons mots with brief thoughts. He does not coin a philosophy. He does not arrogate, by concise formulae, that abrupt abil-ity to make assertions that haughty, skeptical, and bitter moralists use to make their doubts categorical. What he wrote he wrote almost every day, dating it and not giving it any remarkable reference point other than this date, or any other perspective than the movement of the days that had brought it to him. That is how one should read him. It is not only because André Beaunier offered us, for the first time, the integral publication of Joubert's reflections (altered more or less by the preceding editors, but never very seriously—only grouped according to an order that distorted them) that we then had the revelation of an entirely different Joubert: it is because he gave them back their diaristic quality. Thoughts recover once again their dailiness and touch ordinary life, liberate themselves from it, and liberate from it another day, another clarity that shows through here and there. This perspective changes everything. Just as the numerous collections of Joubert's *Pensées* [Thoughts] seem to assert a delicate, cautious, but indifferent wisdom, so the *Carnets*, as they were drafted in the course of an entire life and as they have been restored to us, mingled according to the chance and pressure of life, offer themselves passionately to our reading, lead us by their haphazard movement toward an end that reveals itself only at rare moments, in the brief rift of a clarity.

"Joubert's diary," the subtitle given to the *Carnets*, is not misleading, even if it takes us in. It is indeed with the most profound intimacy, with the search for this intimacy, for the path to reach it and the space of words with which this intimacy must in the end mingle, that his narrative is formed for us. "And may everything come from the entrails, everything down to the least expression. That is perhaps an inconvenience, but it is a necessity: I put up with it." Joubert suffered from this necessity. He would have liked not to be one of "those minds that delve or get too involved beforehand with what they believe," a failing that is, he says, that of his century, but a privileged fault whose language he only tries, sometimes, to preserve. Then, one day, he must sadly write us this note: "I have no more surface." This, for a man who wants to write, who above all can only write by art, by the contact with images and by the space with which they put him in contact, is a difficult assertion. How can one speak from profundity alone, in that state of deep embeddedness in which everything is arduous, fierce, irregular? Something interior, embedded. "When one paints an inward thing, one paints an embedded thing. Yet that which is hidden in the depths, however illumined it may be, can never offer the uniform, lively clarity of a surface." Joubert loves this surface clarity, and so he never stops trying to conceive of this great profundity to which he descends, from which he rises up, as yet another surface, continually added to itself.

In this *Journal*, there are few details touching on what we call private life or public life, but, here and there, there are some discreet allusions that still have a certain force of evocation. In 1801: "That young man whom you call Bonaparte." On the death of his mother: "At ten o'clock in the evening, my poor mother! my poor mother!" In January: "The white spots of snow, scattered here and there on the greenery in the thaw."

In May, at Hyères: "The coolness during the summer." In October: "The cry of the chimney sweep; the cicada's song." Sometimes, there are outlines of thoughts still mixed with circumstances: "Pleasure of being seen from afar." "The occupation of watching the time flow by." Or images, impregnated with their secret origin: "The black hair in the tomb." "The mobile path of the water. . . . A river of air and light. . . . Layers of clarity. . . . And it is from this point of earth that my soul will fly away." He also speaks of himself, not of what he does or what happens to him, but what is in his depths, the demands of his mind, and, behind his mind, of what he calls his soul. It is an intimacy, though, that is barely his own, that remains always distanced from him and distanced from this distance, forcing him to observe himself often in the third person and, when he has noted: "I do not have a patient mind," to correct himself immediately: "He does not have. . . ." Even rarer, although there are numerous notes, dry but precise, on his health, which laboriously preoccupied him, the words of distress in which he seems to reach his limits, he who deems it necessary always to stop his mind before its limits to prevent it from being limited; little phrases that make us pause: "I no longer have any vast thoughts." ". . . incapable of writing." "(Unable to go on.)" That is in parentheses, not long before his death.

WHY DOESN'T HE WRITE?

Why doesn't Joubert write books? Early on, his attention and interest are only on that which is written and is to be written. As a young man, he is close to Diderot; a little later, close to Restif de la Bretonne, both prolific men of letters. His maturity gives him almost exclusively famous writers for friends, with whom he lives in the midst of literature, friends who, moreover, recognize his accomplished talents of thought and form, and gently push him out of his silence. Finally, he is in no way a man paralyzed by any difficulties of expression: his letters, numerous and lengthy, are written with that aptitude for writing that is as it were the gift of that century, and to which he adds sparkling nuances and charming phrases that show him to be always happy to speak and happy with words. Yet this extremely capable man, who almost every day has a notebook near him in which he writes, publishes nothing and leaves nothing to publish. (At least, not according to the customs of his time; even the publication after his death that Chateaubriand undertakes of some of his thoughts is a private edition, reserved for his friends. In our time, he would perhaps no more have resisted solicitations from outside than Valéry did Gide. Fontanes wrote to him in 1803: "I urge you to write every evening, going over the meditations of your day. You will select, after some time, from these fantasies of your thought, and you will be surprised at having made, almost without your knowing it, an extremely fine work." It is to Joubert's credit to have refused to make this extremely fine work.)

One might reply that he is one of those writers whom their journals sterilize by giving them the pleasure of a false abundance and the appearance of words in which they wallow without self-control. But nothing could be more foreign to Joubert. If his *Journal* is still grounded in the days, it is not a reflection of them, but instead strives for something beyond them. Furthermore, he comes late to this habit of the *Carnets*, and it is later still that he gives them the importance and direction that, through the vicissitudes of quite varied reflections, affirm the constancy of his care. It even seems that, up to the age of forty, he still feels ready to produce fine written works like so many others: on universal Benevolence, on Pigalle, on Cook, even a novel, the projects of which we have fragments. Then, there are no or few *Carnets*, which impose on him only when he begins to *think* of writing and when, in this thinking, he recognizes his calling, the attraction he must undergo, the movement by which he will find fulfillment, sometimes sadly, with the regret of not having "emptied all his shells," but also without regret, sure of his preferences and of not having failed them.

"But what in fact is my art? What goal does it propose? What does it produce? What does it cause to be born and to exist? What is my aim, and what do I want to do in exercising it? Is it to write and to assure myself of being read? Only ambition for so many people! Is that what I want? . . . That is what must be examined, carefully and for a long time, until I know." That is written on October 22, 1799, when Joubert is forty-five. One year later, on October 27: "When? you say. I answer: When I have circumscribed my sphere." This questioning is pursued from day to day, from month to year, during his entire existence, but one would be mistaken if one thought him another Amiel who exhausts himself in examination. He knows wonderfully—he is one of the first to know it—that the impulse to which he must answer is one for which reasoning is insufficient and dangerous, for which it is not even suitable to say true things,

for it is as if it is outside of strict truth, calling into question that part of illusion and that environment of the imagination with which hard, firm
reason does not have to comply. Joubert, who seems to draft nothing but
extremely abstract reflections, does not doubt, author without a book as
he is and writer without writing, that he is already dependent on art.
"Here, I am outside of civil things and in the pure region of Art." He has
his moments of doubt, but what strikes him is above all the confidence of
his progress and the certainty that, even if he does not answer with any
visible work to the "When?" of his friends, it is because he is occupied by
something more essential, which interests art more essentially than a book
could.[1]

With what, then, is he occupied? Perhaps he would not like us to say
that he knows. He knows rather that he seeks what he does not know, and
that the difficulty of his research and the felicity of his discoveries stem
from that: "But how can one look where one must when one does not
even know what one is looking for? And that is what always happens
when one composes and when one creates. Fortunately, wandering in this
way, one makes more than discoveries, one has fortunate encounters." We
often have the impression that, if he has a work in mind, it is to envelop
with this commonplace aim and hide from his own eyes the more secret
aim, difficult to grasp and to convey, for which he feels responsible. It is
an almost mythic work to which allusion is made, every now and then,
whose nature, he says, is such "that the very name of the subject must not
be in the title." After which, he adds: "I will entitle it: 'On Man.'" Or
again he answers the reproaches that his friends, or perhaps his executive
mind, make of him: the reproach of lacking variety and of being interested in only one thing—"If he turns in the same circle? That is the horizon of his subject. Add: the circle of immensity." Reproach of not knowing how to conclude anything: "Conclude! What a word. One does not
conclude when one stops and declares oneself finished." Then the more
serious reproach of having finished before any beginning: "When the last
word is always the one that offers itself first, the work becomes difficult."
Difficulty of giving his "ideas" a resting place that resembles them, that is
made of their very freedom, that respects and preserves in them their simplicity of images, their figure of invisibility, and their refusal to associate
with each other like reasons: "My ideas! It is the house in which to lodge
them that I struggle to build."

A work whose subject is quite other than the obvious subject, that must not conclude and cannot begin, a work that is seemingly in default to itself, distanced from what it expresses, so that what it expresses blossoms in that distance, settles there, preserves itself there, and finally disappears there. In 1812—he is almost sixty years old—this is how he describes this "house" that he struggled to build seven years earlier: "Having found nothing that was worth more than emptiness, he leaves the space vacant." On the threshold of old age, is that an avowal of abandon, the confession of failure, to which his excessive demand might have led him? This may not be a triumphal assertion, yet everything shows that he in no way deems it negative and that, if he resigns himself to it, it is because he prefers to hold himself rigorously to this discovery rather than to develop it by approximations that betray it. *Space*—that, in effect, is the heart of his experience, what he finds as soon as he thinks of writing, what he finds close to any written work, the wonder of intimacy that makes literary language [*parole*] at once a thought and the echo of that thought (for him, not a weakened thought, but more profound, since more tenuous, although redoubled, more distant, closer to that distance it designates and from which it flows), turned at the same time toward that reserve of ease and indeterminacy that is in us and that is our soul, and toward that weft of light, air, and infinite space that is above us and that is the sky and that is God.

It is difficult to know what the point of departure for this "experiment" of Joubert was. In a certain way he thinks of everything all at once, all the more so when he has to express himself in isolated thoughts, in the interval of which he perhaps does not exist. It seems, however, that the one who, having just reached maturity, wrote: "Poets should be the great study of the philosopher who wants to know man," received first from poetry and, more precisely, from the strangeness of literary writing the surprise of what he will have to think about his entire life, a sphere where his most varied reflections on man, physics, cosmology, or theology will henceforth embrace their form, while still helping to keep it in movement. When he writes "to represent with air, to circumscribe in a small amount of space great emptinesses or great fullnesses, what am I saying? Immensity itself, and all matter—such are the unquestionable wonders, easy to verify, that perpetually operate by speech and writing," he designates, still confusedly but already with confidence, the point to which he will keep returning: that ability to represent by absence, and to manifest by distance, which is at the center of art, an ability that seems to distance things in order to say them, to keep them apart so that they can be illumined, a capability of transformation, translation, in which it is this very apartness (space) that transforms and translates, that makes invisible things visible and visible things transparent, thus makes itself visible in them and is revealed as the luminous heart of invisibility and unreality from which everything comes, and where everything is completed.

It is a surprising experiment, and sometimes seems to us close to being confused with Rilke's, which is also like an anticipation of Mallarmé's research; however, as soon as one tries to keep them both in focus at once, it sets itself apart all the more as it comes close, by nuances that perhaps illuminate for us the center of gravity of each.

2. An Early Version of Mallarmé

Georges Poulet, speaking of Joubert in one of his best essays, evoked the poetic experience of Mallarmé, toward which, in fact, Joubert's thinking often directs us.[2] And between the two figures are only similarities: the same discretion, a sort of fading of the person, the scarcity of inspiration, but all the strength of this seeming weakness and a great rigor in research, a lucid obstinacy in carrying on toward the unknown goal, an extreme attention to words, to their symbolism, to their essence; and, finally, the feeling that literature and poetry are the locus of a secret that should perhaps be preferred to anything else, even to the glory of making books. Sometimes, in one phrase or another in the *Carnets*, it is almost Mallarmé's voice we think we are hearing. On June 8, 1823, less than a year before his death: "Spaces . . . I would almost say . . . imaginary, so much the existence of them is." Mallarmé would no doubt have stopped himself at "imaginary," but is it not already he who is speaking, with that suspended language, those silences that shape the air and that way of holding back the word so that it can escape and rise up, on its own, to its point of apparency? That is troubling.

What matters to us, though, in this precocious presence of Mallarmé, is that such a resemblance of locutions and thoughts forces us to see them above all in whatever distinct quality they have, and to ask ourselves why similar meditations, the presentiment of the same ways, and the summons to the same images lead them so far from each other. The points of departure are almost the same. Both have a profound experience of the "distance" and the "separation" that alone allow us to speak, to imagine, and to think. Both feel that the force of poetic communication comes not from the fact that it makes us immediately participate in things, but rather from the fact that it gives them to us outside of their range. Only Joubert, a less exclusive mind and perhaps deprived of certain demands that make Mallarmé a poet, did not separate the two regions: on the contrary, he saw in separation—that fabric of absence and emptiness that he calls space—the common share of things, of words, of thoughts, and of worlds, of this sky above and of this transparency in us that here and there are a pure expanse of light. When he discovers that, in literature, all things are spoken, made to be seen, and revealed with their true form and their secret measure, as soon as they are distanced, spaced out, subside and finally spread out into the uncircumscribed and indeterminate void for which one of the keys is imagination, he boldly concludes that this void and this absence are the very ground of the most material realities, to the point, he says, that if one squeezed the world to make the void come out, it would not fill one's hand.

BY DISTANCE AND BY EMPTINESS

"This globe is a drop of water; the world is a drop of air. Marble is thickened air." "Yes, the world is gas, and even clear gas. Newton calculated that the diamond had [ ] times more vacuums than plenums, and the diamond is the most compact of substances." "With its gravitations, its impenetrabilities, its attractions, its impulsions, and all those blind forces about which scholars make so much noise . . . , what is all matter but a grain of emptied metal, a grain of glass made hollow, a bubble of blown water in which light and shadow play; a shadow, finally, where nothing weighs except on itself, is impenetrable except (for) itself." There is, with Joubert, an entire physics and cosmology of dream (which are perhaps not far from the assertions of more modern science) where he ventures forth, pushed by the necessity of reconciling the real and the imaginary, which tend less to negate the reality of things than to make them exist starting from almost nothing—an atom of air, a sparkle of light, or even only the emptiness of space that they occupy: "Observe that everywhere and in everything, what is subtle carries that which is compact, and what is light holds suspended all that is heavy." We see clearly, then, why poetic language can revive things and, translating them in space, make them apparent through their distancing and their emptiness: it is because this distance lives in them, this emptiness is already in them; thus it is right to grasp them, and thus it is the calling of words to extract the invisible center of their actual meaning. It is by shadow that one touches substance, it is by the penumbra of this shadow, when one has arrived at the oscillating limit where, without disappearing, it is fringed and penetrated with light. But, naturally, for the word to attain this limit and represent it, it also must become "a drop of light," and become the image of what it designates, image of itself and of the imaginary, in order finally to be confused with the indeterminate expanse of space, while still raising to the roundness of a perfect sphere the moment that, in its extreme lightness, it carries and, by its transparency, defines.

"The transparent, the diaphanous, the thin crust, the magical; the imitation of the divine that made all things with little and, so to speak, with nothing: that is one of the essential qualities of poetry." "There must be, in our written language, a voice, a soul, space, open air, words that survive all alone, and that carry their place with them." "The force of communication. . . . It is of a subtle, fine nature, whose existence makes itself felt and does not show itself. As is that of ether in electricity." "A poetic vapor, a dense cloud that resolves itself into prose."

However ethereal he wanted language to become, we must note that Joubert never invested it with this power of negation—an overreaching toward, by and through nothingness—that poetry appointed Mallarmé to explore. If the modesty of the word establishes between us and things this distance without which we would be exposed to the stifling silence, this is not by *negating* things, but by opening them up and, by this opening, freeing the part of light and the interval that form them, or by making what is beyond the body perceptible, by consenting to that *beyond* by means of which each body asserts itself, by welcoming the fore-body [*l'avant-corps*] that is "the secret prolongation of its substance." The word does not negate, but consents, and if it sometimes seems an accomplice of nothingness, this "nothingness," says Joubert, is nothing other than "the invisible fullness of the world," whose apparency must be brought out in the open by language, an emptiness that does not let itself be seen but is luminous presence, a fissure through which invisibility spreads.

Around 1804, under the early influence of Malebranche, by the analogy that he perceives between the language of this philosopher and his own, and moreover by the extension of his literary experience into a religious experience, Joubert, having pushed as far as he could the hollowing-out of things and the excavation of reality, finds in God the goal and support of all this emptiness, and makes Him the space of space, as others make Him the thought of thought. It would be easy to think that the name of God comes here, usefully, to plug the big hole that, in his yearning for alleviation and respite, he ends up recognizing and establishing in all things. Without this name (or if it were only a name) wouldn't everything fall back into the nothingness it brushes against, tames, and tastes, like the ineffable contact with any visible or invisible certainty? That could well be. But let us accept his experience as he felt it and represented it. What must be noted to judge it correctly is that he has such a strong feeling of the impalpable, and such a sure understanding of this emptiness he calls space, that he never seems to fear that all things might disperse and be annihilated in it. From the immensity of space, as Georges Poulet notes very well, he extracts not anguish, as Pascal does, but the exaltation of a calm joy, and if God comes to him, it is not like the end of a chain of reasoning, but like the extremity of this joy, of which God will make Himself the only object.

THE BOOK, THE SKY

On his nights of insomnia, Joubert goes outside and contemplates the sky. "*Insomni nocte* [on a sleepless night]." "Insomnia, 5 o'clock in the morning."[3] What do these nighttime thoughts bring him? The same thing that is inside him, but realized outwardly: the supreme book that it seems he will never write, and that he writes as if without knowing it, while *thinking* about writing it. Above there is space, and, farther and farther away, a condensation of space into light, a unified and ordered solitude of points, in which each seems to be unaware of the others, although there is composed with some of them a representation of which one has a premonition, along with all the unrepresentable wholeness of their dispersion. Joubert likes the stars, but even more than the stars, which often sparkle too brilliantly, he likes great, radiant space, the diffuse light that is slowly revealed in it and that reveals that easy simultaneity of distinct perfections, synthesis of the vague with the precise. In a note from his early adulthood, we see him trying to compose a cosmology rather close to that of Cyrano de Bergerac and the ancient authors, in which the stars are only holes in the sky, voids by which the enigma of a hidden light is collected and poured: space hollows, space no longer condensed but subtracted and diminished to the point of rupture, where it is made into clarity.

These metaphorical contemplations, which send us back to nocturnal space as if to a great text of silences, and to the book as if to an immobile sky of stars in movement, may seem within reach of everyone, but for Joubert they open up as the demanding expression of what he must accomplish.[4] An ambitious model, but one that does not crush this modest genius, for what is written on high guarantees him that he can represent it by means of art, if it is true that, withdrawn from ourselves, we can find in ourselves the same intimacy of space and light into which we must henceforth put all our cares so that our life will correspond to it, our thinking preserve it, and our works make it visible.

"And all my stars in one sky. . . . All space is my canvas. II. It falls to me from the stars of the mind."

It would be tempting, and would glorify Joubert, for us to imagine in him an untranscribed first edition of [Mallarmé's] *Un coup de dés* [A throw of the dice] which, as Valéry said on the day he was introduced to the secret thoughts of Mallarmé, "finally [raised] a page to the power of the starry sky." And there is between Joubert's dreams and the work realized a century later the foreshadowing of related demands: with Joubert, as with Mallarmé, the wish to replace ordinary reading (in which one must go from section to section) with the spectacle of simultaneous utterance, in which everything would be said at once, without confusion, in a "total, peaceful, intimate, and finally uniform splendor."[5] This supposes both a way of thinking completely different from that of logicians, who make their way from proof to proof, and also a language completely different from that of discourse (essential preoccupations for the author of the *Carnets*). Further, this more profoundly supposes the encounter with or creation of this space of vacancy where, no single thing coming to break the infinite, everything is present there as in nullity, a *place where nothing will take place except place*, the final goal of these two minds.

But there the community of intentions stops. Even if you look at it only from outside, the poem is given over in the immobility of its assertion to a prodigious movement that Joubert would do anything to avoid: movements of "retreats," "prolongations," "flights," movements that accelerate and slow down, divide and superimpose by a burgeoning animation all the more difficult to the mind since it does not unfold, does not develop, and, refusing the alleviation of succession, forces us to support all at once, in a massive though spaced effect, all the forms of the anxiety of this movement. Nothing could undermine Joubert's spiritual design more than this proliferation in the heart of absence, this infinitely undertaken going-and-coming that is the emptiness of indeterminate space.

Undoubtedly in *Un coup de dés*, as in the sky, there is a secret order that Joubert could welcome, but this order imitates chance, tries to enter into the intimacy of the game of chance, perhaps to penetrate its rules, perhaps to carry the rigor of words and the precision of thoughts to the point where the most determinate referent can integrate indeterminacy. No doubt there is, in the sky that is the poem, the still future and always uncertain brilliance of the "Constellation" that the poem will perhaps also be, at the altitude of exception. But Joubert could never accept the preliminary shipwreck in which nothing must be given so that something *could exist* other and purer than that which is. He would never regard as the descent toward "the unchanged neutrality of the abyss" the movement of incompleteness by which, in all things, we seek a void to find light.

Even the word "chance" is foreign to him. And the dramatic conjunction of the throw of dice and chance would seem to him incapable of representing thought at the level at which it meets poetry. That is the very point where his reflections are firmest. Joubert wants thought not to be determined, as reason can be. He wants it to rise above the constraint of reasoning and proof, he wants it to be finite thought starting from the infinite, just as he wants poetic language, in the perfection of its completion, to carry and support the vagueness, duplicity and ambiguity of several meanings, in order the better to represent the between-meaning and beyond-meaning toward which it is always oriented. But this indeterminacy is not chance. Chance has to do with that part of reality, vain and obvious, that reason—which is content only with proofs and wants to reduce everything to accounts—seeks to master by calculation.[6] The space in which Joubert ends is without chance and without determinacy, and literature, which is space turned into the ability to communicate, is this ordered sky of stars where the infinity of the sky is present in each star and where the infinity of stars does not hinder but rather makes perceptible the freedom of the infinitely empty expanse.

Such is the firm contradiction he sees harmoniously resolved up above, which he keeps coming up against and which, without reducing him to silence, will hold him back from any completed work. It is his merit to have recognized first in art and poetry a way of affirmation that neither an over-mediate reason nor too-immediate sensibility can vindicate. Poetry and art give him a presentiment of an entirely different possibility that he will seek all his life to clarify: a necessity of relationships even more rigorous than those of reason, but pure, light, and free; a contact with profound intimacy more acute than that of sensibility, and yet distanced, for that which is intimately touched by this unique point is distance itself experienced as our intimacy, and the distant in us experienced as our center. Relationships, then, that escape whatever temporal regularity there might be in the logical relations of reason, but that nonetheless do not escape the instantaneous shocks of perceptible presence: communication, at a distance and through distance, of the immediate; the finite, almost localized, affirmation of infinite immensity.

But how can one pass from the sky to the star, from the poem, unlimited fabric of space, to the pure and unique word where it must be assembled? Or from the beautiful, which is indeterminate, to the rigor of the perfection of the beautiful?[7] More than the solutions that Joubert sometimes proposes,[8] it is the care he always kept not to step aside from the opposing necessity of these two movements, even if it was at his own expense, that makes him important and sometimes exemplary. He seems to have been a failure. But he preferred this failure to the compromise of success. Outside of any aim of completion, he suffered considerably because of his devotion to the *intermittency* that he makes the *continuous* basis of the soul but which he must experience, in him, as a cessation of mind, a painful interruption of all ability, a fall into nothingness and no longer into the beautiful silent void. The confidences he shared are rare, but are there to be known (especially in letters: to Molé, to Fontanes, to Mme de Vintimille). And the *Carnets* gathered together the images under which he tried to approach his difficulties: "I am, I will admit, like an Aeolian harp, which makes some beautiful sounds but does not play any tune." "I am an Aeolian harp. No wind has breathed on me." The Aeolian harp: we understand that he welcomes this symbol derived from the Ossian craze, for it is like space itself, turned into both instrument and music, an instrument that has all the expanse and continuity of great space, but a music made of always discontinuous, disparate, and divided sounds. Moreover, it explains the breaks of his meditation and the blanks that interrupt his sentences by the tension he must maintain in his strings so that they resonate as they should, by the easing that results from this harmony, and by the long time he needs to "wind up and retune."

This collaboration of time, this encounter (necessary for him to be able to write) of inner space with outer space, is what led him to think only in the framework of a journal, relying on the movement of the days and requiring of this movement the passage from himself to himself—to the expression of himself—of which he is the patient, often disappointed, expectation, just as the harp is the silent expectation of the wind. Responding, once again, to the impatience of his friends, he finds this new reason for his delay: "And, moreover, my clouds must be allowed to amass and condense." That is indeed the problem of the sky and the star, the great enigma of *Un coup de dés*, which must be at once the identical neutrality of the abyss, the high vacancy of the sky, and the constellation that, at the altitude of a perhaps, is projected there. And in order for clouds to amass and condense, there must be time, there must be a double labor of transformation by time: first that time transmute events and impressions into the distance of memory (and Joubert says: "One must not express oneself as one feels, but as one remembers"), then that it concentrate the vague distance of memory into the starry essence of a pure moment, which is no longer real and which is not fictive (and Joubert says: "My memory now preserves only the essence of what I read, of what I see, and even of what I think"). This is a metamorphosis that he cannot hurry by the force of his will, for it does not depend on this imperious "I" that it must precisely lighten and hollow out so that the intimacy of the outside and the space of the inside can meet there in a unique contact. Joubert thus lies in wait, expecting from time the passage to space, and also expecting from time the concentration of space into a pure, essential moment, into that drop of light that will become word and that, in the sealed transparency of the word, will collect in one unique saying the entire expanse of all language.[9] It is an expectation in which, at the same time, he must not lose interest, in which he must cooperate by an interior labor in which his whole life participates and, even more, by a great intimacy with words, since it is perhaps in them—limit of time and space— that we can most truly act, there where, he says profoundly, "there is . . . at once potency and impossibility."

REST IN LIGHT

If Joubert abandoned nothing that seemed to him necessary, it still must be added that he knew how to interpret this situation so as to find in it, in the end, wisdom, calm, and perhaps appeasement. In that, he followed the inclination of his cautious genius, without disturbing too much the course of his researches. When he writes: "The revolution drove my mind out of the actual world by making it too horrible to me" (he was first a revolutionary—without excess—and atheist—without a crisis of conscience), he also points out why he always sought to establish between himself and things that "zone of contemplation" "where everything passes, is calmed, slows down, becomes tranquil, and subdues its own excesses." Now it is no longer as if to a difficult demand that he exposes himself to separation and distance, but to make himself an "enclosure" that protects him, a quietness that "cushions the ramparts," "an alcove," a defense "to deaden shocks" and "to put the heart at rest." "Rest [*repos*]"—this word accompanied him all his life. As a revolutionary, he seeks rest in negation. To Mme de Beaumont, he says: "Have rest in love, in worship." Then the great theme to which he will direct his thought is this: "Rest in light." He formulated it at the beginning of the *Carnets*. He says it at the end and sometimes repeats it from day to day in the manner of a prayer or a magic spell: "(Bitter. Bitter pains.) Wisdom is rest in light" (October 22, 1821). October 24: "And for the last time, I hope. Wisdom is rest in light." Why this obsessive repetition? It is because there, in the density of a few words, can be found the two trends of his thought, and also the ambiguity of a thought with two trends, for rest in light can be, can tend to be, peace by means of light, a light that calms and gives peace, but it is also rest—privation of all aid and outer impulses—so that nothing can come to disturb or pacify the pure movement of light.[10]

Need for light, great need for daylight, for this spacious opening that is the day ("Without space, no light") and for this point of unique clarity that makes the day and gives day ("Luminous point. Seek it in everything. It's never just in one word in a sentence, just in one idea in a conversation"). Aversion for everything that is obscure, impenetrable, opaque: "An obscure point in his mind is as unbearable to him as a grain of sand in his eye." "Narrow? Yes, I am narrowest in the part of the head destined to receive things that are not clear." Too narrow perhaps, for it is this distancing from obscurity that makes him also turn away from the day, from whatever there is that is too lively in the dawning day, to which he prefers, he will say in a revealing thought, half-light: "Half-light is charming, for it is a gentle and diminished day. But dawn is less so, for it is not yet day. It is still only a beginning or, as the excellent idiom goes, 'the tip,' at break of day."[11] What he wants is "a medium light," an expression in which he lingers to confirm his taste for measure, but that he also seeks to make more profound, calling it medium not only because it is measured, but also because we always lack half of it: it is a divided light, then, and one that divides us, so that it is in this painful division of ourselves that we must repose our contentment.

Rest in light: is that the sweet appeasement by light? Is it the hard privation of oneself and of all movement, position in light without rest? A mere nothing [*un rien*] separates here two infinitely different experiences. It is still Joubert's fascination to remind us, by his privileged example, how essential, but difficult, it is always to maintain firmly this *nothing* that divides thought.

§ 7 Claudel and the Infinite

I do not know who this Claudel is, the man his reputation tells us of: this simple man, one of the Men of Old, indissolubly linked to an unwavering faith, without secret and without doubt, elemental genius that asserts itself impetuously within the bounds of a public functionary lavished with honors.

Man of old? He is an almost exaggeratedly modern man. All modern thought, from Descartes to Hegel and Nietzsche, is an exaltation of wanting, an effort to make the world, to complete it and dominate it. Humankind is a great sovereign power, capable of the universe and, by the development of science, by the understanding of the unknown resources that are within us, capable of making everything and of making all. These formulae charged with audacity, before which today we recoil, remained familiar to him till the end (more Renan than Renan in this), and when Amrouche questions him on his need to be understood, "integrated" into creation, Claudel rudely answers: "Well, *my* idea has always been that we were not made to be included, as you say, within creation, but to conquer it. . . . It is, rather, a struggle: it seems to me perfectly possible and natural to gain the upper hand, not to be included but to surmount." The man who speaks thus from the depths of his being is a man in whom the Middle Ages have been silent for centuries.

He does not want to be conquered. He has a great terror, not ruthless but almost timorous, almost pathological, of the conquered. Those who fail and are lost awaken in him almost a memory of shame and a feeling of unease that makes him tremble: Nietzsche, Villiers, Verlaine and, closer to him, his sister, and even closer, in himself, that failure always possible for the man on whom the misfortune of being an artist has fallen. As if to fail were the real sin, the essential evil. To succeed is the law of his being and the sign of the amplitude of his affirmation. He is neither a Renaissance man, happy to be a brilliant and transient individual, nor a Romantic, who is content to desire in vain and aspire without fruit. He is the modern man, the one who is certain only of what he touches, cares not about himself but rather about what he does, wants not dreams but results, for whom nothing counts except the work and the decisive fulfillment of the work. He must have proofs of this success. He is not a man to solicit them, but he suffers if they are lacking; he cannot be satisfied with an inner certainty: what good is a masterpiece no one knows anything about? So he is wounded by silence, battered by incomprehension, happy with the evidence of fame, but even happier with whatever solid and palpable quality this fame has. Possessions, honors, all that attaches him to reality and helps him make what he has made into a sure, complete, verifiable world—that is what matters to him, not the great enchantments of literary vanity and the apotheoses that he welcomes but which please him only very briefly.

Success simplifies. To the elusive diversity of Gide, some have been pleased (and Gide above all) to contrast the monolith, the being without joints and almost without parts, which at any moment could have made Claudel into a static explosion and a motionless fury. Did he himself like this image? There is none more picturesque, and none more wrong. What strikes one about him is an essential dissonance, the powerful, contained, poorly contained, clash of impulses without harmony, a formidable mixture of contradictory needs, contrary demands, mismatched qualities and irreconcilable aptitudes. Impetuous, but very slow; as void of patience as he is gifted with obstinacy; as abrupt as he is prudent; without method and intimately ordered; without moderation but excess is unbearable to him; a man of crises: in an instant, in his life, everything takes shape, and is undone; in an instant, he converts; later, when he wants to break with his career and his work, one single instant, one single word, the "No" he thinks he hears, are enough to drive him back into the world; not long afterwards, the meeting with Ysé, passion, the jubilation of sin, all history at the quickness of a storm: it is a lightning decision, the edge of the moment. This man of crises, then, never going back, is converted once and for all, but he needs four years to begin to learn that he is, twelve years to take possession of this change and to expose himself to the radical rupture that this conversion demands. Similarly, he will need twenty-five years to assimilate what plays out in a few instants on the bridge of a boat, and to succeed in calming its violence. He is, certainly, essentially an inspired poet, whom the wild visit of the undisciplined Muse awaits and surprises, without whom he can do nothing, and yet it is with the greatest regularity that he writes, with the application of a man who reasonably does his duty and almost, as he says, with the assurance of a bureaucrat.

Tempestuous genius, utterly divided, yet he does not seem torn apart. What divides him increases him and, even more, increases his faith in himself, in his growth. But does this happen without a struggle? Without difficulties? Is there no suffering? Is he only this man of certainty, with a hard, firm optimism, that he gives the appearance of being? A large part of his life was without happiness and without grace. He has said that his youth was unhappy, marked by the knowledge of death and the feeling of abandonment. He has said that, utterly eager to travel the world and break all ties with his family and acquaintances, he nonetheless suffered a great deal from this rupture and, having left, suffered from being ever after in exile everywhere, at home as well as abroad. He is a man profoundly alone, "without wife and without son," for a long time unable to enter into society with others and perhaps with himself. In *Tête d'or* [Golden head], we hear only the song of exaltation of wanting and of young desire, a song, in effect, of conquering ardor; but this ardor is somber, the essence of this wanting is foreign to the happy immensity that it uselessly attains. *Partage de midi* [Break at noon] left us with the image of a separated man, "sinister," who does not find companionship with men, is not in harmony with himself, and remains in the embarrassed rigidity of his great strengths without employment, his great eagerness useless, entrenching himself fiercely, proud and poor, without knowing that he must be broken to become himself.

If he gives the impression that only impersonal feelings are close to him, that he is, like nature, a living force, almost deprived of intimacy and always occupied with expressing this movement of life and feeling it, not as a suffering, but as an infinitely increasing fullness, if he seems, to a surprising degree, foreign to the alienated consciousness that for 150 years has marked our time, our believing time and our nonbelieving time, that does not prove that he knew, from the beginning, how to live and speak without difficulties and without divisions, as a man of faith for whom all problems are resolved, poet whom instinct and talent wonderfully carry and

transport. He is not so. But it remains true that, far from willingly keeping himself close to himself, he on the contrary turns away from himself
with resolute aversion. He does not watch himself suffer, and he does not
want others to look at him. He has a horror of this gaze, which is like the
vision of the void and the visibility of nothingness. He seems to know that
the destructive power of conscience, its displaced intervention, its tormented, tormenting curiosity, would be enough to send him to his ruin,
and to undo what he calls with a stubborn, indestructible faith the simple
core of himself under the pressure of his violently divided, contradictory
powers. That is one of his secrets. Problems, difficulties, sufferings, he carries them in himself rather than reflecting on them or feeling them; he undergoes their heaviness, their weight and pressure [*la pesée et la poussée*]; he
lets them develop on their own and he develops in them. Nature must be
left to its work or helped only by that other natural work [*travail*] which
is the poetic work [*oeuvre*] in which the various struggling forms of his
vast divided "I," from which he wishes to take nothing, refuse nothing, always meet, like separate characters who come to life, provoke each other,
and clash against each other.

Obviously, more than anyone else, more than Gide, who was less threatened by the suppleness of his fluid nature, he needed a system capable of
sorting himself out. It is easy, then, to think that, if he clings unwaver-
ingly to a religious dogmatism that surprises even the most fervent believers of today, it is because of this coherence that he finds in it. No
doubt. But let us also think of the man that he is, gifted with the greatest
possessive forces, animated by an extreme energy, who is never content
with promises of a vague beyond, but who wants to see everything, have
everything, and appropriate everything, who is linked to the earth, who
has "in the marrow of his bones" "that obstinacy with earth," "that cold
taste for the earth," that demand for visible things and for the present
universe, who wants to sacrifice nothing of himself, who repels defeat
with all his strength and, with all his strength, aspires to victory and domination—and what is offered to him? A religion of weakness, of the humiliated and the conquered, which recommends asceticism, poverty, the
sacrifice of self, abandonment of the world, and the desire for the infinite.
How will he make do with this gift? It is a grandiose gift, but one that
first proposes to take him radically away from himself, and this at the very
dawn of life, when he was unable to assure himself by proofs of what he
was and what he was worth. A less natural man would have responded

right away, with a sudden impulse, to this sudden call. But Claudel remains as if immobile, seems not to answer, answers with silence, with a sort of sleep that leaves him whole. The works that he writes at the time scarcely bear the trace of this fundamental change. *Tête d'or* pushes away all faith in the beyond, all superhuman illusion. *Connaissance de l'Est* [Knowledge of the East] drops hints so we guess the slowness of the steps he must take to bring himself to the point at which he will have to put himself, and everything, at risk. These descriptive prose pieces, beautiful but hard and imperious, hide an extreme struggle, and they truly hide it. We sometimes get the impression that Claudel is not so much converted as trying to convert his conversion into the resources for his powerful nature: he is a tree struck by lightning but which doesn't burn, which wants only to grow green again through the fire. But is that possible? Crisis is inevitable.

"THE INFINITE, THAT HORRIFYING WORD"

It is inevitable because Claudel, beside this great possessive strength, harbors an exceptional aversion for the limitless and undefined. This is the case to an extraordinary degree. It is all the more remarkable, since he is not weak but powerful, that he should be annoyed by limits and want to take all boundaries in stride. And it is indeed true that he wants everything, nothing more, and in this everything, only each thing, one by one, already formed, already created, a solid reality he can appropriate and know. He wants everything, the certainty of everything, not the origin, not that which is yet to be but the present universe, the world in its limits, closed and circumscribed, where nothing is lost, which he can count, measure, and confirm by his permanent language. Even if he is linked to desire, Claudel is first the present man and the man of the present; he speaks only in the present; there is always for him, in whatever is there, enough of being so that he can rejoice in it, glorify it, and provoke it, by his language, to even more being. But what is this present to which he wants to correspond by tumultuous pressure? Is it the instant, "that hour that is between spring and summer," of which the *Cantate* [Cantata] will sing? Is it the moment of bliss? Of happiness that one seizes and tastes, carefree or in ecstasy? Nothing is more contrary to him, we know well. For he wants the present to be present for him, not to lose himself in it. Just as he has a horror of the indeterminate, he has a horror and loathing of drowning in pantheism; and the present is made not just so one can be absorbed in it and be happy with it, but also so that one can nourish one-self from it, develop it, and surpass it by a progressive growth and ever-widening development. Will he be content, then, with a spiritual appro-priation, possessing each present thing in its form or touching only its surface? He needs more: he wants not only to see but to have, to possess with his entire being the entire being down to its substance. He thus be-comes the elemental poet. "The element itself! The first matter! It is the sea, I say, that I need"—and the solid, primordial earth, the "Earth of Earth, the breast's abundance," "the burning dark blood," "the plasma that labors and destroys, that transports and shapes," the voluminous abundance, all that is enormous, and not only clear flowing water but "the peaty flood," "impregnated with the substance of the Earth," knowl-edge of which the rivers of China brought him, "current that with a heav-ier burden flees toward the deepest center of an ever enlarged circle" (which is the very definition of the present that suits him: the present for him is not a point, but the constant circular flowering of the being in per-petual vibration).

But, if one gives in to this impulse, doesn't he risk getting bogged down in the formless, possessing everything but dissolved at the heart of everything, "Chaos that has not received the Gospel"? Of the ini-tial indistinctness, he wants no more than he wants of nothingness. This profound genius intends, in his profundity, to consent neither to the abyss of the void nor to the uncertainty of origin: to lose noth-ing of the composition of things, all kept together by the powerful agreement of poetic simultaneity, and of such a nature that he can count them in their unity and their relationships, like a Biblical pa-triarch counting the multitude of his herds where he praises the coin-cidence of earthly richness and heavenly benediction. Claudel is a surprising mixture of elemental comprehension and formal prefer-ence: sometimes profound—and he tends to "be drawn into the ele-ment itself,"—sometimes only vast and seeking to win an elevated point (by image or by faith), not to lose sight of finite reality but on the contrary to be able to contemplate it in its entirety and in its de-tails and, "eye fixed like a crow," to study "the contour and structure of the earth, the disposition of slopes and planes." Still, it seems that in him the broad wins out over the deep: in the compact and the ele-mental, there is a possibility of landslide, a loss of proportion that he will never accept without distress.

The "Infinite," that horrifying Word that clashes with life and the bold march of power and the joy of love. Coventry Patmore says this in Claudel's translation. Claudel felt this horror for the infinite, expressed with an impressive constancy and force. "The infinite is everywhere for the mind the same abomination and the same scandal." "Blessed art thou, my God, . . . who made me a *finite* being. . . . You placed in me relation and proportion once and for all." "We have understood the world and we have found that our creation is finite." And to Amrouche: "All that is boundless is destructive." Similarly, the goal of poetry is not what Baudelaire would have wanted it to be—to plunge into the heart of the infinite[1] to find the new—but "to plunge into the heart of the definite to find there the inexhaustible."

Naturally Claudel corrects, with words, the inconvenient quality his refusal of the Infinite entails for religion: "I speak of the Infinite in things that are of finite nature." But the feeling remains. Anguish, the experience of night and even the experience of pure light, like pure Space—that is what finds in his nature a resistance that does not seem able to be broken. He does not shirk the extreme of poetry any less than the extreme of faith. After his conversion and until the time of his crisis, what seems to keep him apart from what he believes is, strange to say, the very certainty of his belief, the fear of being lost, the fear of entering into contact with Evil and, to sum it up, the ignorance of that death that is sin. From religion, he tends, then, to welcome only reinforcing assurances, not shock and ruinous questionings: being, not being that has nothingness for its face.

The prose pieces of *Connaissance de l'Est* show how little by little he is going to be forced, not without a great inner hesitation, to approach and explore these formidable nocturnal regions and the no less formidable ardors of luminous nudity. The ordeal of the sea, with which he feels complicit, plays a role in this struggle against himself. "Pensée en mer" [Thought at sea], "Risque de la mer" [Risk of the sea], "La terre quittée" [Land quitted], "Dissolution"—these titles mark the stages of the secret itinerary by which he learns to know exile, exterior and interior exile, and to discover himself "an intruder in the uninhabitable."[2] Knowledge of nullity by the sea: "Carried away, toppled over in the collapse and tumult of the incomprehensible Sea, lost in the lapping of the Abyss, the mortal man with all his weight seeks whatever is solid to hold onto." "There is no solidity around me, I am situated in chaos, I am lost in the interior of Death. . . . I have lost my proportion, I travel through the Indifferent. I am at the mercy of elations of the depths and of the Wind, the force of the Void." A little later, it is the heart of darkness that he will be close to entering, there where "night takes away the proof we exist," when "we no longer know where we are," and where "our vision has no longer the visible as a limit but the invisible as prison, homogeneous, immediate, indifferent, compact," the indeterminate, then, for which he feels repulsion and anguish, anguish that betrays itself in him only by the refusal and dissimulation of anguish. This proof of himself that the night takes from him is the important moment, for the proof—the possibility of fixing his position at any moment—counts for a lot with him. And no doubt "the risk of the sea" does nothing but lead him back to life, to gratitude for not being dead and for not having drunk the bitter Water. (We should note also how much his language, even when he is approaching cessation, where everything is dissolved, remains firm, closed, all the more categorical since it must serve as a receptacle for limitless and formless dissipation.) Claudel does not abandon himself easily and, moreover, all these movements are secret, scarcely visible under the fabric of a hard, objective prose. And crisis itself, well known as it is to us in its contours, remains today still covered over and hidden.

"I AM THE IMPOSSIBLE"

At a certain moment, Claudel decides to make an end to his career and even to his work, and to renounce this world, the conquest of which he had barely begun. It is an extraordinary decision on the part of such a man, who never believed in the virtue of all-or-nothing. But the most extraordinary thing is that this impressive decision is not essential in the self-transformation to which he is exposing himself. What finally troubles him, tears him away from what he is, leaves him "with an afflicted heart, with a damaged strength," is that this great sacrifice does not *succeed*, it clashes with a superior "No" that echoes in him like the expression of his personal defeat. We could say that for the first time he knows failure. A decision into which he had put his entire being (perhaps with too personal a will, too swaggering)[3] does not reach its goal, and teaches him that he was not capable of reaching the end of what he wants. Thus he discovers destitution and distress, not at having been separated from everything, but at not having been able to separate himself from himself: bitter knowledge of powerlessness, of that nothingness for which he is poorly prepared.

However, it is still a matter here of only passive shadows, of a lack that, leaving him distraught but intact, preserves the form of his powerful personality. The decisive event will be one we know well: the stormy forbidden passion by which he will suddenly, this Mesa, closed to goodness as to a treasure of which he proudly thinks himself the depository, be attacked by active shadows, "shadows that leap on you like a panther" and, with one single movement, seized by perdition, will become guilty and loving. What is wonderful in this story, what demonstrates the magnificence of the Claudelian nature, which we accuse of pharisaism, is that, far from falling into the sorrowful ruminations of remorse at having committed the grievous sin of becoming attached to a woman married to another, the poet in him and, it seems, the believer in him, experiences an intense feeling of jubilation and triumph. He has done what he had never before been able to do. He has confronted night, broken boundaries, thrown himself into the abyss, accepting losing himself to rejoin someone else.

> And I too, I found it in the end, the death that I needed! I have known this woman. I have known the death of woman.

> I have possessed interdiction.

Language of fullness, purer than that of "Cantique de Mesa" [Song of Mesa], in which there were still traces of self-absorption.[4] "I possessed interdiction." That is the point at which everything begins, at which poetry can also begin, return to its source, by fleeing back to the open, empty space, "pure Space where the sun itself is light."

"What do you fear from me since I am the impossible? Are you afraid of me? I am the impossible." That is Ysé's challenge, but it is first of all the challenge and provocation of poetry. In this woman he will come to call false[5] to contrast her with Wisdom, but who alone succeeded in breaking the strongest "I," Claudel immediately recognizes, in a hymn of jubilant gratitude, pure poetic power, the one who does not suffer from limit, Erato:

> O my friend! O Muse in the wind and the sea! O long-haired
>   idea at the prow!
> O grief! O vindication!
> Erato! You look at me, and I read a resolution in your eyes!
> I read an answer, I read a question in your eyes! An answer and a
>   question in your eyes!

Memorable encounter, discovery of the very essence of poetry: the answer that is still a question, the question that always lives again in the answer to keep it open, living, and eternally beginning. This crisis thus concerns poetry no less than faith,[6] and we understand why, for so many years, Claudel will explore it, trying to keep himself at that summit of torment and truth where it placed him. That he resists it is true. That he takes hold again and gets a grip on himself, choosing to be a balanced, prudent, and successful man, he will soon decide on, but he won't be mistaken about the infidelity that a conversion converted into a marriage represents in relation to that great moment. The dialogue of 1907 (when he is already married and established) with *La muse qui est la Grâce* is a dialogue that fortunately will not have an end, even if it increasingly restricts itself to the reserved part of himself, that secret part that does not endure being bogged down in serious duties, or even in a work of knowledge in which, as a writer, he will keep track of only real, true things.

THE OTHER LANGUAGE

This dialogue is the purest—truest—expression of Claudelian division. On one hand, he is a being of power, will, and mastery, who wants the world, who wants to fulfill his duties in the world, intends to make a useful work and a visible work and not to give in to the temptation of a language that might be vain, ruinous, and incapable of being grasped. "I have with difficulty managed to be a man, used to the things that don't come free, / And that one must seize to have them, learn them, understand them [*prendre, apprendre, comprendre*]." "I have a duty that is not fulfilled! A duty toward all things, there is not one / To which I am not obliged," "my duty is not to go away, nor to be elsewhere, nor to let go of any thing that I hold." For this man full of duty, a full, solid, and actual language is suitable: it is a question not of renouncing speaking, but of drawing the poet to consideration of finite things that are the praise of humanity: "Let me sing of the works of men and let each one find in my lines those things that are known to him. . . . For what use is the writer, if not to keep accounts?" Language of domination and energy (a theory of which he will willingly create: for him, the word is essentially a carrier of energy, and is a condensation of the energy of feeling). "Speech is in its place intelligence and will." "I will sing the great poem of man rescued from chance. . . . I will do it with a poem that will be no longer the adventure of Ulysses among the Lestrygonians and the Cyclops, but the knowledge of Earth. . . . "

An important work, then, and one that seems more typically Claudel than others. And yet there is another language: this one gives nothing, brings nothing but solitude, retreat, separation; it is without knowledge, without result; the one who speaks it does not know it, knows only its weight, its pressure, its infinite demand, speech that is not human, that comes not to the capable man, but to the one who sees himself all of a sudden alone, "detached, refused, abandoned." Will Claudel not try to demean this language so contrary to himself, so foreign to what he wants and what he believes? Will he not prove it wrong? He prefers it. He resists it, being unable to renounce himself, and, in the end, dismisses it, but he prefers it. Everything that is poetry in him is complicit with the very thing that he refuses, which is purity, a rigor to which he sees desperately that he cannot conform.

> O part! O reserved one! O inspirer! O reserved part of myself!
>   O anterior part of myself!
> O passion of Speech! O retreat! O terrible solitude! O separation
>   from all men!
> O death of myself and of everything, in whom I must suffer
>   creation!
> O sister! O conductor! O pitiless one, how much more time? . . .
> O work of myself in pain! O work of this world in representing
>   you!
> As on sheets rolling off the press one sees in successive layers
> The separate parts appear of a design that does not yet exist, . . .
> Thus I work and will never know what I have done, thus the
>   mind with a mortal spasm
> Throws speech outside of itself like a spring that never knows
> Anything other than its pressure and the weight of the sky.

And this supplication, in which the Claudelian split is pathetically expressed, through a cry, the opposition, in himself, of one language destined to assert it and of that other language that is the silent expiration, the work of consummation by fire, the extermination of Noon:

> Say only a human word!

My name only in the ripeness of Earth, in this sun of
    Hymenaean night,
And not one of those terrible words without a sound that you
    communicate to me only one
Like a cross so my mind will stay fastened to it!

There we have the highest testimony of Claudel and also the proof that, giving in to himself, returning to earth, it is "desperately" that he returns.

Go away! I turn back desperately to earth!
Go away! You will not take away from me this cold taste for the
    earth. . . .

He chooses, then, not wanting only to be chosen, but he chooses what he does not prefer, without thinking himself justified, and without hoping ever to be at peace. For years he will always have to hear this irreconcilable, irreducible voice; and what does it say to him, each time, "withdrawn down to the solid ground," as he asserts, even in beautiful works, the happiness of contradictions surmounted? "Do not attempt to pull the wool over my eyes. Do not try to give me the world in your place, / For it is you yourself I require. Know my jealousy, which is more terrible than death!" Jealousy of pure light, which can only consume everything, but jealousy also of night itself in the splendor of the work of August. It is on the mysterious understanding of nocturnal profundity that the dialogue is completed, and by an obscure return, obscure perhaps to the poet himself, to the forbidden figure, the silent presence from below, which is neither the solid goodness of the earth nor grace, the desire of the spirit, but the power of dark passion, which alone allowed him before to cross boundaries, joined him to night and gave him, at the same time as the revelation of the impossible, the joy and drunkenness of the unknown:

Who cried out? I hear a cry in the deep night!
I hear my ancient sister of the shadows who comes back up one
    more time toward me,
The nocturnal wife who returns one more time to me without
    saying a word,
One more time to me with her heart, like a meal shared in the
    darkness,
Her heart like a bread of pain and like a vase full of tears.

Profound, eternal call, in the depths of Hell, from Eurydice to Orpheus, call that will not cease and which, even in the bosom of the Enclosed House ["La Maison Fermée"], when he will be watched over by the great foursquare Muses, the four cardinal powers, severe guardians of his doors, he will never be allowed to escape:[7] "Whoever has tasted blood, will never take nourishment again from brilliant water or ardent honey! Whoever has loved a human soul, whoever once has been close to the other living soul, he remains trapped by it forever."

§ 8 Prophetic Speech

The word "prophet"—borrowed from the Greek to designate a condition foreign to Greek culture[1]—would deceive us if it invited us to make the *nabi* the one who speaks the future. Prophecy is not just a future language. It is a dimension of language that engages it in relationships with time that are much more important than the simple discovery of certain events to come. To foresee and announce some future event does not amount to much, if this future takes place in the ordinary course of events and finds expression in the regularity of language. But prophetic speech announces an impossible future, or makes the future it announces, because it announces it, something impossible, a future one would not know how to live and that must upset all the sure givens of existence. When speech becomes prophetic, it is not the future that is given, it is the present that is taken away, and with it any possibility of a firm, stable, lasting presence. Even the Eternal City and the indestructible Temple are all of a sudden—unbelievably—destroyed. It is once again like the desert, and speech also is desert-like, this voice that needs the desert to cry out and that endlessly awakens in us the terror, understanding, and memory of the desert.

THE DESERT AND THE OUTSIDE

Prophetic speech is a wandering speech that returns to the original demand of movement by opposing all stillness, all settling, any taking root that would be rest. André Neher notes that the return to the desert glimpsed by the prophets of the eighth century was the spiritual counterpart to the return to the desert practiced by the Rekabites [nomadic sects]

of the ninth century, themselves faithful to nomadic aspirations that have
been transmitted without interruption. This is a unique phenomenon in
the history of civilizations, he notes.[2] And we are not unaware that the
one tribe without territory, the Levites, represented and maintained
among the other, definitively fixed tribes the premonition of a mobile existence. Just as the Hebrews had been only sojourners in Egypt, refusing
the temptation of a closed world where they could have had the illusion
of freeing themselves in situ by a slave statute, and just as they began to
exist only in the desert, freed by having taken to the road in a solitude in
which they were no longer alone, so it was necessary that, having become
in turn possessors and dwellers, masters of a rich space, there would always be among them a remnant that possessed nothing, that was the
desert itself, that place without place where alone the Covenant can be
concluded and to which one must always turn as to that moment of
nakedness and separation that is at the origin of true existence.

Neher profoundly connects this nomadic spirit with the refusal to "val-
orize space" and with an affirmation of time that would be the mark of
the genius of Israel, since its relations with God are not timeless relations
but make place for history, are history. No doubt, but we wonder if the
experience of the desert and the recollection of nomadic days when the
land was only promised might not express a more complex, more anguishing, and less determined experience. The desert is still not time, or
space, but a space without place and a time without production. There
one can only wander, and the time that passes leaves nothing behind; it is
a time without past, without present, time of a promise that is real only in
the emptiness of the sky and the sterility of a bare land where man is never
there but always outside. The desert is this outside, where one cannot remain, since to be there is to be always already outside, and prophetic
speech is that speech in which the bare relation with the Outside could be
expressed, with a desolate force, when there are not yet any *possible* relations, primal powerlessness, wretchedness of hunger and cold, which is
the principle of the Covenant, that is to say, of an exchange of speech
from which the surprising justice of reciprocity emerges.[3]

Prophets are indeed constantly mingled with history, whose immense
measure they alone provide. There is nothing symbolic, nothing figurative
in what they say, no more than the desert is an image, but the desert of
Arabia, a place that is geographically localized, while still being also the
way out without a way out to which the exodus always leads. If prophetic

speech is mixed, however, with the fracas of history and the violence of its movement, if it makes the prophet a historical character charged with a heavy temporal weight, it seems that it is essentially linked to a momentary interruption of history, to history become an instant of impossibility of history, a voice where catastrophe hesitates to turn into salvation, where in the fall already the ascension and return begin. Terrible passage through negation, when God himself is negative. "For you are Not-My-People, and I am Not-God for you." And Hosea engenders non-children who, later on, become children again. When everything is impossible, when the future, given over to the fire, burns, when there is no more rest except in the land of midnight, then prophetic speech, which tells of the impossible future, also tells of the "nonetheless" that breaks the impossible and restores time. "Indeed, I will hand over this city and this country to the hands of the Chaldeans; they will enter it, they will set it on fire and reduce it to ashes, and *nevertheless*, I will bring back the inhabitants of this city and this country from all the countries where I have exiled them. They will be my people, I will be their God." *Nevertheless* [*pourtant*]! *Laken*! Unique word by which prophetic speech accomplishes its work and frees its essence: it is a sort of eternal sending on a journey, but only there where the journey stops and it is no longer possible to go forward.[4] So we can say: speech prophesies when it refers to a time of interruption, that *other* time that is always present in all time and in which people, stripped of their power and separated from the possible (the widow and the orphan), exist with each other in the bare relationship in which they had been in the desert and which is the desert itself—bare relationship, but not unmediated, for it is always given in a prior speech.

"MY INCESSANT SPEECH"

André Neher has gathered together the most persistent traits of prophetic existence: scandal and argument. "No Peace," says God. The "No-Peace" of prophecy contrasts as well with spatial priesthood—the sort that knows only the time for rites, and for which the earth and the Temple are places needed for the Covenant—as with profane wisdom. It is a speech that is thus scandalous, but that is scandal first for the prophet. Suddenly a man becomes other. Jeremiah, gentle and sensitive, must become a pillar of fire, a rampart of bronze, for he will have to condemn and destroy all that he loves. Isaiah, decent and respectable, must strip off his clothes: for three years, he walks naked. Ezekiel, scrupulous priest who was never lacking in purity, feeds himself on food cooked in excrement and soils his body. To Hosea, the Eternal says, "Marry a woman of whoredom; let her give you a prostitute's children, for the country is prostituting itself," and this is not an image. Marriage itself prophesies. Prophetic speech is heavy. Its heaviness is the sign of its authenticity. It is not a question of letting one's heart speak, or of saying what pleases the freedom of the imagination. False prophets are pleasant and agreeable: amusers (artists), rather than prophets. But prophetic speech imposes itself from outside, it is the Outside itself, the weight and suffering of the Outside.

Thence the refusal that accompanies the calling. Moses: "Send whomever you want. Why have you sent me? Erase me from the book you have written." Elijah: "Enough." And Jeremiah's cry: "Ah, ah, Eternal Lord, I do not know how to speak, I am just a child.—Do not tell me 'I am just a child.' But go where I sent you and speak as I command." Jonah's refusal is pushed even further. It is not only the calling that he flees, it is God, dialogue with God. If God tells him: rise and go toward the East, he rises and goes toward the West. In order better to flee, he takes to the sea, and to hide himself better, he goes down into the ship's hold, then he sinks into sleep, then into death. In vain. Death is not an end for him, but only a form of that distance he sought in order to distance himself from God, forgetting that distance from God is God himself.[5] If the prophet does not feel prepared to be so, he sometimes has the troubling feeling that God is not ready either, that there is "a sort of divine lack of preparation." Defeat in the face of the absurdity of what he says, what happens and what is linked to that time of interruption and alteration where everything that happens, the impossible, always is already changed into its opposite. He repeats: "Why?" He experiences tiredness, disgust and, says Neher, an actual nausea. There is in the prophet a strange revolt against the lack of seriousness in God: "And it is thou, Eternal Lord, who tells me that!"

Prophetic speech is originally dialogue. It is so in a spectacular manner when the prophet converses with God and when God "confides in him not only his message but his anxiety." "Am I going to hide from Abraham," says God, "what I am going to do?"[6] But it is dialogue in a more essential way, in that it only repeats the speech confided to it, an affirmation in which by a beginning word something that has actually already been said is expressed. That is its originality. It is first, and yet there is always before it already a speech to which it answers by repeating it. As if all

speech that begins began by answering, an answer in which is heard, in order to be led back to silence, the speech of the Outside that does not
cease: "My incessant Word," says God. God, when he speaks, needs to
hear his own speech—thus become response—repeated in the man in
whom it can only assert itself and who becomes responsible for it. There
is no contact of thoughts or translation into words of the inexpressible divine thought, only exchange of speech.[7] And no doubt it is a matter of
God, but *Exodus* says: "As a man speaks to another man!"

The relationship of God to a man by a speech that is repeated and yet
entirely other, having become its own answer, the understanding of itself
and its infinite realization, perpetually in movement, introduces into
prophetic language an ensemble of contradictory qualities from which it
draws the extent of its meaning: relationships bound and free, a word that
is eaten, a word that is a fire, a hammer, a word that seizes, devastates, and
engenders, but at the same time a word that is spirit and the maturity of
the spirit, a true speech that one can hear or refuse to hear, that demands
obedience and questioning, submission and knowledge, and in the space
of which there is the truth of an encounter, the surprise of a confrontation, "as of one man with another man." What Neher calls the *ruach* (the
spirit and the breath), whether its mystery is to cover all levels of signification, from supreme spirituality to physical emanation, from purity to
impurity—the *ruach* of God is pathetic—is no less true for the mystery of
speech, *davar*, while still making it an essentially spoken relation, from
which inner magic and mystical fusion are almost excluded. Language
that is not spiritual and that nonetheless is spirit. Speech of movement,
powerful and without power, active and separate from action, in which,
as in Jeremiah's dream, nothing outlines the future if not the rhythm of
the march, the men en route, the immense motion of an impossible return.[8] Language of transport and of being carried away. Something here is
unfurling in the abrupt, rending, exalting, and monotonous violence of a
perpetual taking-to-task of man in the confines of his power.

TO THE LETTER

To what extent can we welcome this language? The difficulty is not only
in translation. If it is of a rhetorical nature, it is because its moral origin,
linked to an implicit obligation, even for unbelievers, of believing that
Christian spirituality, Platonic idealism, and the whole symbolism with
which our poetic literature is impregnated give us the right of possession

and interpretation of this language that might have found its completion not in it but in the advent of better tidings. If what the prophets announce is actually Christian culture, then it is perfectly legitimate to read them starting from our own sense of delicacy and security, most notably that truth is henceforth sedentary and firmly established. The peasant wisdom of Alain rejoiced that the Bible was unknown to Catholics, and the exceptional injustice that Simone Weil shows with regard to Jewish thought—that it does not know, does not understand and yet judges with a harsh firmness—is certainly revelatory.[9] For if she feels profoundly that speech is originally in relation to the void of suffering and linked to the demand of a primitive poverty—which the reading of the Bible would also have taught her—the aversion she feels for the anxiety of the time without repose, her refusal of movement, her faith in a timeless beauty, the fascination that makes her turn to all the forms of time in which time is renounced—cyclical time (Greek and Hindu), mathematical time, mystical time—above all her need for purity, the horror she could not help but feel instinctively for a God who cares not about purity but about sanctity, who does not say: be pure because I am pure, but "be holy, as I am Holy," God whose pathos endlessly puts prophets to the test in a familiarity without relationship, all these strong incompatibilities, which make her condemn the speech of the Bible without hearing it, must also act in us and act in translators by an obscure urge not to translate but to complete and purify.

Symbolic reading is probably the worst way to read a literary text. Each time we are bothered by language that is too strong, we say: it is a symbol. This wall that is the Bible has thus become a tender transparency where the little fatigues of the soul are colored with melancholy. The coarse but prudent Claudel dies devoured by the symbols he interposes between Biblical language and his own. Actual sickness of language. Yet, if prophetic words reach us, what they make us feel is that they possess neither allegory nor symbol,[10] but that, by the concrete force of the word, they lay things bare, in a nudity that is like that of an immense face that one sees and does not see and that, like a face, is light, the absolute quality of light, terrifying and ravishing, familiar and elusive, immediately present and infinitely foreign, always to come, always to be discovered and even provoked, although as readable as the nudity of the human face can be: in this sense alone, figure.[11] Prophecy is living mimicry.[12] Jeremiah does not content himself with saying: you will be bent under the yoke; he gets hold of some cords and goes under a wooden yoke, a fire yoke. Isaiah does not just say: do not count on Egypt, its soldiers are conquered, taken, led "barefoot, bare-bottomed," rather he himself takes off his sack and sandals and goes naked for three years. The prophet brother of Ahab demands that a man strike and mutilate him in order better to portray the verdict he wants the king to understand. What does that tell us? That we must take everything literally; that we are always given over to the absolute of a meaning, just as we are given over to the absolute of hunger, of physical suffering, and of our body of need; that there is no refuge against this meaning that everywhere pursues us, precedes us, always there before we are, always present in absence, always speaking in silence. Impossibility for man to escape being so: "If they burrow down into Sheol, my hand will seize them; if they rise up to the heavens, I will make them come down; hidden under Carmel, already I find them there; if they think to take refuge in the deepest depths of the seas, there I make them bitten by the Serpent." Terrible curse of speech that makes death vain and nothingness sterile. Uninterrupted speech, without void, without rest, that prophetic speech seizes and, seizing it, sometimes succeeds in interrupting to make us hear it and, in this hearing, to awaken us to ourselves.[13]

It is a speech that takes up all of space and that is still essentially not fixed (thus the necessity for the Covenant, always broken, never interrupted). This harassment, this assault by movement, this rapidity of attack, this indefatigable overleaping—that is what the translations, even the faithful ones, tangled up in their fidelity, have so much difficulty in making us feel. We owe much, then, to the poet whose poetry, translated by the prophets, knew how to transmit the essential to us: this primal eagerness, this haste, this refusal to be delayed and attached.[14] Rare and almost threatening gift, for he must above all make perceptible, in all *true* speech, by the devotion to rhythm and primitive accent, that speech always spoken and never heard that doubles it with a pre-echo, rumor of wind and impatient murmur destined to repeat it in advance, at the risk of destroying it by preceding it. So prediction, using as support the anticipatory intensity of diction, seems to keep trying finally to produce its rupture. Thus Rimbaud: that genius of impatience and haste, great prophetic genius.

§ 9   The Secret of the Golem

The word *symbol* is a venerable word in the history of literature. It has rendered great services to the interpreters of religious forms and, these days, to the distant descendants of Freud, to the close disciples of Jung. Thought is symbolic. The most limited existence lives on symbols and gives them life. The word "symbol" reconciles believers and nonbelievers, scholars and artists.

Perhaps. What is strange in the use of this word is that the writer to whose work we apply it feels while he is engaged in this work very remote from what such a word designates. Afterwards, it is possible that he is grateful for it, and lets himself be flattered by this fine name. Yes, it is a symbol. But in him something resists, protests and secretly asserts: it is not a symbolic manner of speaking, it was only real.

This resistance merits attention. Yet we have indeed perfected the thought of the symbol. Here mysticism has contributed (before any scholarly study by specialists) more clarity and rigor. The first development was made through the need to rescue the symbol from allegory. Allegory is not simple. If an old man with a scythe or a woman with a wheel signifies time or fortune, the allegorical relationship is not exhausted by such meanings alone. The scythe, the wheel, the old man, the woman—each detail, each work in which allegory has appeared and the immense history that hides in it, the emotional powers that have kept it active and above all the manner of expression represented, expand the meaning toward an infinite network of correspondences. From the beginning, we have the infinite at our disposal. But it is an infinite that is precisely accessible. Allegory develops the tangled vibration of its circles very far, but without changing its level, conformable to an abundance that could be called horizontal: it keeps itself inside the limits of measured expression, representing, through something that is expressed or represented, some other thing that could also be directly expressed.

SYMBOLIC EXPERIENCE

The symbol's aims are entirely different. From the start, it wants to jump outside of the sphere of language, of language in all its forms. Its goal is in no way expressible; what it offers to sight or hearing is not susceptible to direct understanding, or indeed understanding of any kind. The plane it makes us leave is only a trampoline to lift us or precipitate us toward another region that lacks other access. Through symbol, then, there is a leap, a change of level, sudden and violent change, there is exaltation, there is falling, a passage not from one meaning to another, from a modest meaning to a vaster richness of significations, but to that which is other, to that which seems other than all possible meanings. This change of level, a dangerous movement downward, even more dangerous upward, is the essential nature of the symbol.

All this is already difficult, promising, and rare, such that speaking about the symbol should not be done without precautions. But other singularities ensue. Allegory has a meaning, much meaning, a greater or lesser ambiguity of meaning. Symbol does not mean anything, expresses nothing. It only makes present—by making us present to it—a reality that escapes all other capture and seems to rise up, there, prodigiously close and prodigiously far away, like a foreign presence. Might symbol then be an opening in the wall, the breach by which what is otherwise concealed from all that we feel and know might suddenly become perceptible to us? Is it a graph traced on the invisible, a transparency in which the obscure can be guessed in its obscurity? It is none of that, and that is how it keeps such a great attraction for art. If symbol is a wall, then it is like a wall that, far from opening wide, not only becomes more opaque, but with a density, a thickness, and a reality so powerful and so exorbitant that it transforms us, changes instantly the sphere of our ways and habits, takes us away from all actual or latent knowledge, makes us more malleable, moves us, turns us around, and exposes us, by this new freedom, to the approach of another space.

There is unfortunately no precise example, for as soon as symbol is particular, closed and usual, it is already degraded. But let us admit for a moment that the cross, as religious experience vivifies it, has all the vitality of the symbol. The cross directs us to a mystery, the mystery of the Passion of Christ, but for all that it does not lose its reality as a cross or its nature of wood: on the contrary, it becomes all the more a tree, and closer to a tree since it seems to rise up into a sky that is not this sky and to a place beyond our access. It is as if the symbol were always more turned in upon itself, upon the unique reality it possesses and its obscurity as thing, by the fact that it is also the place of an infinite force of expansion.

It must briefly be said, then: every symbol is an experience, a radical change that one must live, a leap one must make. There is no symbol, then, but rather a symbolic experience. The symbol is never destroyed by the invisible or the unspeakable for which it tries to aim; on the contrary, in this movement it reaches a reality that the current world never granted it, all the more tree since it is a cross, more visible because of this hidden essence, more eloquent and expressive through the inexpressible, close to which it causes us to rise by an instantaneous decision.

If we try to apply this experience of the symbol to literature, we see, not without surprise, that it uniquely concerns the reader, whose attitude it transforms. It is for the reader alone that the symbol exists, it is the reader who feels linked to the book by the movement of a symbolic search, it is the reader who, faced with the narrative, experiences a power of assertion that seems to go infinitely beyond the limited sphere where this power is exercised, and thinks: "It is much more than a story, there is the premonition of a new truth, a superior reality; something will be revealed to me that this wonderful author destines for me, that he has seen, that he wants to make me see, only on the condition that I not let myself be blinded by the immediate meaning and the pressing reality of his work." Thus the reader is close to uniting with the work through a passion that sometimes reaches illumination, one that most often disappears in subtle translations, if it is a question of a specialized reader, happy to be able to shelter his little light in the hollow of a new profundity. These two ways of reading are illustrious and took birth many centuries ago: to cite only one example, one led to the rich commentaries of the Talmud, the other to the ecstatic experiences of prophetic cabalism linked with the contemplation and manipulation of the letters of the alphabet.

(But perhaps we must recall: reading is a pleasure that requires more innocence and freedom than consideration. A tormented, scrupulous reading, a reading that is celebrated like the rites of a sacred ceremony, places beforehand on a book the seals of respect that lock it closed. The book is not made to be respected, and "the most sublime masterpiece" always finds in the humblest reader the just measure that makes him equal to it. But naturally, the ease of reading is not itself of easy access. The readiness of the book to be opened and the appearance it keeps of being always available—this book which is never there—does not mean that it is available to us, but signifies rather its demand for our complete availability.)

The result of symbolic reading is sometimes of great consequence for culture. New questions are raised, old answers silenced, humankind's need to speak is nobly nourished. But the worst part is that a sort of bastard spirituality finds its resource in it. What is behind the scene, behind the narrative, of which one has had a vague premonition like an eternal secret, is reconstituted into an actual, autonomous world, around which the mind is stirred in the dubious happiness always procured for it by the infinity of the "more-or-less."

The end result of this for the work is its destruction, as if it had become a sort of screen, tirelessly bored through by the insects of commentary, with the aim of facilitating the view over this hinterland that is always too poorly seen and that we try to bring closer to us, not by adapting our sight to it but by transforming it according to our gaze and our experience.

Thus it is to a double alteration that symbolic research almost necessarily leads by its gravity. On one hand, the symbol, which is nothing if not a passion, if it doesn't lead to this leap that we have described, turns back into a simple or complex possibility of representation. On the other hand, instead of remaining a vehement force in which two contrary movements are joined and confirmed—one expansion, the other concentration—it passes little by little wholly into what it symbolizes, tree of the cross that the greatness of the mystery has gnawed and used fiber by fiber.

WHY THERE IS NO PURE ART

Still, on this point, we have made progress, we are more alert, more attentive. We feel that the work in which a symbolic life seems to be animated will approach us all the more from the "outside" if we let ourselves be more completely enclosed in it. It will tell us what it does not tell us on condition that it say nothing but itself, and it leads us elsewhere only if it leads us nowhere, not opening up but closing all exits, Sphinx without a secret, beyond which there is nothing but the desert that it carries in itself and transports into us.

The beyond of the work is real only in the work, is nothing but the unique reality of the work. The narrative, through its movements of a labyrinthine nature, or through the breaking of level that it produces in its substance, seems drawn outside of itself by a light whose reflection we think we surprise here and there, but this attraction that carries it out toward a point infinitely exterior is the movement that carries it back toward the secret of itself, toward its center, toward the intimacy from which it is always engendered and that is its own and eternal birth.

So when we come to speak to a writer about the symbol, he might feel distance from the work with regard to itself, a moving, living distance, center of all life and movement in it, like that distance that the symbol brings with it, proof of a void, of an insurmountable gap that nonetheless must be surmounted, a summons to leap, to shift levels. But for the writer it is in the work that this distance exists. It is only by writing that he gives himself over to it and exposes himself to it to keep it real. It is inside the work that the absolute outside is encountered—radical exteriority, through experience of which the work is formed, as if that which is the outermost of the work were always, for the one writing it, the most intimate point of the work, so that he must, by a most dangerous motion, bring himself endlessly toward the extreme limit of space, comport himself as if at the end of himself, at the end of the genre he thinks he is following, of the story he thinks he is telling and of all writing, there where he can no longer go on: that is where he must remain, without giving in, in order that there, at a certain moment, everything can begin.

But at that point and at that instant, it also seems to him that it is a question no longer of this work that he has undertaken to write but of what no longer has any relationship to it, either to it or to anything whatsoever: it is, he believes, something entirely different that he has seen in it, an unknown Land, a *Mare tenebrarum* [Sea of shadows], a point, an ineffable image, a supreme "meaning," and being haunted by it is henceforth all that animates him. Does he then renounce his own task, his own work, and his own goal? Yes, it is so. Everything occurs as if the writer— or the artist—could not pursue the accomplishment of his work without giving himself, as object and alibi, the pursuit of something else (that is undoubtedly why there is no pure art). To exercise his art, he must have a distortion by which he can hide what he is and what he does—and literature is this dissimulation. Just as Orpheus, when he turns back to Eurydice, stops singing, breaks the power of the song, betrays the rite

and forgets the rule, so at a certain moment the writer must betray, renounce everything, art and the work and literature that now seem like
nothing compared to the truth he glimpses (or to the people he wants to
serve), to the unknown he wants to grasp, to Eurydice, whom he wants to
see and no longer to sing of. It is only at the price of this disavowal of the
work that such a work can acquire its greatest dimension, which makes it
more than a work. And it is often at this price that it gets lost, and also
when it seems most to give nourishment and justification to the symbol.

What does this notion of symbol offer to the writer? Perhaps nothing
but forgetfulness of his failure and a dangerous tendency to delude himself through relying on a language of mystery.[1] If he were forced, in order
to specify the experience that is unique to him, to use another word, it
would rather be the simple word *image*, for often he is like a man who has
encountered an image, feels himself linked to it by a strange passion, has
no other existence than to remain near it, a dwelling that is his work.

HAPPINESS AND UNHAPPINESS OF THE IMAGE

In Bioy Casares's narrative, *Morel's Invention*—which Borges has assigned a place among the great successes—we are told the story of a man
who, fleeing political persecution, finds refuge on an island where he is
safe because a kind of plague has left it deserted. A few years before, a rich
man, with some friends, had built a hotel there, a chapel, and a "Museum," but the epidemic seems to have chased them away. Thus the exiled
man lives there for some time in the anguish of extreme solitude. One day
he sees a young woman, and then some other people, who reoccupy the
hotel and lead, in this wilderness, an incomprehensible life of amusement.
So he must again flee, he must hide himself, but the attraction of this
young woman whom he hears called Faustine, the enchanted indifference
she shows him, this world of celebration and happiness seize him. He approaches, he speaks to her, he touches her, he appeals to her—all in vain.
He must come to a decision: he does not exist for her, he is as if dead in
her eyes, and might he not be dead, in fact? Let us advance to the climax:
the organizer of this little company is a scholar who has succeeded in winning from persons and from things an absolute image, one that strikes all
the senses as an identical and incorruptible double of reality. The scholar,
without their knowing it, has "filmed" his friends, in each instant of their
lives, for a week that will be eternal and that begins again each time the
tides set in motion the mechanism that runs the projectors. Until now, the

narrative is only ingenious. But a second denouement is reserved for us, in which the ingenuity becomes moving. The fugitive lives, then, close to the images, he lives close to the fascinating young woman to whom little by little he feels attached but not attached enough; he would like to enter into the circle of her indifference, enter into her past, modify the past in accord with his desire. A plan comes to him: to adapt his gestures and words to the gestures and words of Faustine, so that they can respond to each other like an allusion to what a spectator would think was their happy intimacy. Thus he lives for an entire week during which, putting the image-taking machinery into movement, he causes himself to be re-produced, with her and with everyone, becoming in his turn an image and living wonderfully in this imaginary intimacy. Naturally, he hastens to destroy the version of the week in which he did not exist. From now on he is happy, in a sort of heaven—happiness and eternity for which he must pay (for this is the price) with his death, for the beams are mortal.

Happiness, unhappiness of the image. In this situation, might the writer not be tempted to recognize, rigorously described, many of his dreams, his illusions, and his torments, up to the naïve, insinuating thought that, if he dies of them, he will pass on a little of his life into the figures eternally animated by his death?

This is the drift of allegorical reverie, and since this commentary has already slipped into it, it is another allegory. We remember the Golem, that rudimentary mass that received life and power from the letters its creator mysteriously knew how to inscribe on its forehead. But tradition wrongly attributes to it a permanent existence, like that of other living beings. The Golem was animated and lived with a prodigious life, superior to any we can conceive of, but only during the ecstasy of its creator. He had to have this ecstasy and the sparkle of ecstatic life, for he himself was only the instantaneous realization of the consciousness of ecstasy. Thus, at least, he was at its origin. Later, the Golem changed itself into an ordinary magical opus, it learned how to last like all works and like all things, and it then became capable of exploits that caused it to enter into fame and legend, but also to abandon the true secret of its art.

§ 10 Literary Infinity: The Aleph

Speaking of the infinite, Borges says that this idea corrupts others. Michaux evokes the infinite, enemy of man, and says of mescaline, which "refuses the movement of the finite": "Infiniverted [*infinivertie*], it detranquilizes."

I suspect Borges of having acquired the infinite from literature. This is not to suggest that he has only a calm knowledge of it drawn from literary works, but to assert that the very experience of literature is perhaps fundamentally close to the paradoxes and sophisms of what Hegel, to distance it, called the evil infinite [*le mauvais infini*].

The truth of literature might be in the error of the infinite.[1] The world in which we live and as we live it is, fortunately, limited. A few steps are enough for us to leave our room, a few years to leave our life. But let us suppose that, in this narrow, suddenly dark space, suddenly blind, we were to wander astray. Let us suppose that the geographic desert becomes the Biblical desert: it is no longer four steps, no longer eleven days that we need to cross it, but the time of two generations, the entire history of all humanity, and perhaps more. For the moderated and moderate man, the room, the desert, and the world are strictly determined places. For the man of the desert and the labyrinth, devoted to the error of a journey necessarily a little longer than his life, the same space will be truly infinite, even if he knows that it is not, all the more so since he knows it.

THE MEANING OF BECOMING

The error, the fact of being on the go without ever being able to stop, changes the finite into infinity. And to it these singular characteristics are added: from the finite, which is still closed, one can always hope to escape, while the infinite vastness is a prison, being without an exit—just as any place absolutely without exit becomes infinite. The place of wandering knows no straight line; one never goes from one point to another in it; one does not leave here to go there; there is no point of departure and no beginning to the walk. Before having begun, already one begins again; before having finished, one broods, and this sort of absurdity (consisting of returning without ever having left, or of beginning by beginning again) is the secret of "evil" eternity, corresponding to "evil" infinity, both of which perhaps contain the meaning of becoming.

Borges, an essentially literary man (which means that he is always ready to understand according to the manner of comprehension that literature authorizes), is constantly grappling with evil eternity and evil infinity, the only ones perhaps we can be sure about, until the glorious reversal that is called ecstasy. The book is in principle the world for him, and the world is a book. That is what should make him serene about the meaning of the universe, for one can doubt the reason of the universe, but the book that we make—and in particular those cleverly organized books of fiction, like perfectly obscure problems to which perfectly clear solutions suffice, such as detective novels—we know to be penetrated with intelligence and animated by that power of arrangement that is the mind. But if the world is a book, every book is the world, and from this innocent tautology, formidable consequences result.

This first of all: that there is no longer a limit of reference. The world and the book eternally and infinitely send back their reflected images. This indefinite power of mirroring, this sparkling and limitless multiplication—which is the labyrinth of light and nothing else besides—will then be all that we will find, dizzily, at the bottom of our desire to understand.

Then this: that if the book is the possibility of the world, we should conclude that at work in the world is not only the ability to make [*faire*], but that great ability to feign [*feindre*], to trick and deceive, of which every work of fiction is the product, all the more so if this ability stays concealed in it. *Fictions, Artifices* risk being the most honest names that literature can be given; and to reproach Borges for writing narratives that fit these titles too well is to reproach him for that excess of frankness without which mystification is taken ponderously at its word (Schopenhauer, Valéry, we see, are the stars that shine in this sky void of sky).

The word *trickery*, the word *falsification*, applied to the mind and to literature, shock us. We think that such a genre of deception is too simple, we think that if there is universal falsification, it is still in the name of a truth that is perhaps inaccessible but worthy of veneration and, for some, adoration. We think that the hypothesis of the evil genius is not the most dreadful: a falsifier, even an all-powerful one, remains a solid truth that excuses us from thinking further. Borges understands that the perilous dignity of literature is not to make us suppose a great author of the world, absorbed in dreamy mystifications, but to make us experience the approach of a strange power, neutral and impersonal. He likes it to be said of Shakespeare: "He was like all men, except for the fact that he was like all men." He sees in all authors one single author, who is the unique Carlyle, the unique Whitman, who is no one. He recognizes himself in George Moore and in Joyce—he could say in Lautréamont, in Rimbaud—able to incorporate into their books pages and figures that do not belong to them, for the essential thing is literature, not individuals, and in literature the essential thing is that it be impersonally, in each book, the inexhaustible unity of one single book and the weary repetition of all books.

When Borges suggests that we imagine a contemporary French writer writing, starting with thoughts that are his own, some pages that would textually reproduce two chapters of *Don Quixote*, this memorable absurdity is nothing other than that which is accomplished in all translation. In a translation, we have the same work in a double language; in the fiction of Borges, we have two works in the identity of one single language and, in this identity that is not one, the fascinating mirage of the duplicity of possibilities. Yet where there is a perfect double the original is erased, and even the origin. Thus, the world, if it could be exactly translated and copied in a book, would lose all beginning and all end and would become that spherical, finite, and limitless volume that all men write and in which they are written: it would no longer be the world; it would be, it will be, the world corrupted into the infinite sum of its possibilities. (This perversion is perhaps the prodigious and abominable Aleph.)

Literature is not a simple deception, it is the dangerous ability to go toward what exists, by the infinite multiplicity of the imaginary. The difference between the real and the unreal, the inestimable privilege of the real, is that there is less reality in reality, being only unreality negated, distanced by the energetic labor of negation and by the negation that labor also is. It is this minus, a sort of thinning, a slimming of space, that allows us to go from one point to another according to the fortunate way of the straight line. But it is the most undefined essence of the imaginary, which prevents K. from ever reaching the Castle, as for eternity it prevents Achilles from catching up with the tortoise, and perhaps the living man from meeting up with himself in a point that would make his death perfectly human and, consequently, invisible.

§ 11 The Failure of the Demon: The Vocation

Goethe loved his devil; he allowed him to end well. Virginia Woolf struggles all her life against the demon that protects her; finally she triumphs over it, in an obscure gesture that perhaps consecrates the truth of her vocation. This struggle is strange. The one who tricks us saves us, but by making us unfaithful to ourselves, too prudent and too wise. In the journals published after her death, it is the peripeteia of this combat that we seek, while still deploring the limits of its publication: twenty-six volumes that have been changed into one single volume; literary conventions demanded it so. It remains a deeply disturbing document, as it reflects the attitude of the writer, with here and there a gleam illuminating the happiness, the unhappiness of her labors.[1]

Deeply disturbing, but often difficult to read. Readers who are not indulgent risk being irritated in seeing the Virginia they love so taken with success, so happy with praise, so vain about a moment of recognition, so wounded at its lack. Yes, that is surprising, painful, almost incomprehensible. There is something enigmatic in these distorted reports that place a writer of such delicacy in such gross dependence. And each time, with each new book, the comedy, the tragedy is the same. This repetition, of which she is very aware—who was more lucid?—is made even more annoying by the abridgements of the *Journal*, but these errors of perspective also have their truth. And suddenly the outcome: that death she chose, which comes to take the place of the public, and which finally gives her the true answer for which she has never stopped waiting.

THE GREAT AGONY

That Virginia Woolf is sensitive to the point of being visibly so, we should not hold against her. That she is sometimes jealous, misjudging Joyce and Katherine Mansfield because of their merits, we regret, but she sees this and regrets it too. That she owes to the aristocracy of writers and artists among whom she was raised, remarkably free-spirited though they were, her own quite dependent relationships with criticism—this is more serious. When she is writing, she brings to mind what some of her friends will think, all specialists, critics, poets, novelists of the first order. When she is done writing, she awaits their judgment (sometimes she awaits it by fleeing it). If it is good, she is happy, for a moment; if it is not altogether good, she is devastated for a long time. Is that healthy? I see, I admire the ever-so-fruitful relationships (so they say) that united Roger Martin du Gard and Copeau and Gide and the whole Bloomsbury milieu of the N.R.F.[2] But doesn't a writer have a great need for anonymity? Doesn't he entertain an illusion when he supposes himself writing about friendly faces and sensibilities he knows? Even Goethe could do nothing for Schiller. And was Virginia Woolf helped by all these admirable writers who were her companions? Assuredly, they helped her; but she also carried, like a burden, the weight of their praise and their encouragement.

That remains superficial. If she is vulnerable, she is not so out of simple immodesty, out of the wish to be "famous" or "great," or out of the anxious concern to please excessively perceptive friends. These ways of being weak allow her only to leave a more essential weakness a little farther away from her, an insecurity she does not escape. This weakness lies within her talent itself. "Perhaps I am not sure of my gifts." We may admire the fact that she can doubt herself, after having already published her most important books (*Mrs. Dalloway*, *To the Lighthouse*, *The Waves*). But we should remember how Goethe, at the age of forty, already a famous writer, suddenly finds himself on the roads of Italy, wondering if he is not a painter or a naturalist rather than a poet. Virginia Woolf surely knows that the most gifted artist, each time he becomes involved in a new work, is as if stripped of himself, devoid of himself. The positive and sturdy Claudel, having finished *L'ôtage* [The hostage], writes to Gide: "Past experience serves nothing; each new work poses new problems, before which one feels all the uncertainties and all the anguishes of a beginner, along with some treacherous abilities that one must brutally dominate." And Péguy: "I never attack a new work without trembling. I live in the trembling of writing."[3]

But even this uncertainty that causes the vocation—and the very existence of the poet—each time to be solved like an enigma by the affirmation of the poem is perhaps not the essential point. In Virginia Woolf's case, one could say that it is the art in her that makes a profound weakness necessary, demanding that she abandon her most natural resources of life and expression. (That is perhaps what Jacques Rivière also meant to express, when he said of Alain-Fournier: "He is himself and finds all his strength only in the moment he feels himself abandoned by all he still needs.") There are in Woolf's journals notes that speak, sometimes with deep seriousness, about the failing to which her work leads her: "I shall make myself face the fact that there is nothing—nothing for any of us. Work, reading, writing are all disguises; & relations with people. Yes, even having children would be useless."[4] This is not a way of thinking inherited temporarily from her milieu; it is a conviction that she feels intimately linked to the truth of her task: she must encounter the void ("the great agony," "the terror of solitude," "the horror of contemplating the bottom of the vase") in order, starting from this void, to begin to see, even if it be the humblest things, and to grasp what she calls *reality*—the attraction of the pure moment, the insignificant abstract scintillation that does not last, reveals nothing, and returns to the void that it illumines. It is the experience of the instant, and what could be easier, we might think; but I don't know how easy it is, demanding as it does such a separation from oneself, such a grave humility, such a complete faithfulness to a limitless power of dispersion (the essence of unfaithfulness) that one sees clearly what risk must finally be run.

"REALITY"

The art in Virginia Woolf is shown to be what it is, of a terrible gravity. Cheating is not allowed. How tempting it would be to try to translate into a great revelatory affirmation those brief illuminations that open and close time and that, well aware of their cost, she calls *moments of being*.[5] Won't they wonderfully, once and for all, change our lives? Do they bear that power of decision and creation capable, as happens in Proust, of making possible the work that must be assembled around them? Not at all. "Little daily miracles," "matches unexpectedly struck in the dark," they speak of nothing but themselves. They appear, they disappear, brilliant fragments that blot out with their saturated purity the space of transparency.[6]

At the same time, and although the misunderstanding is constantly to be feared, what these cores of moving clarity let her see in a necessary dispersion must not be confused with the play of appearances. They are not "impressions," even if they have the modesty of them, and we could not be more mistaken than by describing her writing as impressionist. Virginia Woolf knows that she must not remain passive before the instant, but answer it with a brief, violent, obstinate, and yet thought-out—pensive—passion. "The idea has come to me that what I want now to do is to saturate every atom. I mean to eliminate all waste, deadness, superfluity: to give the moment whole; whatever it includes. Say that the moment is a combination of thought; sensation; the voice of the sea."[7] Appearance, the living, life are not enough and guarantee nothing: "It is a mistake to think that literature can be taken directly from life. You must go out of life. . . . You must go out of yourself, and concentrate as much as possible on one single point. . . . " "I realize that it is true, that I do not have the gift of 'reality.' I deliberately disembody up to a certain point, for I mistrust reality. . . . But in order to go further." And what does she find further on? Speaking in 1928 of the gravest experience she ever had, for which she resorts to unusually strong words—terror, horror, agony—she adds this: "That is one of the experiences [that made me aware] of what I call 'reality': a thing I see before me: something abstract; but residing in the downs or sky; beside which nothing matters; in which I shall rest and continue to exist. Reality I call it. And I fancy sometimes this is the most necessary thing to me: that which I seek."[8]

There, then, while the capricious fire burns, is all that is given to her, to which she must remain faithful, renouncing all the rest—*something abstract, residing in the downs or sky*. A life of courage, years of work, days of despair, of expectation, of sterile pursuit, and the solitary fear of the end, without any justification other than the promise of this little sentence, whose possible trickery she immediately denounces: "But who knows—once one takes a pen and writes? How difficult not to go making 'reality' this and that, whereas it is one thing."[9] Thus Proust deemed the little section of wall so nicely painted yellow equal to the weight of a life.

PERFIDIOUS CALLING

When one looks at the pathetic face that this life grants her over the course of years, a face that is little by little effaced, one has the impression, beyond the melancholy that is all that makes it still visible, that all the exterior strength and personal energy on which we must sometimes fall back to persevere have abandoned her. From what, then, does she draw, until the end, those almost unreasonable possibilities of work, rewriting each of her books I don't know how many times, supporting them, maintaining them above her discouragement, to which she never surrenders them? That is where the indomitable strength unique to her weakness lets itself be felt, as if, when we can do nothing more, sometimes the resource of an entirely different power emerges. But in what insecurity she remains. To link oneself to dispersion, to intermittency, to the fragmented brilliance of images, to the shimmering fascination of the instant, is a terrible movement—a terrible happiness, especially when finally it must give way to a book. Is there a way to gather together what is dispersed, to make continuous the discontinuous and to maintain the wandering in a nonetheless unified whole? Virginia Woolf sometimes finds it, in that moving language that is like dream and the imagination of water, but, in the novelistic plotting from which she cannot entirely free herself, sometimes does not find it. Her last book, on its last pages, only repeats these two words: "Unity—Dispersity... Un... dis... " "All that we can see of ourselves are pieces, debris, fragments." "Now we are dispersed, we who used to be together." "We are dispersed. . . . " "Unity, dispersion." One must be separate.

Virginia Woolf's suicide is so close to her that we prefer to put it aside and forget it, ignore it, though still knowing it to be necessary, but—who knows?—still avoidable. How can we dare link it with her creative life? How can we see in it the completion of her destiny? What is fitting in this most unsuitable end? And in case, as has been suggested, fidelity to her calling had demanded it, what does the word *calling* [*vocation*] signify here? Ortega y Gasset has asserted that each person has an essential— perhaps unique—goal that he devotes his existence to refusing or to accomplishing, nonetheless struggling almost always against it in an obscure, desperate and living fight. Such, he says, was Goethe, who passed his illustrious life in betraying his authentic calling. And every life is ruin, every brilliant achievement a heap of rubble through which the biographer must search for what the living person should have become. For one, his truth was to be a thief, and he falsified his life by virtuously succeeding in not becoming one. For another, to be Don Juan and not a saint. For Goethe, not to fall into the sad history of Weimar, "the greatest misunderstanding of literary history," and not to transform himself into a statue. This thesis, upheld with authority,[10] is hard to endure and troubling. What is this secret, elusive, and inexistent aim whose constant pressure is, in fact, exercised on humankind, and particularly on problematic beings, creators, intellectuals, who are almost at every moment accessible and dangerously new? The idea of a calling (of a fidelity) is the most perverse that can afflict a free artist. Even and especially apart from any idealistic conviction (in which this idea is more easily tamed), we feel it close to each writer like a shadow that precedes him and that he flees, or that he pursues, deserter of himself, imitating himself or, worse, imitating the inimitable idea of the Artist or of the Man he wants spectacularly to present.

The perfidious side of the calling is that it is far from moving by necessity in the direction of the artists' aptitudes, since it can on the contrary demand a renunciation of natural talents, as we see from so many artists who were facile to begin with, who became what they are by ceasing to be themselves, ungrateful then for their spontaneous gifts. With Goethe, it is the very multiplicity of aptitudes that may have altered the calling, while we see Pascal, scholar, writer, religious genius, finding himself only in a difficult conflict, until the moment at which the calling ends in conversion. Calling has the perverse quality of supposing an exclusive demand, a movement toward an always more determined figure, the choice, among many possibilities, of one single one that, even while remaining enigmatic, asserts itself as essential and such that one cannot distance oneself from it without the certainty—imperious, indecipherable—of an error. One must then irrevocably decide, limit oneself, liberate oneself from oneself and from all the rest in view of that unique "reality" (in the sense that Virginia Woolf understands it). But what is peculiar to the writer is, in each work, to keep indecision in decision, to preserve the limitless alongside the limited and to say nothing that does not leave intact all the space of language or the possibility of saying everything. And at the same time he must say one single thing and say nothing but it.

When T. S. Eliot makes this remark: "It is my experience that towards middle age a man has three choices: to stop writing altogether, to repeat

himself with perhaps an increasing skill of virtuosity, or by taking thought
to adapt himself to middle age and find a different way of working,"[11] he
is well aware that it is not only in the middle of his life but at each turn of
himself, and at each new work, at each page of the work, that one of these
three choices—to speak only of them—would present itself, if a sort of
dexterity did not fortunately allow one, each time, to anticipate them.
Virginia Woolf, so anxious, so uncertain, had this dexterity. Nothing
weighs in her, and rarely was so heavy an anguish so apparently light.
While she writes—and even when "writing is despair itself"—she is carried by a prodigious movement, an exultant harmony with her "calling"
that seems to be the attraction of this *something abstract, residing in the
downs or sky*, in which she has, for herself, with a precise imprecision, enclosed her secret. It is only after each book that the obscure unhappiness
seizes her. In vain, she seeks to alleviate it by asking for a favorable judgment from some and by awaiting from others the wound of criticism that
would let her localize her torment. "And no one knows how much I suffer, all along this road, struggling with my anguish as I did after the death
of my only brother, struggling all alone against something. But at that
time, I was struggling against a demon, and now against nothing." She
suggests that after almost all of her books she has contemplated suicide,
particularly after *To the Lighthouse*, which was nonetheless the novel about
which she had the least reason to doubt. We could readily explain this by
saying that she pays for the excessive tension her work has demanded with
great exhaustion. That is one aspect of the thing. She herself, though, expresses it quite otherwise: "Directly I stop working I feel that I am sinking
down, down. And as usual, I feel that if I sink further I shall reach the
truth. That is the only mitigation; a kind of nobility. Solemnity."[12]

"I FAIL"

When she dies, her final novel (*Between the Acts*) ends without having
been finished. That is the most perilous instant: the book abandons her,
the strength that came from it is withdrawn, leaving her faced with the
task without resources and without faith: "There is some check in the flow
of my being; a deep stream presses on some obstacle; it jerks; it tugs; some
knot in the centre resists. Oh, this is pain, this is anguish! I faint, I fail."[13]
She fails. What is striking in this failure, affirmed by her voluntary death,
is the scandalous act that it introduces into the course of an existence that
until then had been so perfectly respectable (as she herself qualified it with

an ironic regret). Thus it is certainly true that, if he is linked to civilized customs that require he do nothing shocking, for a writer faithful to the "calling," there always comes a time when customs are broken. We understand better now the words of the young Goethe—"For me, there could be no question of ending well"—a certainty that accompanies him during his whole youth until the day he discovers and accepts the demoniacal power that must protect him, he thinks, against the fear of losing himself. This power did protect him, true, but then began his infidelity to himself, and the glorious decline from which Virginia Woolf preferred to escape by sinking.

PART III

On an Art Without Future

§ 12 At Every Extreme

Is art reaching its end? Is poetry perishing for having looked itself in the face, just as he dies who has seen God? The critic who considers our time, comparing it to the past, can only express doubt and, on the subject of artists who despite everything still produce, a despairing admiration. But when someone proves, as Wladimir Weidlé does in a book of culture, reason, and regret, that modern art is impossible—and this proof is convincing, perhaps too flattering—is one not emphasizing the secret demand of art, which is always, in every artist, the surprise of what *is*, without being possible, the surprise of what must begin at every extreme, the work of the end of the world, art that finds its beginning only where there is no more art and where its conditions are lacking? We do not have to go too far into doubt. That is the way, or one of the ways, of going further into the wonder of the indubitable.

In his book *Les abeilles d'Aristée* [The bees of Aristaeus], Weidlé writes, "Mallarmé's error,"[1] and Gabriel Marcel says, "The Mallarméan error. . . . " Obvious mistake. But is it not obvious, too, that to this mistake we owe Mallarmé? Every artist is linked to a mistake with which he has a particular intimate relation. There is the mistake of Homer, of Shakespeare—which is perhaps, for both, the fact of not existing. Every art draws its origin from an exceptional fault, every work is the implementation of this original fault, from which come to us a new light and a risky conception of plenitude. Is that a concept unique to our time, this time in which art has stopped being a communal affirmation, a tranquil collective wonder, and is all the more important since it is more improbable? It may be. But what was it formerly? And what is this vague "formerly" when everything seems to us to have been so easy, so sure? At least it is today that concerns us and, for today, we can resolutely assert: an artist cannot be too mistaken or link himself too much to his mistake, in a serious, solitary, perilous, irreplaceable embrace in which he hurls himself, with terror, with delight, at the excess that, in himself, leads him outside himself and perhaps outside of everything.

(The disciples, the imitators are those who, like critics, make a mistake into a rule, rationalize it, stabilize it, but thereby give it value so that it becomes visible, and it is then easy for critics to show the mistake and show to what impasse it leads, with what failure success pays for itself, and even the failure that was the success.)

This link with error, this relationship so difficult to attain, more difficult to sustain, which clashes with a doubt, with a disavowal in the very one whom the mistake holds under its fascination, this passion, this paradoxical progress also affects the novel, the happiest of genres, about which nonetheless we have always heard it said that it has reached its end. And this assertion was made not when great works were no longer produced, but every time that great writers wrote great novels, unanimously recognized as books of considerable literary value. That is because each time these authors seemed to have broken something: they did not exhaust the genre, as Homer did for the epic, but they altered it with such an authority and such a cumbersome, sometimes encumbered, power, that it no longer seemed possible to return to the traditional form or to go further in the use of the aberrant form, or even to repeat it. That was said in England about Virginia Woolf or Joyce; in Germany about Broch, Musil, and even [Thomas Mann's] *The Magic Mountain*. In France, the situation is a little different. The shock provoked by Proust was immediately covered over with such a wave of universal admiration that this unique phenomenon (one of the earliest) seemed only to prove Proust's genius, while leaving the traditional horizon of the novel intact. Similarly, *Les faux-monnayeurs* [The counterfeiters] makes us reflect on the novelistic genius of Gide rather than on the novel itself, while later, *La nausée* [Nausea] shows Sartre's gifts without calling into question the verities of the novel, his book being categorized (wrongly) sometimes as a form of ideological narrative, sometimes naturalistic. Besides, by Sartre's time, the damage is done. The novel, which absorbs and concentrates almost all the efforts of all the writers, seems also an art henceforth without a future.

THE EXCEPTION AND THE RULE

In this extremely cursory view of things, there must be some truth. Certainly Balzac, creating a monstrous body of work, also powerfully deforms the very genre that he introduces to literature. But Balzac has a posterity. There is a Balzacian novel. All those authors we have named engender nothing. Whatever one says, neither Proust nor Joyce gives birth to other books that resemble them; they seem to have no other power than to prevent imitators and to reward similar attempts with despair. They close a door.

But this result is not only negative. If it is true that Joyce breaks the novelistic form by making it aberrant, he also gives us a premonition that it perhaps lives only on its transformations. It might be developed, not by engendering monsters, shapeless works, without law and without rigor, but uniquely by provoking exceptions to itself, which form a law and at the same time suppress it.

This situation is all the more difficult to untangle when the novel, thus understood, asserts itself solitarily and silently apart from that enormous mass of books written with talent, ingenuity, and generosity, in which the reader is invited to recognize the vitality of an inexhaustible genre. Shouldn't we think that all these good books (sometimes brilliant works among them) represent the rule to which the others would be the exception, thanks to their inimitable originality? From that perspective, the law would be Jules Romains, the exception would be Joyce. But the opposite seems to be the case. We must rather think that, each time, in these exceptional works in which a limit is reached, it is the exception alone that reveals to us this "law" from which it also constitutes the unusual and necessary deviation. It seems then, in novelistic literature, and perhaps in all literature, that we could never recognize the rule except by the exception that abolishes it: the rule, or more precisely this center, of which the certain work is the uncertain affirmation, the already destructive manifestation, the momentary and soon negating presence.

It is not a question of newness at any price: technical newness or newness of form or vision. Nor is it always a question of imposing and successful works, revealing those great individuals for whose return the admired name of Balzac and the beloved name of Stendhal make us wish in vain. Naturally, talents are very useful; the creative power, sometimes annoying, is an aid that one cannot do without, even if only to go beyond it. But what is at stake is something else, an excessive demand, a rigorous and exclusive assertion that is directed in one single direction, with the passion that makes the impossible attempt necessary. Nathalie Sarraute, like Virginia Woolf, speaks of "reality"; she says that the novelist "seeks to bring to light that portion of reality that is her own."[2] Let us say reality, then. But as this reality is not given in advance, neither in other books— not even qualified masterpieces—nor in the world that our day-to-day gaze opens, as it endlessly escapes us, elusive and almost hidden by what reveals it, it is a reality that is as simple, but also as exceptional, as the book that will make it shine for an instant in our eyes.

When we think about a novelist's attempt and learn that it leads to an impasse, that is perhaps not enough in itself to make it valid, but each time that in some new book we grasp again the solitary and silent assertion of the novel understood as the exception, even if it is poorly arrived at from an endlessly compromised law, a moment already disappearing with a greater movement into the future, we experience the feeling of a promise and the exultant impression that a new writer, having touched a limit, has succeeded in displacing it and perhaps in fixing it farther ahead. That is what counts, first of all. Each writer feels himself in solidarity with this new affirmation, even if it does not excuse him from the one he must assert (that would be too good) and even if he opposes it. There is no progress here from which he can benefit, any more than there is a surer and purer understanding of the novelistic form; everything, on the contrary, is made more difficult and less certain. And these works are rare, fugitive. They are not always written by Proust, they are tortured, "clumsy," held back by conventions that they do not dare to renounce; sometimes exaggeratedly conscientious. Some are modest. But all, even the ones that efface themselves, have this strength that comes from a new contact with "reality."

§ 13 Broch

1. The Sleepwalkers: Logical Vertigo

His oeuvre does not include many works. He is not a writer like
Thomas Mann, whose creative generosity is deployed on many levels and
who endlessly renews for himself the celebration that is narration. Few
books, but ample ones and, by their mass, imposing. In that respect he is
already close to Joyce, who was his model. Before the war, the trilogy of
The Sleepwalkers (1928–31). In 1945, *The Death of Virgil.* Then a series of
stories, *The Innocents*, which, some say, marks the extreme limit of his investigations and perhaps the decline of his means. The publication of his
complete works, however, comprises eight volumes. That is because in
addition to a posthumous novel, *Der Versucher* [The seducer], and a volume of poems, three books of critical and philosophical essays show to
what point the aims of Hermann Broch were carried. But it would not be
right to speak of the variety of his gifts and of the breadth of his preoccupations. He was not a novelist on one hand, a poet on the other, and, at
other times, a writer of thoughts. He was all those things simultaneously,
often in the same book. He felt, as many other writers of our time have,
that impetuous pressure of literature that no longer endures the distinc-
tion of genres and wants to break all boundaries.

THE SCATTERED, FRAGMENTED MAN

He becomes a writer late; it is only little by little, and perhaps against
his will, that he gives in to the excesses of a work that he would have preferred to control fully. Until the age of forty, he attends to an industrial

textile business inherited from his family, an activity he suddenly renounces to study philosophy and especially mathematics. Some German commentators have compared him to Valéry. Like Valéry, he is carried by a sort of passion for mathematics, in which he is ready to seek the most secret—the most dangerous—part of man. But unlike Valéry, he is not a writer devoted first of all to the mind. He feels called by his time, on which impends the threat of approaching catastrophe. The collapse of a single system of values, as existed in the Middle Ages in Christian form, far from freeing the individual, exposes him to an inevitable disintegration. In the Christian system, faith and, at the center of faith, God, a living God, were "the point of plausibility" that stopped the irrepressible force of questions. It is this force that seems especially to interest Broch, that attracts him as much as it terrifies him: logical intolerance, that cruelty within the notion of being. Why does a being tend to "dissolve himself into pure functionality"? Why must the physical image of the world disappear? Why does reality necessarily give way to symbol, and symbol to the symbol of the symbol? What happens when one must decide on abstraction? We live in a prodigious discord. Man is scattered and discontinuous, and not temporarily, as has occurred at other times in history— but now it is the very essence of the world to be discontinuous. As if one had precisely to build a world—the universe, the most total and unified assertion—on the dislocated, discordant, and fragmented quality of being, or on the defects of man.

Broch does not see fewer dangers in pure rationality than in impure irrationality. Both are without style. Nature on one hand, mathematics on the other expose us to the empty demand of infinity. Indeed, every value system seeks to distance the irrational element and to lead earthly existence from its "malevolence" to a higher meaning of reasonableness, to that ensemble of meanings in which "it becomes possible for us instinctively to assign things, as well as actions, their suitable place." To transform what is irrational and without value into a rational absolute—that is the task, one that necessarily fails. For two reasons: what we call "irrational" remains inaccessible; we can only come near to it; we can trace around it always narrower circles, we can integrate it into calculations, but it always hides itself at the end so that we never know anything of the nonmeaning that impregnates our way of acting. "Man knows nothing of 'the intrusion from below' to which he is exposed, and he knows nothing of it, because at each step and at each moment he finds himself inside a system of values that has no other aim than to conceal and tame all the irrational by which our life linked to earth is driven." It is light that prevents us from seeing, it is the ability to give meaning that abandons us to the imperceptible action of what is hidden behind meaning and acts through this very dissimulation.

But there is something even graver: reason, deductive or dialectic, moved by the irrepressible force of questions, leans toward the absolute. The rational wants to become the super-rational. Logical impulse supports neither pause nor point of equilibrium; it no longer tolerates form, dissolves all content, organizes the cold, dreamlike reign of abstraction. It is a radical moment of evil, for pure reason, once it has become autonomous, is even more "malevolent" than the irrational: it introduces its own dissolution, everything dissipates into an abstract fog in which there is no longer a center of values, and the human individual, given over to the empty game of intolerant conventions, wanders amidst phantoms of reason that he continues to cherish as superior certainties. He is then a man of nothingness, metaphysically excluded and physically dispossessed, a sleepwalker who wanders in his dream and, chased from the dream, is thrown back into the anguish of the night from which he cannot awaken, in which he cannot sleep.

These thoughts (the origins of which one can easily recognize) have this special characteristic: they develop, in their abstract form, side by side with the narrative course of the novel, which, in the three books of *The Sleepwalkers*, leads us from imperial Germany, brilliant and conventional, to the collapse of 1918. The theme of this vast novel is not hidden. Broch has the skill to foreground the theoretical notions that we would otherwise look for inside his stories: the titles already tell all: *Pasenow, or Romanticism, 1888; Esch, or Anarchy, 1903; Huguenau, or Realism, 1918;* and, above these three names, the nocturnal word that is not even an image here, but a diagnosis: *Sleepwalkers.* Novel of the decadence, which still does not teach us about it, as a didactic novel would do, does not even describe it, but mimics it by opening itself up, even in form, to deprecatory forces. When Broch tells us the story of the Pomeranian country squire, Lieutenant Pasenow, there is none of that sympathy of imagination and even of origin on the part of the writer for his character that linked Thomas Mann to *Buddenbrooks,* which is also the narrative of a destiny that is exhausted, but without any denigrating intention. If we think with unease about Pasenow, that poor young man, about his empty attachment to an empty ideal, about his impotence, which does not allow him to open his eyes to himself and which he naïvely hides, even when it exposes him to the embarrassments of a failed wedding night, it is the form of the narrative that is responsible for it. It is classic, even conventional. Broch takes pleasure in narrating as a novelist of the era he evokes might have been able to do, and he is quite at ease in this half-objective, half-psychological narrative form, but already there is a fissure between behavior and thought. Both have something mechanical that we perceive only when a slight gap opens between them. With whom are we dealing? What is there behind this thin layer of events and words? In the end, the author brutally intervenes to finish destroying the fiction; one feels he is impatient to rescue himself from the nullity he has represented, and also to save the reader from it. But books are sleepwalkers that must not be awakened.

MANY WRITERS IN ONE

Broch is closer to Esch, the character in the second book, an average German, first a little accountant whom a refined mixture of abstract ideas about justice, the desire for order, and the desire for a bad conscience lead, by a zigzag of mediocre associations, seedy love affairs, and petty intrigues pursued to the edge of more profound movements represented by revolutionary currents, to a position as a major accountant in a Luxemburg business. It is a very convincing tale. Its movement is swift. The sentences are short, detached. Actions, deeds, thoughts follow each other or, better, are juxtaposed with a dry haste, a sort of mechanical fever, of sterile precipitation that is the truth of this novel. Now is the time to admire (and to be surprised at) the extreme diversity of languages, styles, and even syntaxes of which Broch is capable. If someone were to discover at the bottom of some jar Broch's central work, *The Death of Virgil*, in which there are also planned changes of rhythms, but in which an immense sentence still dominates, with endless repetitions and the solemn amplitude of a boundless space of words, and if he then encountered the novel *Esch*, with its skipping sentences and its frenzied pace, he could only imagine two writers unknown to each other or enemies of each other—and perhaps he would be right. Certainly, just as there are in modern society particular value systems—economical, religious, military—that subsist side by side, separated by impenetrable bulwarks, although each one also tries to dominate the others, so is the writer fragmented into distinct modes of expression, into languages without a common measure, without contact, and almost untranslatable, between which he must seek an equilibrium that will allow him to avoid disintegration, or to direct it.

This diversity of styles and languages is unsettling for our old romantic convictions, which make us look, in the writer's tone, for something unique, the expression of his secret truth or his immutable soul; thence the suspicious gaze with which we ponder the great demiurgic artists who, like Joyce or Picasso, pass from one language to another, without caring about letting themselves be recognized. Broch, by the discontinuity of form, does not just seek to make a world of pieces and debris more obvious. Nor is he interested in technique for its own sake (although, like many novelists of the time, he feels obliged to call into question anew the novelistic genre and to reinvent it), but since he is desperately trying to learn where this world is going and to anticipate its fate, he gives himself over to all modes of expression—narrative, lyrical, and expository—so that his book can arrive at a more central point, which he himself, in his small individual consciousness, does not discern.

The third volume of *The Sleepwalkers* describes what happens in 1918. Its essential part, though, is no longer in the intertwining of episodes: the story of the positive man, Huguenau, and how he ends up ruining, then killing, Esch by running him through with a bayonet; or the poetic story of the poor girl of the Salvation Army. The heart of the book is the logic itself, whose controlling force the *Logische Exkurse*, the "Logical Digressions," try, in lengthy passages that interrupt the narrative ten times, to grasp again.

FATE IS LOGIC

In *War and Peace*, Tolstoy also sought to crown a novelistic work with an interpretation of history. But his final commentary did not succeed in undoing the novel, or in lowering the prodigious reality of the figures whose insignificance he was trying to demonstrate to us. In *The Sleepwalkers*, we are present at the appearance of a new form of destiny: this fate is logic. These are no longer struggling men or clashing events, but values of which the characters are the unconscious protagonists. No more faces, but masks; no more facts, but abstract powers according to which beings act, like figures in a dream. Huguenau's crime is a logical crime. Not because he kills for ideological motives or for cold reasons well thought out and pursued to their end. He kills by chance, by grasping the occasion offered him by the disorder of the days of rioting. But there is no chance in this abstract desert, where men are agitated and where the meanest values necessarily prevail over vaster and more complex values. In the world that is his, Huguenau, the man of success, can only destroy what impedes him. He will have neither regret nor even memory of his act. At no time does he see its irregular nature. He is not a Dostoyevskian hero, and the time of the Demons is past. In Huguenau we have the first of those ordinary men who, sheltered by a system and with its justification, are going to become, even without knowing it, bureaucrats of crime and accountants of violence.

It seems that Broch, in this final volume of *The Sleepwalkers*, has sought to create, like a new novelistic genre, a sort of novel of thought. Thought—logic—is represented in it as it acts, not in the particular conscience of men, but in the enchanted circle where it invisibly attracts the world to submit to the necessity of its infinite questions. If he nonetheless fails in his aim, if he renounces it without even daring to become aware of doing so, it is because he is afraid of letting his own thinking slip into that somnambulistic element that can become, according to him, the secret heart of reason. So he remains distanced from what he thinks, and his digressions now become nothing but commentaries, sometimes pathetic, sometimes pedantic, from which the vertigo of infinity is lacking.

Things will go otherwise in *The Death of Virgil*. Here, thought will join closely to destiny, without reserve and without precaution. It will become involved in the imaginary and aim toward the extremity of itself, that point of freedom, hope, and distress where the sphere that it forms, the supremely rational, suddenly is reversed to become the supremely irrational. How does Broch manage this? How does what had been measured thought, rigorous analysis, cold controlled narration, finally end up in an immense book in which all novelistic prudence and conventions disappear? It is in the prison where he has just been thrown, when he is threatened with a speedy demise, that Broch begins his central work, a narrative that he cannot hope will lead to "good" except in this space of death that opens up to him, by years of survival and calm work. The one who awakens in order to die thus writes the first page of a work whose completion will require ten years. Wonderful challenge, almost terrifying confidence.

2. The Death of Virgil: The Search for Unity

The Death of Virgil had a double birth. In a letter published in America, Broch recounted how he came to think of this work during the spring of 1935. He had proposed to the Austrian radio in Vienna a lecture on the theme "Literature at the End of an Era," and while he was writing it, the name, presence, and fate of Virgil occupied his mind. The Latin poet too was the poet of a civilization at its end. If the Imperium of Augustus raises the sovereignty of Rome and the values that this sovereignty represents to their highest expression, in this Roman writer, who nonetheless supports the great empire with his poem and founds it in antiquity and in beauty, there is some harmonious weakness, some nostalgia for another age, which without troubling his clarity, opens him to prophetic doubts. On one side, the universal empire that is beginning, and the peace, the great peace of Augustus. On the other, the greatest poet of Rome, who like Rome, is always linked to the land and linked to Rome, to its principle and its leader, by the celebration of his songs. There is nothing here that does not betoken the solidity of human things and the assurance of an art devoted to the eternal. Yet, and not only in the famous Eclogue but also in the light that pervades many of his lines, the mysterious approach of the end can be felt. One might say that time turns round in Virgil, this poet of culture, of savoir-faire and perfection, quite distanced, it seems, from any inspired divination.

> . . . in Virgil sometimes
> The line brings at its summit a strange gleam

To this strangeness, Broch, like Victor Hugo, was sensitive. Virgil's second millennium had just been celebrated, but he does not think of the imperial poet, in whom the glory of time and the calm certainty of civilizations are asserted. He recalls the legend of how, as he lay dying, the poet wanted to destroy the *Aeneid*, that still incomplete poem. This is a modern thought. Did he deem his work imperfect? Or did he turn away from it with the same feeling of being at a turning point that shows itself in his poetry, with that mysterious force of the time that seems to reverse itself in him and distance him from himself? What was the end of Virgil? In this way Broch begins his short narrative, entitled "The Return of Virgil," which he reads on the radio in 1935, on Pentecost. To make the Latin poet, his uncertainties and his work, into a representation symbolic of the West—that is the notion with which he is preoccupied. Broch is always the writer who anxiously reflects on his time and, between reason and unreason, looks for a way of passage.

But is Virgil still vivid enough today to bear the gravity of our fate? If in the Middle Ages there was a myth that Dante could reawaken, wouldn't that still belong to a literary tradition so distant and so exhausted that it is no longer capable of telling us even about our own exhaustion? Broch probably encountered this doubt and, although still feeling that the theme had not been followed in him to the end of its resources, he abandoned it to take up a play intended for performance in Zurich as well as other projects.

He should have left Austria. He was Jewish and in danger, but he could not resign himself to leaving. When he was thrown into prison, "the inner preparation for death" suddenly reanimated in him the ancient name, and "the death of Virgil became the image of my own death." The images that he used, particularly in the fourth part of his book, to make the disappearance of the poet the expression of a universal future—Virgil passes through all the stages of creation—were drawn from his own experience: "I had only," he says, "to welcome them." Similarly, his doubts about himself, anxiety about his insignificant body of work and his unjustified life, the certainty of having failed at an essential duty that he is not able to perform, the indictment that brings on him the sufferings of a slave, his soul laid bare, finally the effort to pass through the Gates of Horn of terror, and to seek, as close as possible to nothingness, salvation beyond scattering and dispersion—these are not literary motives but rather the impact of "a primal mystical experience" that remains the center around which the work developed.

THE INTERIOR SPEECH OF THE LAST DAY

Virgil is not, however, a simple alias. The myth protects Broch and allows him to explore what he could not have reached under his name alone. But when Broch writes his book, he does not aim just to make us aware of what he has experienced. It is not his immediate experience that matters to him; he means rather to prolong it, to deepen it, and to find in it a way out that will be his very work, if this work succeeds in raising to unity the violently contradictory movements between which man is divided when he nears the end. That is the majestic ambition of the writer. When he begins his book, he is going to die, just as Virgil is going to die: eighteen hours separate him from the final instant. This book will be "the interior monologue" of the last day, but the monologue is quite different from the form that tradition lends it. It is recast in the third person, and this passage from I to He, far from being a writerly convenience, is linked to the approach of the event, to its impersonal power, to the distance that is its proximity. With what is the monologue filled? Deeds are reduced in it to almost nothing, without becoming negligible. The galley that carries Virgil, the dying poet, enters the harbor of Brindisi and, while sounds of the crowd cheering Caesar are heard, the litter, guided by a young peasant, Lysanias, image of Virgil as a child, must make its way through the most wretched neighborhoods of the city. That is the first part: the *arrival* and the slow rocking of the *water*.

The second part is even poorer in events. Night has come. The dying man is alone, although he is a guest in the imperial palace. At a certain moment, in the anxiety of fever and under the burning of *fire*, he gets up and goes to the window, where he witnesses a drunkards' quarrel, unsteady and sniggering trio, whose laughter is like an outpouring of the abyss, the jovial rupture of the human oath, perjury in which he feels himself implicated, involved, laid bare before himself. Thus begins the *descent* into those regions where he lacks all that had justified him until now: his name, his work, beauty, hope of true knowledge, hope of a time free of fate. Explanation occurs in him and outside of him, an actual examination of consciousness in the heart of which he turns around and turns back, exposed to the formless, betrayed to the anonymous, with the illusion of advancing into profundity, while his fall is only a vain fall into the superficial muddle of an earthly dream. At least, the approach of death, this listening to a self that is dying, this recognition of his condition as an artist, foreign to truth, enclosed in an unreal world of symbols, content with a game and exulting in a solitary drunkenness that has turned him away from his true duty, this ordeal beside terror, silence, and emptiness brings him to the decision: the *Aeneid* must be burned.

The third part is a return to day. It is the *waiting*, the confrontation of truths of the night with certainties of the *earth*, the bringing together of Virgil, who wants to destroy his work, with Virgil's friends, who want to save it; of Virgil, who opens himself to another world, to another time, and of Augustus, who maintains, against the chimera of the prophetic spirit and an imprecise redemption, the values of the State and the importance of the *Aeneid*, which belongs to the State. This chapter, the longest in the work and one in which Broch's technical virtuosity comes to light, is the only one in which historical reality takes on more importance. However, the principle of the interior monologue in the third person is not abandoned. It is in the space of this immense, impersonal way of thinking that the dialogues, precise nonetheless and closely expressed, resound; something vaster than them remembers them. All that could be artificial in them, in the realistic evocation of characters and of an era about which we scarcely care, subsides; without too much implausibility, the long debate between Augustus and Virgil, between the earthly role and the super-earthly role, between temporal Rome and spiritual Rome—with, as stake, under the name *Aeneid*, the fate of the entire West—can represent the more contemporary debate that interested Broch. Can culture be saved? What will be the fate of the work of art, precious fruit of a declining civilization, poetry that ignores the simplicity of the slave, that even ignores the gods and has welcomed only their images, that is finally only "a half-successful counterfeit of the Homeric epic," "a tired nothingness," of this creation that is only a symbol? Mustn't what the poet has written be burnt in the fire of reality? Will he have to abandon himself to the terrifying immortality of the sovereign old men, Homer, Aeschylus? No, the *Aeneid* must be burned. At the end, though, Broch and Virgil save their work and, it seems, save the West. Why? That is not clear.[1] It is like a bet in favor of the future. It is also the premonition of salvation, which, during the fourth part, will allow the monologue to reach its center, the well of simultaneity, the gushing milieu where death and creation coincide, where the end is the beginning and, in the annihilation that seals unity, the word is pronounced in which everything is dissolved, everything is contained, that secret of the power of the word to which Broch entrusts himself to save his work and to save what is at stake, he thinks, in his work: the return to sources, the felicity of unity rediscovered.

THE TEMPTATION OF UNITY

It is in fact toward unity that his book does not stop reaching, through all the despair, uncertainties, and negative experiences. The search for unity was Broch's great passion, his torment, his nostalgia: unity, the hope of reaching the point of the circle's closing, when the one who has gone far ahead wins the right to turn back and to surprise, like a unified whole, the infinitely opposed forces that divide him. *The Sleepwalkers* had described this division: the dispersion of values into irreducible systems, the vertigo of infinity that pushes each one of these values to occupy the entire space and at the same time to disappear into the abstract where it reigns, logic that introduces its own dissolution, the irrational that triumphs under the mask of reason. Yet *The Sleepwalkers* ended with an indecisive promise of salvation: the greater the anguish of man aware of his solitude, the more he aspires to a guide, the bearer of redemption who will take him by the hand and will make him grasp, by his acts, the incomprehensible event of this time. "Such is nostalgia," says Broch, nostalgia for the Führer, whom, starting in 1928, he had reason to be wary of.

But Broch also shares this nostalgia, and he does not shy away from giving voice to the summons of the absolute that he had recognized first in the cold passion of mathematical abstraction. Where is unity? How can the irreconcilable powers that divide the human world assert themselves in an entirety where the secret law of their incessant contrariness would be revealed? *The Death of Virgil* is the answer. Not that this work tells us where unity is, but that it represents it itself: poem, it is that sphere where the forces of emotion and reasonable certainties, form and content, meaning and expression pass into each other. So we can say that what is at stake for Broch in his work is quite a bit more than his work: if he can write it, it is because unity is possible; symbol will become reality, and the poem will be truth and knowledge. Hence the importance that, in the second part, the debate between the poet and his art acquires: will the work of art always be only a symbol? At the farthest frontier, will it still meet only beauty?

It is to answer this doubt and to learn if the work of literature can become the approach to the point where the whole is asserted and not just the power of magnificence that momentarily stops the alternating game of questions and answers, that Broch, breaking with novelistic traditions, demands from lyrical form a new possibility of unity and transforms interior monologue to make it a force of progression. Although he recognized all he owed Joyce, he insisted how few relationships there are between the form of *Ulysses* and the form he used. With Joyce, thoughts, images, sensations are placed side by side, without anything to unify them except the great verbal current that carries them along. With Broch, there is a play of exchanges between the diverse profundities of human reality, at each instant passing from feeling to thought, from stupor to meditation, from coarse experience to a vaster experience comprehended through reflection—then, again, it is immerged into a more profound ignorance, which in turn is transformed into a more interior knowledge.

Broch's ideal would be the ability to express, at once and as if in one single sentence, all opposing movements, to maintain them in their opposition while at the same time opening them up to unity, or even more: to embrace them, at each instant and on the occasion of each event and even each word, in a simultaneity that requires no temporal development, the immensity of the whole, which is his aim. If so many of his sentences become excessively lengthy (specialists claim they are the longest in the German language), it is because each of them wants to exhaust the world, wants to pass through all the levels of experience, wants each time to unite all that clashes—cruelty and goodness, life and death, instant and eternity—but does not manage to end; for the perpetual reversal of pro and con, the effort not to betray incessant drives, the silent work of words against prematurely finished forms, involve him in infinite repetitions and amplifications that his predilection for the use of nouns makes even more massive.

Broch said of such a form of interior monologue: "Something absolutely new was attempted here, what could be called a lyrical commentary on itself." He in effect wants constantly to unite the two possibilities: on one hand, by the exercise of a vigilant thought that is always more internalized without renouncing its power of reflection, to maintain to the end a demand for clarity and truth; on the other hand, by the call to song, to the lyrical powers of rhythm, and above all to musical forms of composition, to transcend, without destroying, the intellectual content of the experience and to assure to the discordant demands of the rational and the irrational a common measure that will reconcile them into a whole. His book always has a double face. It has a logical reality that, even in its most extreme gestures, never endangers comprehension—in that respect he is closer to Proust than to Joyce; but the book is no less expressive by its ability of suggestion, which it owes to its rhythmic structure and to a mode of development intentionally borrowed from music.[2]

The Death of Virgil, says Broch, is "a quartet, or more precisely, a symphony," composed as a musical work might be, on the compositional model known as "theme and variations." The work, like a classical symphony, has four movements, which borrow from the four elements—water, fire, earth, and ether—and from four spiritual attitudes—arrival, descent, waiting, return—the double indication that allows us to situate, in the various worlds, by a game of coordinates, Virgil's exact position in the course of his journey. In each part, the writer imposes a unique rhythm to which corresponds a particular type of sentence, intended to make us aware of the unique thought of the dying man at each stage of his journey. As Jean Starr Untermeyer remarks, the faster the tempo, the more agitated the soul, the shorter the sentence; the more time slows down, the more thought, given over to the movements of aimless inquiry, joins with the perpetuity of night, and the more complicated the sentence is, the longer it extends, repeats itself, fixes itself in a stationary gesture where it seems ready to dissolve itself into the formless. Sometimes, without any break in tone, by a greater concentration of rhythmic elements, the prose becomes poetry, as if, at those privileged moments, the virtue of the work crystallized to become visible to us. Those are the most authentic parts of the book, the ones in which we most feel, beyond the anguish of Virgil, herald of a time he does not know, the hope and despair of the man who "does not yet exist and yet who exists already": waiting without direction, perpetual departure, illusion of return, "oh to return, to return to things, to dream, oh to return once more, oh flight!"

THE CHARACTERISTICS OF THE WORK

If, while making a quick overview of this book, we sought to bring out its main features, we would have to say: like all the great works of this time, those of Proust, of Joyce, of Thomas Mann, not to speak of the poets, *The Death of Virgil* is a work that has possibility as its center. What threatens art, expression, and the affirmation of culture in the West? Suffering. From the first pages on, when he must travel down the alleyway of misery, Virgil feels stripped of himself: shame of becoming attached to his own memories and of celebrating the anniversaries of his beginnings, now as he finds himself faced with this time without past, without future, which is that of the slave-herd, silence formed from voice. What is poetic language, if it remains foreign to what is without memory, without name? Condemnation that is not only a moral condemnation, that affects the work at its roots. There will be no true communication, no song, if song cannot descend, below all form, toward the formless and toward that profundity where the voice outside of all language speaks. It is this descent—descent toward the undetermined—that the dying poet seeks to accomplish by his death. The space of song and the space of death are described to us as linked and embraced by each other.

The other essential trait: like almost all great modern writers, Broch wants to make literary expression an experiment. He believes that interior monologue, having become "a lyrical commentary," will let him reach the point of unique presence where, in absolute simultaneity, the infinity of the past and the infinity of the future will open up to him. He thinks that by the force of musical development, the pathetic elements and the philosophical elements of his work, images of the disparateness of the human soul, will be fully unified. Grand ambition, but does he sustain it to the end? Is he even faithful to the demand of this free movement of discovery that should be the justification of his work? Does he not, on the contrary, give the impression of imposing on us his own preliminary beliefs, particularly in the fourth part, when Virgil enters, dying, into the intimacy of creation, becomes a sort of Adam Kadmon, cosmic Man, the Universe metamorphosed into man and the man who returns harmoniously to the origin, by turns primitive animality, original vegetable density, the primal clay, until, joined with the nothingness of the center, he suddenly sees once again the nothing fill the void and become the whole, conformable to the cyclic hope that wills the end to be the beginning.[3] These are certainly felicitous and harmonious pages. But is musical felicity enough? Is it a guarantee of truth? Does it succeed in convincing us of the reality of this funeral procession and of the redemption it promises us? Aren't we here exactly in the presence of this language of beauty and of that false metaphoric knowledge from which Broch wants to rescue art, and from which death is charged with freeing us?

To that, Broch would undoubtedly have replied that he gave to the agony of the poet, formerly called Virgil, the meaning that eastern concepts have made accessible to his own experience.[4] It is in the space of such imaginations that the event was carried out, and it is by their intervention that we, we others, men of the late West, can best identify with this past that is also our own. *The Death of Virgil*, in fact, is not just the development of a personal experience, but a myth, an effort to represent symbolically the knowledge and fate of all Western civilization. This is the other essential trait. Just as the story of Leopold Bloom must be read in the context of *The Odyssey*, just as the fate of Adrian Leverkühn is a reanimation of Faust, and [Thomas Mann's] *Joseph and His Brothers* an essay to lead narration back to the youth of its mythical sources, so did Broch ask an ancient name and legend for the resources of a narrative able to speak to us about ourselves, beginning with a world that was at once close and foreign to us. His task was not easy. What is Virgil for us? And what is Rome? But as much as he could succeed, he succeeded. His book escapes in part the artifices of historical narrative, and it is with a real force of truth that little by little the great melancholic presence of the poet—the gravity of his fate, his world, the premonition of this return of time, of which we also have the premonition—imposes itself on us.

It would be easy to relate to Broch's origin, born in Vienna, not far from Hofmannsthal, this Latin sensibility that, at the time when Rome's heritage is vacillating, invites him to revive its shadows, to recognize himself in them—for Virgil is Broch—and to assure its salvation, albeit by death. Those who like these explanations will say that Broch owes to his double patrimony—his Viennese past and his Jewish past—the complexity of his gifts and the boldness of attempts that, even in their excesses, a certain classical harmony tempers. Heinz Politzer, who went to see him at Princeton after the war, recognized in him an adviser of the former imperial court of Austria: he had its customs, politeness, elegance, spiritual seduction; but his face, harshly sculpted, expressed the painful rigor of a very ancient way of thinking. These opposing traits, more than any prerogative of birth, are the sign of his vocation. Like any modern artist, like Joyce, he had a great devotion to art and a great mistrust of the means of art, he had great culture and a great disgust for culture, an intellectual passion that wants to surpass, surmount intelligence and is exalted in mystical visions. We are told that he was always on familiar terms with death, without pathos and with a light, almost Mozartian feeling, which, even in Hitler's prisons, allowed him to play with it and even to play tricks on it. It is finally this confidence and this gentleness that are expressed in *The Death of Virgil*: funeral song, requiem, but, like the Fauré Requiem, it invites us almost tenderly to force the doors of terror, to descend, preceded by our loving memory, to that point where the happiness or knowledge of the circle is accomplished. Strange happiness, dark knowledge of which Hofmannsthal also spoke to us: "Whoever knows the power of the circle no longer fears death," and Rilke, who is of the same family: "I love when the circle is closed again, when one thing merges in the other." "There is nothing wiser than the circle." "The ring is rich by its return."

§ 14 The Turn of the Screw

When one reads Henry James's *Notebooks*, one is surprised to see him preparing his novels by very detailed plans, which he of course modifies when he writes the book, but which he sometimes follows faithfully.

If one compares the *Notebooks* to those in which Kafka sketched out his stories, the difference is striking: in Kafka's *Notebooks*, there is never a plan or any preliminary analysis; there are many drafts, but these drafts are the work itself—sometimes a page or a single sentence, but this sentence is involved in the profundity of the story, and if it is an experiment, it is an experiment of the story itself, a way that the unforeseeable movement of the novel's prose can alone open up. These fragments are not materials that are later used. Proust uses scissors and glue; he "pins here and there an additional leaf," the "*paperoles*" with which he puts his book together, "not with myriad details, like a cathedral, but quite simply, like a dress." For other writers, the story cannot be composed from without: it loses all strength and all reality if it does not contain within itself the forward movement by which it discovers the shape of its completion. And that does not necessarily signify, for the book, an obscure and irrational coherence: Kafka's books are, in their structure, clearer than James's, less difficult and less complex than Proust's.

"THE SUBJECT IS EVERYTHING"

The example of James is still—be it understood—not as simple as it seems. In his *Notebooks*, he accumulates anecdotes, sometimes interesting, sometimes extremely mediocre, that he collects in the salons. He must have subjects. "The subject is everything—the subject is everything," he writes with timorous confidence. "The further I go, the more intensely I realize that it is on the solidity of the subject, the importance, the capacity of emotion of the subject, on that alone, hereafter, that I should dwell. Everything else crumbles, collapses, comes to a sudden end, turns out poorly, turns out badly—betrays you miserably." That also surprises us. What is the "subject"? A writer as refined as Borges asserts that modern novelistic literature is superior not because of the study of characters and the development of psychological variety, but when it invents fables or subjects. It is an answer to Robert Louis Stevenson, who observed sadly, against himself—around 1882—that English readers disdained the novelist's plotting, and preferred the cleverness of writers able to write a novel without a subject "or with a tiny, atrophied subject." Ortega y Gasset declares, fifty years later, that it is "very difficult, today, to invent an adventure that can interest our superior sensibility." According to Borges, our superior sensibility is more happily satisfied than it has ever been. "I think I am free from any superstition of modernism, from any illusion that yesterday differs profoundly from today or will differ from tomorrow, but I think that no other era possesses novels of a subject as admirable as *The Turn of the Screw*, *The Trial*, or *Le voyage sur la terre*; or as the novel that, in Buenos Aires, Adolfo Bioy Casares has achieved" (*Morel's Invention*). The love of truth ought to have led Borges to name in the privacy of his memoir also his own *The Circular Ruins* or *The Library of Babel*.

But what is a subject? To say that the novel is valuable because of the rigor of its plot, the attractive power of its motives—this assertion is not as reassuring for tradition as tradition would like to think; it is saying, in fact, that it is not valuable because of the truth of its characters or for its realism, psychological or physical, that it should not count on imitation, either of the world or of society or of nature, to retain interest. A story with a subject is thus a mysterious work, removed from all matter: a narrative without characters, a story in which the storyless day-to-day and eventless intimacy, those resources always at hand, stop being a resource. Moreover it is a story in which what happens is not content with occurring through the play of superficial or capricious succession, episodes that would follow episodes, as in picaresque novels; rather it forms a unified whole, rigorously ordered according to a law all the more important because it remains hidden, like the secret center of everything.

"The subject is everything—the subject is everything," this cry of James, is pathetic, and the help that Borges generously offers him is not

easily used. When Borges names *The Trial* among the modern works more
admirable for their subject than any other, that makes us reflect. Is the
subject of this novel of such a surprising invention? Vigny had already formulated it in a few grave lines, as had Pascal, and perhaps each one of us.
The story of a man grappling with himself as with an obscure tribunal before which he cannot justify himself because he cannot find it is indeed
worthy of interest, but it is scarcely a story, even less a fiction and, for
Kafka, it was the given of his life: this guilt that is all the heavier because
it was the shadow of his very innocence.

But is that the subject of the *Trial,* this abstract, empty theme, this dry
sentence with which we summarize it? No, certainly not. What is a subject, then? Borges cites *The Turn of the Screw,* a narrative that seems to us
in fact to shine, starting with an impressive and beautiful story that would
become its subject. In the *Notebooks,* three years before writing the work,
James happens to report the anecdote that gives him the idea for it. It is
the Archbishop of Canterbury who tells it: "very vague, confused sketch,
without details," that the bishop himself has from a lady who had neither
gift of expression nor clarity. "The story of young children (number and
age undetermined), confided to servants in an old manor house in the
country, no doubt upon the death of their parents. The servants, mean
and depraved, corrupt and deprave the children; the children are bad, full
of evil to a sinister degree. The servants die (the story is vague about the
way of it) and their apparitions return to haunt the house and the children, to whom they seem to beckon, whom they invite and solicit, from
the depth of dangerous recesses—from the deep ditch of a sunk fence,
etc.—so that the children may destroy themselves, lose themselves by
obeying them, by placing themselves under their domination. As long as
the children are kept far from them, they are not lost; but these evil presences tirelessly try to get hold of them, and to draw them to where they
are." James adds this remark: "All that is obscure and imperfect—the
scene, the story—but there is, inside that, the suggestion of an effect, a
strange shiver of horror. The story must be told—tolerably obviously—by
a spectator, an observer from outside."

Is that the subject of *The Turn of the Screw?* Everything is found in it,
and above all the essential part: some children, linked by a dominating relationship with figures that haunt them, that draw them, by the memory
of evil, toward that space where they must lose themselves. Everything is
in it, and even the worst part: that these children are perverted, but that
they are, also, innocent ("as long as the children are kept far from the

specters, they are not lost"). From this motif, James will draw one of his cruelest effects: the ambiguity of this innocence, an innocence that is the purity of evil in them, the secret of the perfection of the lie that hides this evil from the honest people close to them, but that is perhaps also the purity that evil becomes when it touches them, the incorruptible ingenuity that they contrast with true evil, that of adults; or the very enigma of these apparitions that is lent them, the uncertainty that weighs on the story and makes us wonder if it is not entirely projected on them by the hallucinating mind of their governess—who torments them with her own hauntings until death.

When Gide discovered that *The Turn of the Screw* was not a story of phantoms but probably a Freudian narrative in which it is the female narrator—the governess with her passions and her visions—who, blind to herself and terrible with her lack of awareness, ends up making the innocent children live in contact with terrifying images that, without her, they would not have suspected, he was amazed and overjoyed. (But naturally a doubt remained in him that he would have liked to see dissipate.)

Would this, then, be the subject of the story, to which the archbishop would no longer have any rights as author? But is this indeed the subject? Is it even the one that James consciously decided to treat? The editors of the *Notebooks* fasten on this anecdote to claim that the modern interpretation is not definitive, that James indeed wanted to write a ghost story, with, as postulated, the corruption of children and real apparitions. Of course, the uncanny is evoked only indirectly, and the terrifying element there is in the story, the shiver of unease that it excites, comes less from the presence of specters than from the secret disorder that results, but this is a rule for which James himself gave the formula in the preface to his ghost stories when he emphasizes "the importance of presenting the wonderful and the strange by limiting oneself almost exclusively to showing their repercussion on a sensibility and by recognizing that their principal element of interest consists in some strong impression that they produce and that is perceived with intensity."

THE CUNNING HEART OF EVERY STORY

It is, then, quite possible that James was unable to answer Gide or to confirm him in the pleasure of his discovery. It is almost certain that his answer would have been witty, evasive, and deceptive. In truth, if the Freudian interpretation were imposed as an obvious decipherment, the narrative would gain nothing from it except a momentary psychological

interest, and it would risk losing everything that makes it a narrative—
fascinating, indubitable, elusive—in which truth has the slippery certainty
of an image—close, like it, and like it inaccessible. Modern readers, so
cunning, have all understood that the ambiguity of the story is explained
not just by the abnormal sensibility of the governess but also because this
governess is also the *narrator*. She is not content with seeing ghosts by
which the children might be haunted; she is the one who speaks of them,
drawing them into the uncertain space of the narration, into that unreal
beyond where everything becomes phantom, everything becomes slippery,
fugitive, present and absent, symbol of Evil under the shadow of which
Graham Greene sees James writing and which is perhaps only the cunning
heart of every story.

After having noted the anecdote, James added: "The story should be
told—with a sufficient amount of plausibility—by a spectator, an observer from outside." One can thus say that all he lacked was the essential
part, the *subject*: the female narrator who is the very nucleus of the narrative, though it is true that her essence is an alien one, a presence that tries
to penetrate to the center of a story where she remains nonetheless an intruder, an excluded witness, who imposes herself by violence, who distorts
the secret, invents it perhaps, perhaps discovers it, in every way forces it,
destroys it, and reveals to us only its ambiguity, which hides it.

Which brings us back to saying that the subject of *The Turn of the
Screw* is—simply—James's art, the way he has of always circling round a
secret that, in so many of his books, some anecdote sets in operation, and
that is not only a real secret—some fact, some thought or truth that can
be revealed—that is not even a detour of the mind, but one that escapes
all revelation, for it belongs to a region that is not that of light.[1] Of this
art, James has the liveliest awareness, although he remains strangely silent
in the *Notebooks* on this awareness, aside from a few exceptions, like: "I see
that my leaps and shortcuts, my drawbridges and my great comprehensive
loops (in one or two lively, admirable sentences) should be of an impec-
cable, masterly boldness."

One can, then, wonder why this art, in which everything is movement,
effort of discovery and investigation, fold, refold, sinuosity, reserve, art
that does not decipher but is the cipher of the indecipherable, instead of
beginning from itself begins often from an extremely coarse schema, with
halting items, with numbered sections; why, also, he must start with a
story to tell, which exists for him even before he tells it.

To this peculiarity, there are undoubtedly many responses. And this one first of all: that the American writer belonged to a time when the novel was written not by Mallarmé but by Flaubert and Maupassant; that he is preoccupied with giving his work an important content; that moral conflicts count for a lot with him. While this is true, there is something else. Obviously, James is afraid of his art; he struggles against the "scattering" to which James's art exposes him, rejecting the need to say everything, to "say and write too much," which risks dragging him to prodigious lengths, while he admires above all the perfection of a neat form. (James always dreamed of a popular success. He also wished to find this success in the theater, the models for which he seeks in the worst French theater. It is true that, like Proust, he has a taste for scenes, for the dramatic structure of works; this contradiction maintains equilibrium in him.) There is, in the form that is unique to him, an excess, perhaps a touch of madness against which he tries to protect himself, because every artist is frightened of himself. "Ah, to be able simply to let oneself go—finally." "The result of all my reflections is that I have only to give myself free rein! That is what I have told myself all my life. . . . Yet I have never fully done that."[2]

James fears beginning: this beginning, where the work is all ignorance of itself, is the weakness of that which is without weight, without reality, without truth, and yet already necessary, of an empty, ineluctable necessity. Of this beginning, he is afraid. Before giving himself over to the force of the narrative, he must have the security of a framework, a work that clarifies and plots the subject clearly on a graph. "God save me—not however that I am inclined to it! heaven is my witness—from relaxing from my profound observance of that strong and salutary method that consists in having a structure that is solidly constructed, strongly built and articulated." Through this fear of beginning, he comes to lose himself in preliminaries that he develops more and more, with a detail and detours where his art is already insinuating itself: "Begin, begin, don't delay by talking about it and detouring around it." "I have only to bite down and to put one word after another. Bite down and line up words, the eternal recipe."

THE "DIVINE PRESSURE"

However, that does not explain everything. As the years pass and as James moves in a more deliberate way toward himself, he discovers the true significance of this preliminary work that is precisely not a work.

Endlessly, he speaks of these hours of preparation as "blessed hours," "wonderful, ineffable, secret, pathetic, tragic" instants, or even as a "sacred" time, when his pen exercises "an enchanted pressure," becomes the "deciphering" pen, the magic needle in movement, whose turns and detours give him a premonition of the innumerable paths that are not yet traced. He calls the principle of the plot "divine," "divine light illuminating the ancient holy little virtualities," "divine ancient joy of the plot that makes my arteries throb, with its little sacred, irrepressible emotions." Why this joy, this passion, this feeling of a wonderful life, which he cannot evoke without tears, to the point that his notebook, "the patient, passionate little notebook becomes . . . the essential part of my life"? It is because in these hours of confiding in himself, he is grappling with the fullness of the narrative that has not yet begun, when the still undetermined work, pure of any action and any limit, is only possible, is the "blessed" drunkenness of pure possibility, and we know how the possible—this phantasmal and unreal life of what we have not been, these figures with whom we have always had an appointment—exercised over James a dangerous attraction, sometimes almost mad, that perhaps art alone allowed him to explore and plot. "The further I go, the more I find that the only balm, the only refuge, the true solution to the powerful problem of life consists in this frequent, fertile, intimate struggle with the particular idea, the subject, the possibility, the place."

We can say, then, that if this moment of preliminary work, so wonderful in his memory, is so necessary to James, it is because it represents the moment when the work, approached, but not touched, remains the secret center around which he devotes himself, with an almost perverse pleasure, to investigations that he can stretch out even more when they let loose the narrative but do not yet commence it. Often, all the anecdotal precisions that he develops in his plans not only will disappear from the work itself, but will be found again, in it, as negative values, incidents to which allusion is made as to that which precisely has not occurred. By these means, James produces the experience, not of the narrative that he must write but of its reverse, from the other side of the work, the one that the movement of writing necessarily hides and about which he is anxious, as if he had the anxiety and curiosity—naïve, moving—about what there is behind his work, while he writes.

What can then be called the passionate paradox of the plan with James is that it represents, for him, the security of a composition determined in advance, but also the opposite: the joys of creation, which coincide with the pure *indeterminacy* of the work, which put it to the test, but without reducing it, without depriving it of all the possibilities that it contains (and such is perhaps the essence of James's art: each instant to produce the entire work present and, even behind the constructed and limited work that he shapes, to make other forms felt, the infinite and light space of the narrative as it could have been, as it is before any beginning). Yet this pressure to which he submits the work, not to limit it but on the contrary to make it speak completely, without reserve in its nonetheless reserved secret, this firm and gentle pressure, this pressing solicitude—what does he call it? With the very name he chose as title for his ghost story: *The Turn of the Screw*. "What can my case of K. B. [a novel that he will not finish] give, once submitted to the pressure and to the *turn of the screw*?" Revealing allusion. It confirms to us that James is certainly not unaware of what the "subject" of his story is: this pressure that the governess makes the children undergo in order to tear their secret from them and that they also perhaps experience on the part of the invisible, but that is essentially the pressure of the narration itself, the wonderful and terrible movement that the deed of writing exercises on truth, torment, torture, violence that finally lead to death, in which everything seems to be revealed, in which everything, however, falls back again into the doubt and void of the shadows. "We are working in darkness—we do what we can—we give what we have. Our doubt is our passion, and our passion, our task. The rest is the madness of art."[3]

§ 15 Musil

1. The Passion of Indifference

I fear that Robert Musil's great work, made accessible to French readers by the efforts of a courageous translator, will be blindly praised. I also fear the opposite: that it will be more commented on than read, for it offers critics, by its rare aim, its contradictory qualities, the difficulties of its accomplishment, the profundity of its failure, everything that attracts them; it is so close to commentary that it often seems to have been commented on rather than written, as if it could be analyzed instead of read. With what wonderful, insoluble, inexhaustible problems this great attempt delights us. And how it will please us, as much by its first-rate defects as by the refinement of its qualities, by the excessiveness and, in its excesses, the restraint it has; finally by its imposing failure. Here is another immense, unfinished, and unfinishable work. Here again is the surprise of a monument admirably in ruins.

Maybe it is pleasant for us to see a misunderstood author and an unknown "masterpiece" suddenly emerge from obscurity, but at the same time to know that they were as if in reserve. Our era, which knows everything and knows it right away, loves these injustices that it puts right and these rediscoveries that it manages to make with fanfare after having neglected them with such indifference, despite the advice of a few enlightened men. It is as if, in its universal knowledge, our age were happy not to know everything, and to be able to preserve invisible, capital works about which only some lucky chance will alert them. This faith in unknown masterpieces is accompanied by an unusual confidence in posterity. We continue to believe with the force of an invincible prejudice that what the present rejects the future will necessarily welcome, as little as art wants it to. And there is scarcely an artist, even without a taste for heaven, who does not die always certain and always happy about that other heaven with which the future must recompense his poor shade.

If we regard as abnormal the writer who disappears forgotten and content at being so—although this disappearance probably has cogent meaning—Robert Musil will then seem to us quite classic. His unfortunate fate did not please him, and he did not seek it out. He often judged the great writers of his time with whom he thought himself equal, but whom he did not equal in fame, with an almost aggressive harshness. He was scarcely unknown, though. He himself said that his fame was that of a great poet who had only limited publication: he lacked only number and social clout; he also said that the knowledge people had of him was equal to the ignorance, "as known as unknown, which does not mean half-known, but produces a bizarre mixture." First, as author of a brilliant novel that brought him two prizes and some reputation, he immerses himself methodically in an excessive work on which he labors for forty years, almost his entire creative life, a work that is for him the equivalent of his life. During his lifetime, in 1930, he publishes the first part of it, which does not bring him the glory of Proust but produces the impression of a work of first importance; not long afterwards, in 1932, he quickly publishes the first volume of the second part, as if to warn of the upheavals whose danger he feels. Success did not come to him. What did come was rupture with the future, poverty, deterioration of the world, finally exile. Of course, he is not the only writer in the German language to know the difficulties of emigration. Others were physically more threatened, underwent more atrocious ordeals. Musil lives poorly in Geneva, certainly very isolated (but having beside him Marthe Musil, his wife), but in an isolation he knows he complains about after having sought it out: in his journal, he notes around 1939: "Interior opposition to my friends and my enemies; desire to be neither here nor there, and yet regret and complaint, when they reject me from here and there." It is not doubtful that, during the last ten years—approximate number—he changes, not only because of events but also with regard to his work, which itself changes, while he pursues it obstinately, slowly, while maintaining with great difficulty the great lines of the original project (often modified, however). I think that one cannot ignore the profound trouble that comes to him from this book that he does not entirely master, that resists him and that he also resists, seeking to impose on it a plan that perhaps is not suitable for it. His sudden death, which he had not foreseen, always granting himself twenty years more, comes to surprise him, then, at the darkest moment of the war and of his creative task. Eight people accompany him to the last exile. Ten years later, when a devoted friend, continuing the work of Mme Musil, publishes the definitive edition, he is saluted as the equal of Proust, of Joyce. Five more years go by, and now it is translated into French.[1] Rather than his obscurity, it is the promptness and fanfare of his fame that almost surprises me. The posthumous irony we continue to attribute to Musil could not fail to marvel silently at it.

Even if we know nothing about him except for his novel and his recently published journal, we would be immediately taken, seduced, sometimes surprised by this complex figure. A difficult man, capable of criticizing what he loves and of feeling close to what he rejects; in many respects, a modern man who welcomes the new era as it is and lucidly foresees what it will become, a man of knowledge, of science, an exact mind, and in no way ready to condemn the formidable transformations of technology, but at the same time, a man of an earlier era, of a refined culture, almost an aristocrat. If he paints a strongly satirical portrait of the old Empire of Austria-Hungary, which he calls Kakania (it would be better to call it *Cancania*),[2] we must not think that he feels foreign to this world of decadence, a world of an old-fashioned civilization still capable of an intense creative life, if we recall that not only was Musil a Cancanian, but so were Hofmannsthal, Rilke, Freud, Husserl, Trakl, Broch, Schoenberg, Reinhardt, Kafka, and Kassner—these names alone suffice to show us that dying cultures are very apt to produce revolutionary works and talents of the future.

Musil is a man of Cancania—we cannot neglect this trait; just as, in his book, we should not content ourselves with looking for Musil's mind in the discoveries of the protagonist, but should look also in the movements in counterpoint that the other figures perform, sometimes caricatures but in no way foreign to his ironic sympathy. The entire fantastic and ridiculous history of the Parallel Campaign—which serves as a high point in the first part of the book—shows not only the efforts of some puppets of high society to celebrate the apogee of an Empire that already is touching the abyss; it also has a serious meaning, secretly dramatic: that of learning if culture can acquire an ultimate value or if it can do no more than march about gloriously in the void from which it protects us by hiding it from us.

Man of the past, wholly modern man, almost classical writer, although his language is intentionally bare and of a light and refined stiffness with occasional illuminating images, writer who nonetheless is ready to dedicate everything to literature (to the point of formulating this pathetic alternative: "commit suicide or write"), but also to make it serve the spiritual conquest of the world, to lend it ethical aims, to assert that the theoretical expression of the essay has in our time more value than aesthetic expression. Like Valéry and Broch, he drew from his knowledge of the sciences and above all of mathematics an ideal of precision, the absence of which makes literary works scarcely bearable for him. The impersonality of knowledge, the impersonality of scholarship, reveal to him a demand with which he feels dangerously in agreement and about which he will try to discover what transformations it might bring to reality, if only the reality of the time were not a century behind the knowledge of the time.

THE CENTRAL THEME

The central theme, if there is one in this essentially bipolar book, is represented to us exactly by its title, *Der Mann ohne Eigenschaften* [The man without qualities]. This title passes with difficulty into our language. Philippe Jaccottet, as exact a translator as he is an excellent writer and poet, certainly weighed the pros and cons. Gide jokingly proposed a Gidian title, *L'homme disponible* [The available man]. The journal *Mesures* cleverly offered us *L'homme sans caractères* [The man without characteristics]. I think I would have stopped at the simplest translation, the one closest to the German and the most natural in French: *L'homme sans particularités* [The man without particularities]. The expression "the man without qualities," although elegantly worded, makes the mistake of not making immediate sense and of losing the idea that the man in question has nothing that is unique to him—he has no qualities but no substance either. His essential particularity, says Musil in his notes, is that he is nothing in particular. He is any man whatsoever, and more profoundly he is the man without essence, the man who does not accept being crystallized into a character or fixed in a stable personality: a man indeed deprived of himself, but because he does not want to welcome as particular to him this ensemble of particularities that comes to him from outside and that almost all men naïvely identify with their pure secret soul, far from seeing in it a foreign inheritance, accidental and overwhelming.

But here we must immediately enter into the mind of the work, which is precisely mind under the form of irony. Musil's irony is the cold light that invisibly changes, instant by instant, the lighting of the book (above all in the first part) and, although often indistinct, does not let us settle in the distinctness of a precise meaning, or one given in advance. Assuredly, in a tradition like that of German literature, in which irony was elevated to the seriousness of a metaphysical category, the ironic investigation of the man without particularities is not an absolute creation; moreover it comes after Nietzsche, whose influence Musil welcomed even while rejecting it. But here, irony is one of the centers of the work, it is the relationship of the writer and the man with himself, a relationship that occurs only in the absence of all particular relationships and in the refusal of being someone for others and something for oneself.[3] It is a poetic gift and it is a methodical principle. If one looks for it in words, one will rarely find it, or find it ready to be distorted into satirical traits. It lies rather in the very composition of the book; it is in the way certain situations turn on themselves, in the fact that the most serious thoughts and the most authentic impulses of the hero, Ulrich, will then play themselves out a second time in other characters, where they take on a pitiful or comic aspect. Thus the effort to associate the ideal of exactitude with this void that is the soul—one of Ulrich's main concerns—has as a counterpart the love affair of Diotima, the beautiful soul, and Arnheim, powerful industrialist, scheming capitalist, and idealistic philosopher, for whom Walther Rathenau provided an example. Thus too, the mystical passion of Ulrich and his sister is reduplicated and sadly repeated in the relationships of Ulrich and Clarisse, experiences straight out of Nietzsche that end in sterile hysteria. The result is that events, by changing from echo to echo, not only lose their simple significance but abandon even their reality and, instead of developing into a story, direct us to the moving field where deeds take place in the uncertainty of possible relationships.

Now we are facing another aspect of the work. The man without particularities, who does not want to recognize himself in the person he is, for whom all the traits that particularize him make him nothing in particular, never close to what is closest to him, never foreign to what is exterior to him, chooses to be this way because of an ideal of freedom, but also because he lives in a world—the modern world, our world—in which particular deeds are always about to be lost in the impersonal conjuncture of relationships, of which they mark only the temporary intersection. In

the world, the world of great cities and great collective masses, it is imma-
terial whether something has truly taken place and in what historical
event we suppose ourselves to be actors and witnesses. What has taken
place remains elusive, and in any case incidental, even null: the only important thing is the possibility of what has happened thus but could have
happened otherwise; all that counts is the general significance and the
right of the mind to seek this meaning, not in what is (which is nothing in
particular), but in the panoply of possibilities. What we call "reality" is a
utopia. History, as we represent it to ourselves and think we live it, with its
succession of calmly linear incidents, expresses only our wish to cling to
solid things, to unquestionable events unfolding in a simple order which
the art of narrative, the eternal literature of nursemaids, highlights, making the most of this attractive illusion. Of this narrative complacency, on
the model of which centuries of historical realities have been invented,
Ulrich is no longer capable. If he lives, it is in a world of possibilities and
no longer of events, where nothing happens that one can *recount*. Strange
situation for the hero of a novel, stranger still for the novelist. And is his
hero himself real, even as fiction? But isn't he more than that: the risky
experiment, whose outcome alone, by assuring him that he is possible,
will finally make him real, but only as possibility?

THE POSSIBLE MAN

We slowly begin to perceive the amplitude of the project that Musil has
sustained for so many years. He himself discerned it quite slowly. He
thought about his book from the beginning of the century onward, and
we find in his journal scenes and situations drawn from adventures of his
youth, which would take place only in the final part of the work (at least
as the posthumous publication restores it to us).[4] We should not forget
this slow maturation, this life that his life lends to the work, and the
strange experiment that makes his existence depend on an endless book,
then transforms it by making it fundamentally improbable. The book is
both superficially and profoundly autobiographical. Ulrich sends us back
to Musil, but Musil is linked anxiously to Ulrich, his truth is only in him
who prefers to be without truth rather than to receive it from without.
There is, then, a foreground where the "man without characteristics" curiously reproduces the givens of a "character" in which we may rediscover
that of the author: the passionate indifference, the distance he puts between his feelings and himself, the refusal to become involved and to live

outside of himself, the coldness that is violence, the rigor of mind and the virile mastery, joined however to a certain passivity to which the sensual subplots of the book sometimes alert us. The man without particularities is thus not a hypothesis that is little by little embodied. He is rather the opposite: a living presence that becomes a thought, a reality that becomes utopia, a particular being progressively discovering his particularity, which is to lack one, and trying to assume this absence, raising it to a quest that makes oneself a new being, perhaps the man of the future, the theoretical man, finally ceasing to be—in order authentically to be what he is: a being who is merely possible, but one open to all possibilities.

Musil's irony is useful to his plan. Let us not forget that this nickname [the man without particularities] is given to Ulrich, as an insult, by his boyhood friend Walter (a boyhood friend of Musil's), who at the time when the book begins, is almost no longer his friend. A man without particularities? *What is that? asked Clarisse, stupidly smiling.* The answer is illustrative of Musil's irony: *Nichts. Eben nichts ist das!*—"Nothing, precisely nothing at all!" And Walter adds: "There are millions of them today. That is the kind our time has produced." Musil does not himself endorse this judgment, but he does not reject it. The man without particularities is then not only the free hero who refuses any limitation and, refusing the essence, feels that he must also refuse existence, replaced by potentiality. He is first the ordinary man of great cities, the interchangeable man, who is nothing and looks like nothing, the ordinary impersonal "Anyone" (*On*), the individual who is no longer a particular but is confused with the icy truth of impersonal existence. Here, the Musil of a bygone era does not hold back from taking to task the Musil of today, who, believing in the impersonality of science and in the strangeness of his own being, tries courageously to discover in the nothingness that he is—*Nothing, precisely nothing at all*—the principle of a new morality and the beginning of a new man.

The dangerous quality in this search does not escape him, just as he is far, as I said, from separating his destiny from that of the former Cancania, of which his efforts can only mean the ruin, which will also necessarily be his own ruin. If, though, he forges ahead, in a majestic effort to follow, even as a novelist, the boldest path of experimentation, it is from his horror of illusion and his concern for precision. Even before 1914, he saw that truth condemned his world, and he preferred truth to anything. The strange thing is that this love of truth, of which he developed a notion

and a passion in the course of a brief career as engineer, logician, mathe-
matician, and almost professor of psychology, finally makes him the man
of letters who risks everything on the bold stroke of a novel—and of a
novel that, by virtue of one of its essential aspects, could easily be called
mystical.

2. The Experience of "the Other State"

When, in 1930, the first part of *The Man Without Qualities* appeared, I
doubt whether the most ingenious reader could guess what would follow
it. He read, with timidity and surprise, a novel in classical language and
disconcerting form, which sometimes resembled a novel, sometimes an essay, sometimes evoked Wilhelm Meister, sometimes Proust, Tristram
Shandy, sometimes Monsieur Teste; if he was sensitive, he was happy to
have a work that he readily saw eluded him, although it continued to be,
by a false appearance, its own commentary. But the reader was sure of two
things: one, that Musil described, with irony, coldness, and feeling, the
fall of the House of Usher, the one that sheltered men's illusions on the
eve of 1914; the other, that the protagonist of the book, Ulrich, was a hero
of the mind, pursuing an entirely intellectual adventure by seeking to live
according to the dangers of exactitude and the impersonal force of modern reason.

Was the reader of 1932—when the first volume of the second part was
published—disconcerted? But Musil's fate was already being fulfilled, for
there were hardly any readers. Moreover, this volume, which only began
the second episode, ended so neatly and so unhappily that the publication
seemed almost complete, and the new theme seemed to have reached its
conclusion, whereas in the several hundred pages by which it would continue with an often desperate momentum, the same story would be lifted
to entirely different interior events, resulting in an alteration of meaning
that, even today, still troubles us, as I think it troubled Musil. We also
sense that he is, starting from that point, engaged in a huge creative task,
and perhaps in an experiment that surpasses his anticipations. Everything
becomes more difficult, less certain, not more somber (for what reaches us
is often a sensitive and simple light) but more foreign to the willed accomplishment he pathetically persists in obtaining by himself. Something
escapes him, and he is surprised, frightened, rebels before these excesses—
excesses of sensibility, excesses of abstraction—that the rigorous writer he

is, always driven to write not at all rather than to flatter illusions, tries in vain to introduce into the framework of a premeditated plan.

THE DOUBLE VERSION OF THE MODERN MAN

What is exalting is that the unforeseeable continuation of the book is not only linked to the development of its theme but made necessary by the mythology peculiar to the writer and the coherence of some obscure dream. We come face-to-face with an adventure as motivated as it is unjustified. When Ulrich, the indifferent one who refuses the stable world of particular realities (the security of particularized differences), meets his sister Agathe next to the coffin of their father, a man whom they do not like, an old pedantic and late-ennobled man, this meeting is the beginning of the most beautiful incestuous passion of modern literature. It is passion of a singular form, for a long time and almost till the end unaccomplished, while still being the freest and most violent, at once methodical and magical, principle of abstract investigation and of mystical effusion, union of the two in the between-vision of a supreme state, the *other* state, the millenary Reign whose truth, in the beginning accessible to the privileged passion of the forbidden couple, in the end will extend perhaps to the dangerous universal community.

Naturally, there is nothing arbitrary in what it would be deceptive to represent as a romantic survival.[5] That Ulrich, the man without particularities, in whom the impersonal impulse of knowledge is awakened, the neutrality of great collective existences, the pure force of Valéry-like consciousness, which starts only by refusing to be anything whatsoever, the man of thought, a theory of himself and an attempt at living in the mode of pure abstraction, now opens himself up to the vertigo of mystical experiences—that is surprising, but necessary; it belongs to the meaning of his impulse, that impersonality he deliberately welcomes, which he lives sometimes as the sovereign indeterminacy of reason, sometimes as the undetermined void, reversing itself into fullness, of mystical existence. Thus the refusal to be with others and with himself in relationships that are overdetermined, particular—source of the attractive indifference that is the magic of Ulrich (and of Musil)—gives way to this double version of the modern man: capable of the highest exactitude and of the most extreme dissolution, ready to satisfy his refusal of fixed forms as much by the indefinite exchange of mathematical formulations as by the pursuit of the formless and the unformulated, seeking finally to suppress the reality of existence in order to stretch it between the possible, which is meaning, and the nonmeaning of the impossible.

Ulrich meets Agathe. Since his childhood, he has almost forgotten his sister. In the funereal house, the way they rise up before each other, surprised at their similar traits and even their similar clothes, the surprise of their still unperceived relationship, the return of an unreal past, the complicity of certain gestures (when they replace the true decorations on the dead man's uniform with false ones; later, Agathe will falsify the will to wrong her husband), the childlike freedom with which, trying to find some last present to give him, the young woman takes off the large ribbon of her garter to slip into the old man's pocket, many other details expressed in a style of spellbinding restraint preparing, in a half-nocturnal, half-diurnal atmosphere, the scene to which we are all anxious to consent, like the brother and sister, but which in truth does not occur, will occur only much later, when our expectation and theirs will perhaps no longer be satisfied by it. Is this out of respect for the forbidden? Only to a certain extent, and without any moral prejudice; but neither Ulrich nor Agathe mean to exhaust too quickly the chance that the dangerous adventure of their new relationship offers them, which is to be impossible.

THE UNFULFILLED FULFILLMENT

"What had almost occurred and yet did not occur," "what had truly happened, without anything having happened," "what took place, but did it take place?"—this present, real, and unrealizable event, neither wished for nor rejected, but close, of so ardent a proximity that reality is not enough, which opens the realm of the imaginary, gives the impossible an almost bodily form in which the brother and sister unite with each other in strange movements, as pure as they are free, whose description constitutes the latest experiment of the work. It must be added that this wonderful passion, so long deprived of body, has talk as its principal intermediary. This is deliberately sought by Musil: "In love, conversations play almost a greater role than all the rest; love is the most conversant of all passions, and it lies mainly in the happiness of speaking. . . . To speak and to love are essentially linked." I will not say that this very Musilian idea can convince us outside of the work of Musil; nor will I say that it is only a stratagem to justify the long theoretical discussions of which his book is composed. One must, in order to evaluate the transformation that the abstract language undergoes at the approach of "the wonderful, boundless, incredible, and unforgettable state in which everything wants to unite into one single Yes," try to find, in the drunkenness of emotions and the mastery of words, a common relationship that transforms them both, making the abstract aridity into a new state of passion, and the emotional ardor a higher sang-froid. These conversations, though, do not occur without a great need for silence. In the Ulrich-Agathe couple, the silent part is felicitously represented by the young woman, and it is not without an incisive ulterior motive that she, emerging from her state of spiritual dissolution and physical distress, thinks sadly, before the articulate passivity of her brother: "He should have done something besides talking."

One day, Agathe will go as far as preparing to commit suicide, and this crisis will give the love affair a new turn. "We will not kill ourselves before having tried everything." Then begins "the voyage to paradise," represented, according to Goethian tradition, by the voyage to the South. But this decision, well thought out, comes very late. Eight hundred pages of a dense text have already reunited those who remain intimately separated, carrying them, beyond all sentiment and in the very fatigue of feeling, to actions of slow and profound metamorphosis, similar in every way, we are told, to those of mystics. It seems, then, that in advance that absolute had been attained, and that Ulrich's attempt, in the unfulfilled fulfillment, had already found its end.

That is because the strange relationship of the brother and sister—very distanced in one sense, but only in the sense of Byronic perversion and defiance—signifies precisely what the man without particularities seeks vainly and can meet only by default: by uniting with this sister, who is like his most beautiful and most sensitive Self (the incarnate body that he lacks), he finds in her the relationship to himself of which he is deprived, a certain tender connection that is self-love, *Eigenliebe*, the particular love of self, that a man without particularities cannot know, unless he encounters in the world his identity wandering in the form of his double, the little sister-wife, the eternal Isis who gives life and fullness to the scattered being whose dispersion is the infinite wait for gathering, fallen endlessly toward the void.

Of course, if Agathe is Ulrich, she is as deprived of herself—which is shown by a certain moral recklessness—as he is of himself, and this double lack binds them all the more to each other, a melancholy attraction, like that of Paolo and Francesca in hell, condemning them to seek out each other in an exhausting and fascinating narcissistic game. The vanity of their union thus forms part of the impulse that determines it. What is unexpected, and what I think surprised and disoriented Musil, is that the extraordinary experiences he draws from it, the delight that leads the two lovers into a garden of light apart from the world, on the edge of being, the creative generosity that does not allow him ever to end it with this episode, forcing him to pursue it for hundreds of pages as if out of a secret protest against the final disappointment—all these excessive developments, which unbalance the book but give it a new power, far from representing a failure, cause to shine in the impossible love, even if they are only a mirage, a happiness and a truth, an illusion, against his expectation and against his plan, that Musil cannot make up his mind to destroy.[6]

Strange concern on his part. One might think that Musil is linked to this fable by personal relationships. Did he have a sister? Yes, one who died before he came into the world (thence the profound forgetfulness he attributes to Ulrich and, perhaps, the ambiance of funereal gaiety at the first meeting). Musil himself certainly wondered about this friend he could have had. Always precise, he says that he devoted a certain cult to her; then he amends: "This sister interested me. Did it not occur to me to think, 'And if she were still alive? Would I be closest to her? Would I identify with her?' There is no motive for that. I recall, though, that at the age of little dresses I would also have liked to be a girl. I could easily see in this trait a reduplication of the erotic."[7] We should take care not to give this single memory a decisive value. I will only recall that Ulrich and Musil are linked by relationships of uncertainty and experience whose development is the very premise of the book. Musil is present in it, but in the impersonal and unreal way that Ulrich tries to assume in accord with the profound impersonality that modern life presents to us as an enigma, a menace, a resource, and even the source of every source. The intimacy without intimacy of twins' passion is a myth that the writer nourishes with himself, which sometimes repels us by its sterility, sometimes attracts us as anything does that, violating prohibitions, promises us *for an instant* access to the absolute.

For an instant: there is the inevitable failure. In a 1926 interview in which Musil imprudently revealed the plan of his book, he said of the episode of the brother and sister (then twins): "The attempt to maintain and fix the experience fails: the absolute cannot be preserved." And the effervescent communication between two people can perhaps be secured even less in a morality capable of opening the commonwealth of the world to a free movement, constantly unusual, renewed and pure. This failure still does not bring an end to the book, for Musil, after having conveyed the marvelous aspect of the "love-ecstasy" complex, intended to make it come near to madness, and not to conceal the attraction that the least pleasing forms of anomaly and aberration exercise over the man without particularities. Madness is one of the themes of the book. The madness of war, the end of this voyage to the edge of the possible, may have constituted the decisive irruption of impersonal power in which the man without particularities, encountering inhuman particularities, accomplished his final and pitiful metamorphosis. Throughout the numerous fragments that allow us to imagine possible ends for the novel, we see Musil trying to complete the destinies implied in whatever narrative survives in its absence of narrative and, especially, pursue to its final dissolution the Parallel Campaign, founded by schemers, idealists, and men of the world—the capitalist aristocracy—to play, on the eve of the war, with the illusion of Universal Peace. He had even foreseen, at least in the 1926 outline, a complicated plot filled with espionage.[8] Yet a curious phenomenon occurs: after the splendor of the novel of Ulrich and Agathe, we no longer manage, nor does, I think, Musil, to resume contact with the story or with the characters of the first book. Even the irony that the writer had to silence during this mystical episode—for "the mystical state is a state without laughter; mystics do not laugh"—no longer manages to rediscover its secret possibilities of creation. Everything occurs as if an extreme point had been reached, which destroyed the normal resources of the work. No denouement is now possible. Agathe and Ulrich had promised themselves death, if they did not succeed. But now they feel that in this adventure even the power to die has been lost, so there is all the more incentive to live, all the more reason for Musil to write. "I can go no further," he notes pathetically. It is perhaps the conclusion that best respects the significance of the book, while still reminding us how far, thanks to it, we have come.

UNDER THREAT OF THE IMPERSONAL

"The story of this novel comes down to this: the story that should be told in it is not told." Musil offers this reflection in 1932, in the midst of his creative work. A little later, he will speak of his refusal of narrative, which is at the origin of his narratives. He will also note: "Draw technique from my inability to describe time passing [*la durée*]." It is slowly, through practice, that he became aware of the necessities of his art and of the form of his book, until the discovery that what he regarded in himself as a lack could become the richness of a new genre and, even more, could give him the key to modern times. It remains for us to study the essential thing: the relationship these themes have with form, and the consequences for the art of the novel that result from it.

It is not conceivable that the man without particularities could reveal himself in a personal form or in the subjective tone of an over-particular "I." Musil's discovery and perhaps obsession is the new role of impersonality. He encounters it, and with enthusiasm, in science; later, with more timidity, in modern society; then, with a cold anxiety, in himself. What is this neutral power that suddenly emerges in the world? How does it happen that, in the human space that is ours, we have to do no longer with distinct people living particular experiences, but with "experiences lived without anyone living them"? How is it that in us and outside us something anonymous keeps appearing while concealing itself? Prodigious mutation, dangerous and essential, new and infinitely old. We speak, and the words, precise, rigorous, do not care about us and are ours only thanks to this strangeness that we have become to ourselves. At each instant, "we are given replies" about which we know only that they are addressed to us and "do not concern us."

Musil's book translates this mutation and seeks to give it form, while still trying to discover what morality could suit a man in whom the paradoxical alliance of exactitude and indeterminacy has taken place. For art, such a metamorphosis does not happen without consequences. Musil remained for a long time uncertain about the form he should choose: he thought of a novel in the first person (when his book was called "Catacombs")[9], but in which the "I" would have been neither that of the fictional character nor that of the novelist, but the relationship of one to the other, the self without self that the writer must become by impersonalizing himself through art—which is essentially impersonal—and in this character that assumes the fate of impersonality. An abstract "I," an empty self intervening to reveal the emptiness of an incomplete story and to fill the between-space of a thought still being tested. Perhaps we should regret that Musil did not finally use this form, whose resources he subtly revealed. But in the end Musil feels more attracted by the "He" of the narrative, that strange neutrality whose perhaps untenable demand the art of the novel constantly tries and constantly hesitates to welcome. The impersonality of classic art tempts him no less, although he cannot accept it as a fixed form, or as an ability to tell supremely well an action that one controls in its entirety. That, too, is because he has nothing to tell, the very meaning of his narrative being that we no longer have to do with events that are actually accomplished, or with people who personally accomplish them, but with a precise and undetermined ensemble of possible versions. How can one say: this took place, then this, and finally that, while the essential thing is that what took place could have taken place otherwise, and consequently did not *truly* take place, in a decisive and definitive way, but only in a spectral way, in the manner of the imaginary? (Here appears the profound meaning of the incest that is fulfilled in the impossibility of its fulfillment.)

We see Musil, then, grappling with these two problems: to seek a language that resembles classical language but that is closer to the original impersonality;[10] to make a narrative with a story in which the time of the story is lacking and which makes us attentive, not to events themselves but, through them, to the infinite series of possible events, to the power of source that procures no fixed result.

LITERATURE AND THOUGHT

Another major problem of Musil's art: the relationship of thought and literature. He understands precisely that, in a literary work, one can express thoughts as difficult and of as abstract a form as in a philosophical essay, but only on the condition that they are *not yet* thoughts. This "not yet" is literature itself, a "not yet" that, just as it is, is accomplishment and perfection. The writer has all the rights, and he can arrogate to himself all the ways of being and saying—except the customary language that aspires to meaning and truth: what is said in what he says does not yet have meaning, is not yet truth—not yet and never more; not yet, and that is the sufficient splendor that used to be called beauty. The being who is revealed in art is always previous to revelation: hence his innocence (for he does not have to be redeemed through signification), but also his infinite anxiety, if he is excluded from the promised land of truth.

Musil was very aware of the experimental nature of literature. The man without particularities is precisely the man of "not yet," the one who considers nothing as firm, stops every system, prevents every fixation, who "does not say 'no' to life, but 'not yet,'" who, finally, acts as if the world— the world of truth—could never begin except on the next day. At heart, he is a pure writer and does not know how to be anything else. The utopia of "the attempt [*l'essai*]" is what he pursues with a passionate coldness.

In all the beautiful parts of his work, Musil succeeded in preserving it as a work of art, expressing thoughts in it but knowing how to distinguish thought that speaks true from thought that gives form. "What in a poetic work passes for psychology is something other than psychology, just as poetry is something other than science." Or again: "One describes men as one thinks they would conduct themselves inwardly and outwardly during the course of action, but even the psychological interior, with respect to the central work of the personality that begins only behind all the surfaces of pain, confusion, passion and weakness, and often after them, is properly speaking only the outward raised to a higher power." Yet he was obsessed by psychology, ethical researches, by the circle of questions that all mean: how can one live?—then obsessed by the fear of having altered art by contact with thoughts, and altered his thoughts by confiding them to art: "The main fault: too much theory." "Shouldn't they just tell me that I simply lacked the courage to represent in a scientific and philosophical way what occupied me philosophically, which continued to lurk behind my narratives and made them impossible?" With lucidity, Musil here blames another cause of incompleteness. It is true: there is in his book an anxious excess of problems, too many imprudent debates on too many topics, too many philosophical conversations on morality, the proper life, love. People speak too much, and "the more words you need, the worse that is." The novelist gives us, then, the terrible impression of employing characters to make them express ideas: a major fault that destroys art and reduces the idea to the poverty of the idea.

To such a critic, one would like to be able to answer that this defect, so obvious, is implied in the theme of the work: the man without particularities is the man who has as his vocation and his torment to live the theory of himself, the abstract man who does not exist and does not realize himself in a sensory way. By accepting the confusion between theoretical expression and aesthetic expression to which he lends himself, Musil could then do nothing but pursue the expression appropriate to him. I do not think so. I see him rather as having been unfaithful to himself by having consented to divide his work into reflections on topics and into concrete scenes, into theoretical discourse and into characters who act, instead of going back to the most original point where, in the choice of a unique form, language that is not yet particularized speaks of the fullness, and of the emptiness, of the one without particularity.

§ 16 The Pain of Dialogue

On the difficult practice of criticism. The critic almost does not read. It is not always because of lack of time; it is that he cannot read while he's thinking only of what he has to write; if he simplifies (sometimes by making more complicated), if he praises, if he blames, if he hastily gets rid of the simplicity of the book by replacing it with the correctness of a judgment or the benevolent assertion of his rich comprehension, it is because impatience pushes him, it is because, being unable to read a book, he must have not-read twenty, thirty, and many more, and because this innumerable non-reading that on one hand absorbs him, on the other eludes him, inviting him to pass always more quickly from one book to another, from a book he scarcely reads to another he thinks he has already read, in order to reach that moment when, having read nothing of all these books, he will perhaps clash with himself, in the lack of anything to do that might finally allow him to begin to read, if he had not long ago in his turn become an author.

That the critic's will to simplify uneasily meets the simplicity of the book, which seems to him always too simple or not simple enough—that is what Marguerite Duras's *Le square* makes us feel. This book is certainly not naïve, and although it touches us in its first few pages by a contact from which we do not shrink—(strange, the sort of loyalty that reading gives birth to in us)—it does not have, it cannot have the simplicity whose appearance it offers, for the hard simplicity of the simple things with which it puts us in contact is too hard to seem simple.

Two almost abstract voices in an almost abstract place. That is what strikes us first, this sort of abstraction: as if these two beings who converse in a square—she is twenty, a servant; he, older, goes from store to store selling things of little value—had no other reality than their voice alone, and in this accidental conversation exhausted whatever a living person still has in the way of chance and truth, or more simply of speech. They have to speak, and these cautious, almost ceremonious words are terrible because of the restraint that is not only the politeness of simple lives, but is made of their extreme vulnerability. The fear of wounding and the fear of being wounded are in the very words. The words touch each other, they withdraw at the slightest contact; they are assuredly still living. Slow, but uninterrupted, never stopping for fear of not having enough time: one must speak now or never; but still without haste, patient and on the defensive, calm too, the way speech is calm that if it did not restrain itself would break out into a cry; and deprived, to a painful degree, of that ease of chatter that is the lightness and freedom of a certain sort of happiness. Here, in the simple world of need and necessity, words are devoted to the essential, attracted only to the essential, and so are monotonous, but they are attentive also to what must be said in order not to avoid the brutal formulations that would put an end to everything.

It is a matter of dialogue. How rare dialogue is; we realize this by the surprise it makes us feel, bringing us into the presence of an unusual event, almost more painful than remarkable. In novels, the "dialogued" part is the expression of laziness and routine: the characters speak to put white spaces on a page and out of an imitation of life, where there is no narration, only conversation; from time to time one must give speech to people in books; the direct contact is an economy and a repose (for the author even more than for the reader). Or, the "dialogue," under the influence of some American writers, can be wrought of an expressive incommunicativeness: more threadbare than in reality, a little below the meaningless speech that suffices for us in current life. When someone speaks, it is his refusal to speak that becomes obvious; his discourse is his silence: closed, violent, saying nothing but himself, his abrupt massiveness, his desire to emit words rather than to speak. Or simply, as happens in Hemingway, this exquisite way of expressing himself a little below zero is a ruse to make us believe in some high degree of life, emotion, or thought, an honest and classic ruse that often succeeds and to which Hemingway's melancholy talent gives various resources. But the three great directions of modern novelistic "dialogue" are represented, in my opinion, by the names Malraux, Henry James, and Kafka.

MALRAUX

In his two great books, *La condition humaine* [Man's fate] and *L'espoir* [Man's hope], Malraux gave art and life to a very old stance, one that, thanks to him, has become an artistic form: the stance of discussion. The hero of this, long ago, was Socrates. Socrates is a man who is sure that it is enough to talk to reach agreement: he believes in the efficacy of speech, as long as it does not contradict itself, and as long as it is pursued long enough to prove and to establish, by proofs, coherence. Speech must necessarily get the better of violence: that is the certainty he calmly represents, and his death is heroic but calm, because the violence that interrupts his life cannot interrupt the reasonable language that is his true life and at the end of which we find harmony, and violence disarmed. No doubt Malraux's characters carry us far from Socrates: they are passionate, active and, in action, given to solitude; but, at instants of illumination that his books preserve for us, they suddenly, as it were naturally, become the voices of the great thoughts of history. Without ceasing to be themselves, they give voice to each side of these great thoughts, to what can be formulated, in ideal terms, in respect to forces battling in some grave conflict of our time—and that is the moving shock of his books: we discover that discussion is still possible. These simple human gods, momentarily at rest on their humble Parnassus, do not swear at each other, do not chat with each other—they discuss, for they want to be right, and this rightness is served by the ardent vivacity of words, which still remain in contact with a thought common to all, the preserved communality of which each one respects. There is not enough time to reach agreement. The lulls when the divided mind of the time speaks come to an end, and violence once again asserts itself, but a violence that is nonetheless changed, because it could not break the discourse or this respect for the communal speech that persists in each of these violent men.

It must be added that Malraux's success is perhaps unique. His imitators have transformed into a commodity of exposition and a procedure of argumentation what, with him, by the reconciliation of art and politics, is an authentic creative manifestation, a lyricism of the intelligence.[1] This is a difficult art, and it so happens that Malraux becomes one of his own imitators, as we see in *Les noyers de l'Altenburg* [The walnut trees of Altenburg].

HENRY JAMES

With Henry James, the role of conversation is one of the great means of his art. It is all the more striking that the discussions emerge directly from the trivialities of every day, "around the tea in the old lady's cup," with which Hawthorne said he was enchanted. But his great works, the ones with majestic proportions, as well as sometimes his more concise works, all have some capital conversations as poles in which the secret, passionate, and fascinating truth, diffused throughout the book, tries to manifest in its necessarily hidden aspect. There are extraordinary explanations in which the protagonists wonderfully understand each other by the intermediary of this hidden truth they know they do not have the right to hear, communicating actually around the incommunicable, thanks to the reserve with which they surround it and the air of understanding that allows them to speak of it without speaking of it, in the manner of an always negative formulation, the only way of knowing the unknown that no one should ever name under pain of death. (In *The Turn of the Screw*, the governess actually kills the child by the terrifying pressure she uses to force him to recognize and say what cannot be said.) James thus manages to make *the third party* in conversations that obscure element that is the center and the stake of each of his books and to make it not only the cause of misunderstandings but the reason for anxious and profound understandings. What cannot be expressed—that is what brings us close and draws our otherwise separated words to one another. It is around what escapes direct communication that their community restructures itself.

KAFKA

To contrast James with Kafka would be arbitrary but easy. For we immediately see that what in James still brings words together—the unknown, the unexpressed—tends now to separate them. There is scission, impassable distance, between the two sides of discourse: it is the infinite coming into play, to which one cannot come close except by distancing oneself from it. Hence the rigor of logic, the stronger need to be right and to speak without losing any of the prerogatives of reasonable discourse. Kafka's characters discuss and refute. "He always refuted everything," one of them says about another. This logic is, on one hand, the obstinacy of the will to live, the confidence that life cannot be wrong. But on the other hand, it is already the force of the enemy in them that is always right. The hero believes that he is still at the pleasant stage of discussion. It is a matter of an ordinary trial, he thinks, and the essential thing in a trial is that at the end of the debate represented by the proceedings and the pleas in which all the arguments are set forth, the verdict must express the agreement of everyone, the proven and recognized speech with which even the party defeated by it is happy, because he at least triumphs in the proof he shares with his adversary. But for K., the trial consists in this: for the law of discourse an Other Law has been substituted, foreign to the rules and in particular to the rule of noncontradiction. Since one does not know when the substitution takes place, one can never distinguish the two laws or know if one has to deal with one or the other; the false duality entrains this consequence: seized by the Law that is above and below logic, it is however in the name of logic that the man remains accused, with the duty to adhere strictly to it and with the painful surprise, each time he tries to defend himself against the contradictions by contradictory means, of feeling guiltier and guiltier. Finally, it is still logic that condemns him, the man whose only support in this whole story has been his little vacillating reason; and it is logic that condemns him as an enemy of logic, by a mocking decision in which he finds the justice of reason and the justice of the absurd allied against him. (At the end of *The Trial*, K. attempts a final appeal: "Was there still recourse? Did there exist objections that had not yet been raised? Certainly there were. Logic is unshakeable, but it does not withstand a man who wants to live." Caught in the net of final despair, the condemned man wants to raise more objections, to argue and refute, that is to say, to appeal to logic one last time, but at the same time he challenges it and, already beneath the knife, invokes against it the will to live, which is pure violence: doing so makes him an enemy of reason and thus with reason condemned.)

It would be a mistake to think that the chill, oscillating space, inserted by Kafka between the words in conversation, only destroys communication. The aim is still unity. The distance that separates the speakers is never impassable; it becomes so only for one who persists in crossing it with the aid of discourse, where duality reigns and where it engenders always more duplicity and those false intermediaries that are its doubles. How, far from being negative, the impossibility of relationships becomes the basis for a new form of communication in Kafka—that is what we must study. At least it remains clear that these conversations are at no time dialogues. The characters are not interlocutors; words cannot be exchanged and, though communal in meaning, never have the same range or the same reality: some are words on top of words, words of a judge, words of commandment, of authority or temptation; others, words of deception, of evasion, of lies, which would be enough to prevent them from ever being reciprocal.

DIALOGUE IS RARE

Dialogue is rare, and let us not suppose it easy or pleasant. Listen to the two simple voices of *Le Square*; they are not trying for agreement, in the manner of conversational words that go from test to test to meet each other through the simple play of coherence. Do they even seek a definitive comprehension that, by mutual recognition, would appease them? That is too distant a goal. Perhaps they only want to speak, using this last ability that chance gives them, and it is not certain that it always belongs to them. It is this final resource, weak and threatened, that from the very first words lends the simple discussion its serious quality. We feel that, for these two people, for her especially, the space and air and possibility of speaking, which there must be, is very close to being exhausted. And perhaps, if it is indeed a dialogue that is at stake, we find its first characteristic in the approach of this threat, a boundary below which wordlessness and violence will enclose the being. One must have one's back to the wall to begin to speak *with* someone. Comfort, ease, mastery raise speech to forms of impersonal communication, in which one talks around problems, and in which each person renounces his ego in order to let the discourse in general momentarily speak. Or rather, on the contrary, if the limit is crossed, we find the speech of solitude and exile, the speech of extremity, deprived of center and thus without orientation, impersonal once again, through loss of person, that modern literature has succeeded in capturing and making understood: a speech of profundity without profundity.

By the extreme delicacy of her attention, Marguerite Duras sought for and perhaps grasped the moment when men become capable of dialogue: there must be the chance of an unexpected encounter and the simplicity of the encounter—in a public square, what could be simpler—that contrasts with the hidden tension that these two people must confront, and that other simplicity, the one that stems from the fact that, if there is tension, it has no dramatic quality and is not linked to a visible event, to some grand misfortune, some crime or notable injustice, but is banal, without depth and without "interest," thus perfectly simple and almost as if effaced (one cannot have dialogue with one great sadness as starting point, any more than two great sadnesses could converse together). And finally, perhaps the essential thing is this: these two people are brought into contact because they have nothing in common except this very fact of being, for very different reasons, separated from the ordinary world where they happen to live.

This is expressed in the simplest and most necessary way, a necessity above all present in each of the young woman's words. In all that she says with extreme moderation and restraint, there is this impossibility that is at the heart of human lives and that her condition makes her feel at each instant: this servant's profession that is not even a profession, that is like an illness, a sub-servitude, in which she has no real tie with anyone, not even the tie a slave has to his master, and not even with herself. And this impossibility has become her own will, the fierce and stubborn rigor with which she rejects all that could make her life easier; yet she would also risk, by this ease, forgetting whatever impossible quality her life has and losing sight of the single goal: an encounter with someone, it doesn't matter who, provided that, when she marries him, he removes her from her condition and makes her like everybody else. Her interlocutor gently points out to her that she will perhaps be very unhappy with no matter who; and won't she choose? Shouldn't she, at the Croix-Nivert dance she attends every Saturday, the only moment of affirmation on which her life is poised, herself look for the one who would suit her best? But how can she choose, when she exists so little, in her own eyes, that in order to make herself exist, she no longer counts on anything but being chosen by someone? "For if I let myself choose, all men would suit me, all of them, just as long as they want me a little." "Common" sense will reply that it is not so difficult to be chosen, and that this twenty-year-old young woman, servant though she is, with beautiful eyes, will not fail to leave her unfortunate condition through marriage, and thus become happy and unhappy like everyone else. This is true, but it is not true for someone who already belongs to the ordinary world. There lies the profound root of the difficulty, and from it comes the tension that shapes the dialogue: when someone has become aware of the impossible, impossibility affects and infects the very desire to flee it by the most normal ways: "When a man invites you to dance, Mademoiselle, do you think right away that he might marry you?" "Yes, that's it. I am too practical, you see, all my trouble comes from that. How can I act otherwise, though? It seems to me that I could not love anyone before I have a beginning of freedom, and that beginning only a man can give me."

From the unexpected encounter in the square might emerge this other form of encounter that is a shared life—that idea comes naturally, in the end, to console the mind of the reader as well, perhaps, as that of the author. We must hope for it, but without much hope. That is because her interlocutor, this little traveling salesman, or rather a peddler, who goes from town to town, led always farther away by his valise, without future, without illusion, and without desire, is a seriously wounded man. The young woman's strength lies in having nothing but desiring one single thing that will allow her to want all the others, or rather to borrow ordinary will from which she will begin to have, or not to have, according to possibilities in general. This fierce desire, heroic and absolute, this courage is for her the issue, but it is also what might close the way out to her, for the violence of desire makes what is desired impossible. The man is wiser, with the kind of wisdom that accepts and demands nothing; this apparent wisdom is about the danger of solitude, which, without making him content, fills him in some way, to the point of no longer leaving him time to wish for anything else. He seems to be, as they say, a déclassé; he has let himself slide into this profession, which is not really one at all, but something imposed on him by that need to wander in which he finds the only possibility left to him, and that embodies precisely what he is. That way, although he expresses himself with all the prudence necessary not to discourage the young woman, he represents temptation for her: the attraction of this future without a future about which she suddenly, silently, weeps. Like her, he is "the last of the last," but he is not only a man deprived of ordinary happiness; he also has had in the course of his travels a few brief, happy illuminations, humble scintillations that he describes to her with good will and about which she questions him, first with a faraway and even disapproving interest and then, unfortunately, with an increasingly awakened and fascinated curiosity. *Private* happiness is there, the one that belongs to solitude, making it for an instant light up and disappear, a happiness that is like the other form of the impossible and that receives from it a brilliance that is perhaps dazzling, perhaps all deception and affectation.

But they do speak: they speak to each other, but without being in agreement. They do not entirely understand each other, they do not share between them the common space in which comprehension is realized, and all their relationship rests only on the very intense and very simple feeling of being both *equally* outside of the ordinary circle of relationships. That is a great deal. It creates an instantaneous closeness and a sort of complete understanding without understanding in which each one offers the other all the more attention and expresses himself with all the more scruples and patient truth since the things to say can be said only once and cannot remain unsaid either, for they cannot benefit from the easy comprehension we enjoy in this ordinary world, this world where the chance and pain of true dialogue are very rarely offered to us.

§ 17 The Clarity of the Novel

Where does the light come from that dominates a story like *Le voyeur?* A light? A kind of clarity rather, but a surprising clarity that penetrates everything, dissipates all shadows, destroys all density, reduces every thing and every being to the thinness of a gleaming surface. It is a total, equal clarity, which could be called monotone; it is colorless, limitless, continuous, impregnating all space, and like space it is always the same, so that it seems also to transform time, giving us the ability to travel through it, responsive to new senses.

It is a clarity that makes everything clear, and since it reveals everything except itself it is whatever is most secret. Where does it come from? From where does it shed light on us? In Robbe-Grillet's book a sense of the most objective description is imposed. Everything in it is described minutely, with a regular precision, and as if by someone who could be satisfied just with "seeing." It is as if we were seeing everything, without anything being visible. The result is strange. Before André Breton reproached novelists for their penchant for describing, their wish was to interest us in the yellow wallpaper of the bedroom, the one with the black-and-white tiled floor, with the wardrobes, the curtains, fastidious details. It is true, these descriptions are boring; there is no reader who does not skip over them, content though that they are there, precisely to be passed over; that is because we are in a hurry to enter the bedroom, because we go straight to what is going to happen. But what if nothing were to happen? If it remained empty? What if everything that happens, all the events that we surprise, all the beings we glimpse, only contributed to making the room just visible, always more visible, more susceptible to being described, more exposed to that clarity of a complete description, firmly delimited and yet infinite? What could be more fascinating, and more singular, or perhaps more cruel? or in any case closer to surrealism (Roussel)?

THE BLIND SPOT

In this detective story, there is neither a detective nor a mystery. Perhaps there is a crime, but it is undoubtedly not the apparent crime of which the story, with too much premeditation, seeks to convince us. But there is an unknown. Among the hours that Mathias, the traveling salesman, has spent in the little country of his childhood selling wristwatches, a dead time has slipped in that cannot be recovered. We cannot directly approach this void. We cannot even situate it at a definite moment of ordinary time, but just as, in the tradition of the detective novel, the crime leads us to the criminal by a labyrinth of traces and indices, so here we suspect the minutely objective description, in which everything is detailed, expressed, and revealed, of having at its center a gap that is like the origin and source of this extreme clarity through which we see everything except itself. This obscure point that allows us to see, this sun situated eternally below the horizon, this blind spot that the gaze is unaware of, islet of absence in the heart of vision—that is the aim of the quest and the setting, the stake, of the plot.

How are we led to it? Less by the thread of anecdote than by a refined art of images. The scene we do not witness is nothing other than a central image constructed little by little by a subtle superimposition of details, images, memories, by the metamorphosis and imperceptible shift of a pattern or scheme around which everything the traveler sees is organized and animated. For instance, when he lands on the island to which he returns for the first time since his childhood to spend a few hours there and sell his watches, Mathias sees, engraved on the harbor wall, a sign in the shape of a figure eight. "It was an eight lying down: two equal circles a little less than ten centimeters in diameter, tangent at the sides. At the center of the eight, a reddish excrescence was seen that seemed to be the linchpin, eroded by rust, of an old iron hook." Nothing could be more objective, or closer to the geometrical purity towards which a description without shadow should strive. But the "eight" will haunt the narrative like an obsessive motif: it will be the shape of the path followed across the island, the sort of double circuit of which one loop is known to us and the other cannot be. On each door he has to open, it will be the two dark circles the wood grain forms, or the paint imitating irregularities and knots. It will be the fourfold iron ring through which the legs and arms of the girl he tortures in reality or in imagination are passed to emphasize the slimness of her body. Above all, it will be the perfect double circle of the eyes that are at the center of this novel of vision, fixing things with the impassibility and cruelty of an absolute gaze, or of that unmoving gaze attributed to certain birds, or that photographs of long ago evoke.

We must not be surprised that the irretrievable hour, subtracted from the enterprises of the day, is filled by the supposed image of torture. Is it true that the traveling businessman has entered a path that does not belong to a normal course, "there under the bend"? Has he looked for and actually found the girl, who may have provoked him by a seeming resemblance to a previous girlfriend? Has he actually tied her up, stripped her, tortured her with slight burns, before throwing her naked body into the sea? Is he Sade, this calm young man? But when did the scene take place? Slowly, with gradual strokes, we see it elaborated well before the actual instant in which it could have been accomplished: it circulates throughout the entire narrative; it is behind each thing and beneath each person's face; it intervenes between two sentences, between two paragraphs, and is the very transparency of this cold clarity to which we owe seeing everything, for it is this clarity, the void in which everything becomes transparency. The scene of violence glimpsed (or imagined) by Mathias at the outset, in an alleyway; the girl he sees on the boat, standing and as if tied up for torture; the movie theater marquee, the empty bedroom with the scene of the little girl kneeling, the newspaper clipping, the play with the cords, then, after the event, the dead body, on the road, "thighs open, arms in a cross" of a little frog: these are the movements by which the central image, which we do not see, which we cannot see, for it is invisible, comes for an instant to let itself be seen in actual circumstances, like a faint specter of clarity. We could say that time, scattered by a secret inner catastrophe, lets segments of the future come to light through the present or enter into free communication with the past. Time dreamed, time recalled, time that could have been, finally the future, are incessantly transformed in the shining presence of space, the place of deployment of pure visibility.

METAMORPHOSIS OF TIME INTO SPACE

That, I think, is where the essential interest of this book lies. Everything in it is clear; everything, at least, strives for this clarity that is the essence of scale, and the narrative itself, as well as objects, events, and beings, all are arranged according to a homogeneous disposition into series of lines, geometrical figures, with a willful art that it would be only too easy to compare to Cubism. Joyce, Faulkner, Huxley, and many others have already tormented time and broken with the habits of ordinary sequence; sometimes they did it for vain technical reasons, sometimes for profound inner reasons and in order to express the vicissitudes of the personal experience of time. But it does not seem that Robbe-Grillet's aim is to portray for us the obsessions of his hero or the psychological itinerary of the project that animates him. If the past, the future, what is ahead or behind, tend in his narrative to settle on the smooth surface of the present by a subtle and calculated game of perspectives and approaches, it is in order to obey the demand of shadowless and shallow space, in which everything must unfurl—in order for everything to be described—as in the simultaneity of a painting, by that metamorphosis of time into space that maybe every narrative attempts with more or less success.

Le voyeur thus instructs us in one of the directions of the genre of the novel. Sartre showed that the novel should answer not to the premeditation of the novelist but to the freedom of the characters. At the center of every narrative, there is a subjective consciousness, that free and unexpected gaze that causes events to rise up through the seeing by which it grasps them. This is the living core that must be preserved. The narrative, always brought close to a certain point of view, should be as if written from the inside, not by the novelist whose art, embracing everything, dominates what it creates, but responsive instead to the spirit of an infinite freedom, but one limited, situated, and oriented in the very world that affirms it, represents it, and betrays it. This is a lively, profound criticism that has often characterized the masterworks of the modern novel. It is still necessary to remind the novelist that it is not he who is writing his work, but that it seeks itself through him and that, as lucid as he wants to be, he is given over to an experience that surpasses him. Difficult and obscure movement. But isn't this the movement of a consciousness whose freedom cannot be challenged? And is the voice that speaks in a narrative always the voice of a person, a personal voice? Is it not first of all (like an alibi for the nonspecific He) a strange neutral voice that, like that of the ghost in *Hamlet*, wanders here and there, speaking from who knows where, as if through the gaps of time that it must not, however, destroy or change?

In an attempt like Robbe-Grillet's, it is a new effort to make the narrative itself speak within the narrative that we witness. The story is apparently told from the sole point of view of the one who has lived it, this businessman *voyeur* whose steps we follow. We know only what he knows, we see only what he has seen, and perhaps what distinguishes us from him is that we know a little less about him, but it is also starting from this "less," from this gap in the narrative, that the clarity that belongs to the narrative takes its origin, that strange, equal, wandering light that sometimes seems to come from childhood, sometimes from thought, sometimes from dream, for it has the precision, the gentleness, and the cruel force of dream.

THE GLIMMER

Coincident with the hero's consciousness, or with the central event of this consciousness, there is in this book a sort of intermittency, a zone from which we are pushed away, from which he too seems pushed away, so that, through this lacuna inside himself, the pure power of seeing can come to light and be exercised: a glimmer [*éclaircie*]. It is true that some attempt to reduce or destroy the value of what is called inwardness seeks to assert itself here; but if the narrative has the fascination and characteristics typical of true enigmas, it is because the cold clarity that takes the place of inner life remains the mysterious opening to that very intimacy, an ambiguous, unapproachable event, that one can evoke only under the guise of an act of murder or torture.[1]

The voyeur's crime is a crime that he has not carried out, that time has carried out for him. Into the day he should have devoted entirely to useful, regularly coordinated deeds (his profession—selling watches—is the convenient symbol for this time without defect), an empty, null time has insinuated itself. But this lost time, hidden from the ordered progression of the ordinary day, is not the profundity of personal, experienced time that Bergson called *durée*. On the contrary, it is a time without profundity, whose action consists rather in reducing all that is profundity—and first of all profound inner life—to surface modifications, as if to allow the movements of this life to be described in terms of space. In this narrative, the same objects are sometimes described, a few pages apart, with almost imperceptible changes. And the central character—the man who makes a business of seeing—when he enters different houses seems to enter the same house, only displaced to slightly different viewpoints, and since everything that is interior—the image of memories, the image of the imagination—is always ready to assert itself in a quasi-exteriority, the hero is also always on the point of passing from the space of his imagination or of his memory to that of reality, for it is as if he has reached the limit where, in an unrepresentable outside, the vast dimensions of being could meet. Thus it is almost beside the point to know if the act of torture was real or imaginary, or if it is the chance coinciding of images come from different regions or from different points of time. We cannot know, and we do not have to know. If it is indeed Mathias's hand that touched the girl, this action is no more susceptible of being recognized than the empty action of time could be, that imperceptible action we never see in itself but which settles visibly on the surface of things, which are thereby reduced precisely to the nakedness of their surface.

We can admire Alain Robbe-Grillet's mastery, the thought with which he sustains new techniques, and the experimental aspect of his books. But I think that what gives them their attraction is first of all the clarity that pierces them, and this clarity also has the strangeness of the invisible light that sheds the light of the obvious on our great dreams. At the resemblance there is between the "objective" space that Robbe-Grillet's gaze seeks to attain, not without risks or adventures, and the inner space of our nights, we must not be surprised. For what makes our dreams tormenting—their power of revelation and enchantment—is that they transport us in us outside ourselves, where what is inside us seems to stretch out into a pure surface under the false daylight of an eternal outside.

§ 18 H. H.

1. The Pursuit of Oneself

These two letters designate the traveler who one day, around 1931, joined the secret association of pilgrims to the East and took part in the vicissitudes of this enchanted pilgrimage. They also designate the initials of characters in two other novels: Hermann Heilner and Harry Haller, the first a young boy who runs away from the Maulbronn Protestant seminary; the other, a tormented fifty-year-old, solitary, wild, and vehement, who around 1926 wanders to the edge of madness in the obscure regions of a big city, calling himself a "wolf of the steppes." Finally, H. H. is Hermann Hesse, noble writer of the German language whom the glory of the Nobel Prize tardily rewarded, still without giving him that youthful celebrity that always attended Thomas Mann.

Hesse is certainly an author of worldwide reputation, who still perpetuates in world literature the figure of the man of great culture, of the creator who cares about wisdom and is capable of thought, whose genus has perhaps disappeared in France with Valéry and Gide. Moreover, Hesse had the merit of not taking part in the passionate mistakes of his time. In 1914 he was treated as a man with unhealthy ideas because he protested earnestly against the war and lamented the debasement of those intellectuals who were content with a conflict whose significance they were incapable of understanding. Of this social rupture, which he feels so cruelly and which resounds in his mind, there lingered a memory of animosity from which, even a long time afterwards, when he had become the famous author of *Demian* and *Steppenwolf,* his country did not release him. It is true that he had abandoned his nationality around 1923. It is also true that he was living on the fringes, sometimes in Switzerland, sometimes in Italy, exiled in himself, always anxious and divided, and thus a man of his time yet very foreign to his time. His fate is a curious one. More than most, he has a right to claim the title of cosmopolitan. First because of his family: his father is an ethnic German from Russian Estonia; his grandmother is a Dubois, speaks French and comes from French Switzerland; his mother was born in India; one of his brothers was English; he himself, although born in Swabia, begins life as a Swiss citizen but, in order to be educated in his native country, must be naturalized a Wurttemberger. Cosmopolitan in his origin, his learning, and even some of his spiritual tastes, he does not enjoy the international sympathy from which a Rilke very quickly benefits. If I say that he failed to be well known in France, it must be understood that he avoided personal contacts with French literature at a time when it was particularly alive, and did so for reasons that are part of his art and of his fate.

Might this art itself be a little marginal, foreign at least to the great innovative forces whose seminal urgency Proust, Joyce, Breton—to choose names at random—immediately evoke? Perhaps. Yet that is not true either. The relationships he forms between literature and himself, between each of his books and the serious crises of his life; the need to write that is linked in him to the anxiety not to sink down, victim of his divided mind; the effort he makes to welcome anomaly and neurosis and to understand it as a normal state in an abnormal time; the psychoanalytic therapy to which he submits and which gives birth to one of his finest novels; that freedom that nonetheless does not free him, but that he would like to deepen by replacing psychoanalysis with meditation, Jung with yoga exercises, and then trying to situate himself in relation with the great interpreters of Taoism, and despite that, despite this wisdom to which he feels allied, the despair that seizes him and that makes him write in 1926 with tremendous literary passion one of the key novels of his time, *Steppenwolf,* in which Expressionism would recognize one of its masterpieces: all that—this linking of literature with a vital quest, the recourse to psychoanalysis, the call of India and China, even the magical and, at least once, expressionist violence that his art could attain—all this should have made his work a representative body of modern literature.

That does actually happen around 1930. Germany withdraws more and more from him, and he himself increasingly takes refuge in a solitude that illness does not allow him to open onto the agitated world of emigration.

He still writes three more books that, far from being the works of a remnant consciousness, express his late mastery and the felicitous reconciliation he finally wins from his talents so long in conflict. The final book, and the most ample, is *The Glass Bead Game*. In progress from 1931, published in 1943, it made a great impression on the little milieu that was still interested in nontopical literature; it made a particular impression on German émigré writers and on Thomas Mann, who had not yet written *Doctor Faustus* but was preparing to write it and who was, he tells us, almost terrified by the resemblance of this work to the one he had in mind. It is, in fact, a curious resemblance, but one that above all reveals the independence of talents, the singularity of works and the incomparable way that related problems seek their solution in literature. It is an important work, one that the war did not manage to stifle, and it is the one the Nobel Prize sought to emphasize. One can certainly read it and be interested in it without caring about H. H., for it is a work that asserts itself by itself around a central, mysterious, and beautiful image, which to be illumined needs only our experience.

Still, this book is not without apparent coldness. Impersonal, it develops with a studied mastery from which the passion peculiar to this writer seems to be missing. Might it be a calm spiritual allegory, composed in a knowledgeable, almost pedantic way, by an author who contemplates the problems of his time without taking part in them? Whoever reads the book well cannot make this mistake. Hesse is still present in it, even in the somewhat constrained effort he makes to be absent from it, and he is especially present in it through the inquiries that always joined, for him, the problems of the work and the demands of his own life. Not all his books are autobiographical, but almost all speak intimately about him. He has said of poetry that today it has no other value than "to express, in the form of confession and with the greatest possible sincerity, personal distress, and the distress of our age" (this, it is true, was said in 1925, at a time when he was particularly in conflict with himself). Always, in a corner of his narratives, there is some H. H., or the initials of his name, sometimes dissimulated, sometimes mutilated. Even when he signs one of his books with a pseudonym, as *Demian* appeared under the pseudonym of Emil Sinclair, it is to find himself again by trying to identify himself magically with a chosen historic personality: Hölderlin's friend, who protected him during the early days of his madness and thus allowed him to live a little while longer in the world.

This pursuit of himself in his work and through it is endearing. It makes for the great interest of this work. It also makes clear its limits. How he succeeds—in part—in freeing himself and mastering himself in his work and, finally, with the same energy, in freeing the work from itself—that is what one could learn from the arc of his existence as writer and what gives *The Glass Bead Game* its most vital truth, the one his whole life seems to have sought, often even at the expense of literature, and which he finally discovers only in an image in which his life disappears for the sake of the work.

His biographers have revealed someone divided between contradictory tendencies: wandering, staying in place, freeing himself almost scandalously from his people and yet faithful to the spiritual tradition of his family, founding a family in his turn, and very soon becoming a wise man who owns his life and leads the calm life of a German bourgeois, but suffering from this security, which he also desires, and suffering too from not being able to endure this life. Similarly, if in 1914 he has the strength to withdraw from the delirium of passions, it is surely because he does not follow the ordinary way and because he is animated by his own energetic sense. But he is not easily satisfied with himself; he tells himself that if he thinks apart from everyone else, that proves that there is in him a dangerous discord, for which he will someday have to pay. And, in fact, one day, when circumstances are aggravated, something in him breaks; it is this 1916 crisis that will bring him to psychoanalysis and will painfully but powerfully transform him, in his mind and in his art.

This crisis, though a sort of second spiritual birth, is in fact only a secondary one. The most serious event of his inner life occurs when he is fourteen, the day when he runs away from the Maulbronn seminary[1] and when he also tries to run away from the family fate, from the rigor of pious disciplines, from the ministerial future in which he was supposed to follow his father and his grandfather. For two days he hides in the forest and almost dies of cold; a gamekeeper finds him and brings him back. How surprised his pious family is. They entrust him to a sort of exorcist who thinks he is possessed but fails to deliver him from his demon, which, according to Hesse, was nothing but the wicked poetic spirit.

One would be tempted to evoke André Gide, also divided by contradictions in ancestry and tendency. But everything is quite different. Hesse's rupture is more painful and more involuntary. What happens to him, that obligation to free himself, is like an incomprehensible unhappiness he will need many years to master and understand. He is not a triumphant rebel. He is linked to what he rejects just as much as he is to the spirit of independence. Not much would be necessary for him, in becoming a poet, to become a gentle, bucolic poet happy with finding in vague romantic effusion the forgetfulness of his difficulties. And this is indeed what is manifested during the first part of his life; only the dreaming part is expressed, forgetful and at peace with himself, the one that establishes his fame with *Peter Camenzind.* In the history of rebellious adolescents, that is peculiar to him. Having succeeded in freeing himself violently in order to make himself a poet, far from giving expression to this rebellion or to the violence of his conflicts, he on the contrary does everything he can to lose sight of them and to reach, through his art, an ideal reconciliation of which Romanticism—for which he has only too many leanings—provides him with obliging examples.[2] Since he rather quickly wins quite an honorable reputation, since he succeeds, poet that he is, in settling into life and into the comfort of life, this success closes, seemingly once and for all, the crisis of his adolescence; but the forces of division that provoked him and of which he refused to become aware are only more dangerously at work and, profiting from the worldwide conflict, they will carry him to the violent upheaval of 1916, from which he will, with lucid courage, win the fairest chances for renewal.

DEMIAN

Demian, which emerged from this crisis, is a magical work in which the writer makes an effort to arrive at himself, even at his original confusion. The young Sinclair tells about his life: how he discovers the division of the world into two zones, one clear, when he's together with his parents and existence is straight and innocent; the other, which is hardly ever spoken about, is the low life of the servants' quarters; whoever passes through it is exposed to powerful evil forces. Mere chance is enough to fall into it, and the young Sinclair does in fact fall into it, led through blackmail by a neighborhood street kid to a cascade of reprehensible actions under the weight of which his childlike world alters and crumbles. That is when Demian appears. Demian is only a classmate of his, a little older. He will not only deliver Sinclair from blackmail but initiate him to the terrifying thought of Evil that no longer opposes good but rather represents the other side, somber and beautiful, of the divine. Demian himself is a strange, fascinating creature. He dares to defy the clergyman by justifying Cain. Sometimes, during class, his face becomes frozen, becomes stone-like, the face of a being without age and as if without appearance. Later, we will learn that he lives with his mother in relations of illegitimate intimacy.

Hesse's aim is visibly the glorification of a demiurgic world, the world in which morality, law, the State, the school, narrow paternal rigor must be silenced, and in which, like a power that authorizes everything, the great fascination with maternal attraction makes itself felt. It is an effort that costs him a lot, for which he uses a little randomly the resources he finds in the Gnostics, the psychoanalysis of Jung, the mediocre theosophy of Steiner. All this would not be enough to make the story enchant us. But the figure of Demian, the glow of this figure, the somber light with which it is illumined and which we welcome, just as in dream we welcome the symbolized meaning of our desires—that is what still seduces us, readers from a later time. The story is simple, almost naïve, as must be the memory of the childlike world at the boundary of which this grave experience takes place. And the author does not try to make us curious about his secrets by hiding them. The name Demian, as well as the name Eva (Demian's mother), tells us right away more than we would like to know. Hesse will always be that way. He will not let the great magical secret to which he is attached gradually rise up from daily reality; instead he starts with the mythical sense he finds immediately in it and presents it to us ingeniously as such, succeeding, by this naïve simplicity, at giving it life in a world that temporarily opens onto our own. He will be reproached with not having the gift of lifelike characters, of day-to-day details, of epic narration. Perhaps; but why ask him to be other than what he is? Why, as he himself says, when you are standing in front of a crocus in a garden, should you reproach it for not being a palm tree? In all his narratives, he says again, it is not a question of story, characters, or episodes: these are all fundamentally nothing but monologues in which one single person tries to grasp his relationships with the world and with himself. Thus in *Demian* we feel that all the figures are only dream images, born from the inner life of the child Sinclair, but it is a beautiful thing that we can welcome this dream and find our own selves through its light.

Hesse accepts the discipline of psychoanalysis while at roughly the same time Rilke and Kafka reject it, although, to overcome their problems, both of them had also considered this method. Rilke fears waking up cured, and cured of poetry: simplified excessively. For Hesse, things never become simpler. On the contrary, he only becomes aware of his complex division, of the necessity he feels of contradicting himself and not renouncing his contradictions. He always wants unity. As a young man, it is a vague unity, of semblance and unconsciousness, that he sought in nature by closing his eyes to himself. Now he sees that this happy unity was built only of his ignorance. During the years that follow, great years of material and moral ordeal (he broke all ties, lived alone in Montagnola in conditions of painful destitution, often having nothing except chestnuts gathered in the forest for a meal), what he wants to attain, to hear and make heard, is the double melody, the fluctuation between two poles, the come-and-go between the pillars of the two principles of the world. "If I were a musician, I could without difficulty write a melody for two voices, that would consist of two lines, in two sequences of sounds and notes, capable of responding to each other, of completing each other, of fighting each other and of holding each other, at each instant and in each point of the series, in the liveliest and most intimate relationship of exchange and opposition. And whoever knew how to read the notes could read my double melody, see and hear in each sound the counter-sound, the brother, the enemy, the antipode. Well, this double voice, this eternal movement of antithesis—that is what I want to express with my words, but I try in vain, I do not succeed."

We understand why he will be tempted by the solutions of Hindu spirituality and even more by the language of Chinese thought, as he never stopped being lured by the great dream of Romantic poetry, which wants to unite magically in itself all times, spaces, and worlds, starting from inner indeterminacy. He will later say: "For me, the highest words of humanity are those pairs of words in which fundamental dichotomy was expressed in magical signs, those few sentences and those secret symbols in which the great oppositions of the world are recognized as necessary and at the same time as illusory." But Hesse is not a dialectic being, or even a man of thought, perhaps not even of that thought that poetry and literature conceal within themselves and that is thought only on condition of remaining hidden. That is why the experiments he undertakes enrich him, but without giving him secure mooring. His aspiration to unity is religious, but art that can only be discordant in a discordant time is also his religion. And what would be the use of saving his soul, of giving it coherence and harmony, when the truth of the world is now nothing but a passionate rending?

Steppenwolf, written ten years after *Demian,* is the expression of this impulse. Despite the despair that is obvious in it and the feeling of unreality that sustains it, it is a strong and virile book. The opening, as often in his narratives, is the truest part of it: it is the portrayal of a solitary fifty-year-old man (Hesse's own age), who one day rents a room in a well-to-do house in a large city and, despite his good manners, arouses a feeling of unease there. Hesse is not very generous with details, but they are enough to impose an image on us: the secret agitation, the nervous movements of the strange tenant, which contrast with his comfortable bourgeois dress; his hesitant, painful walk, and yet his air of hauteur, his careful elocution. Or a scene like this one: one day, the owner's son finds this distinguished man sitting on the landing, breathing its wax smell and nostalgically contemplating the antechamber of the well-polished paradise of the German bourgeoisie. That makes us smile, but it is moving too, for we recognize in it the great need for a home with which Hesse is haunted and that he cannot satisfy: if he possesses it, this enduring resting place, the wanderer in him keeps renouncing it, just as, solitary, he cannot do without friendship, just as the naïve bucolic poet clashes with the writer tormented by problems to the point of self-destruction.

The theme of *Steppenwolf* is that man is not wolf plus man, instinct plus mind, a rigid split inherited from Lutheran thought; we have to unmask and demystify this over-simple dichotomy by descending more deeply into the dispersion of the inner world. The other theme is the desperate attempt to grasp the world again, starting from chaos. The pain of the one who writes the book and the pain of the time in which he writes it should meet each other in the book, as if a writer, enclosed in himself, suffering from his own imbalance, could not become aware of it, introverted as he might be, except through the imbalance of his time. To rejoin the world, even if at the price of the coherence of an illusory self. Does he manage to do this? In one sense, no, and not even in the representation that his book gives of such a reunion. The sort of magical transfiguration by which, describing the lower depths of a large city, he masks the difficulty he experiences in portraying them actually, seems like an alibi. Initiation into sensual life is still nothing but the unfolding of a dream, but here one that is too close to reality, without value if it does not allude to an actual experience. In the end, the solitary man undergoes the ordeal of the "Magic Theater" in which, in the game of mirrors and drunken reflection, he must meet his own subconscious: a modern Walpurgis night, in the course of which H. H. gives free rein to his hatred of machines, while, in the upper regions, Mozart and Goethe, smiling and detached divinities, are present at the hero's collapse to remind him of the existence of a more serene world, the world of aesthetic creation in which technique itself does not arouse condemnation.[3]

Steppenwolf is a grating book in which the imagination, the reality, and the truth of the central character do not manage to correspond to each other. The impression is that of a painfully artificial image of a time itself unnatural. That a writer as alien to excessive expression had to go so far out of himself in order to give his experience its truest form—that is what holds our attention. His friends were surprised with this violence and this discord. He gave them this answer: "It is not a matter for me of opinions, but of necessities. One cannot have the ideal of sincerity and show only the pretty sides, the imposing sides of one's being." And on another occasion: "My friends were right when they reproached my writings for having lost harmony and beauty. These words made me laugh. What is beauty, what is harmony for the one condemned to death who runs between the collapsing walls, searching for his life?"

We get the impression that Hesse actually lost himself. But his destiny is to move in contradictions. Scarcely has he exhausted one experience than this exhaustion drives him toward another extreme. Periods of passionate explosion are followed by times of retreat; delirium is followed by sober will and serene certainty. With *Steppenwolf*, it seems that for the first time he had the strength to go to the end of his most dangerous impulse. The mastery he gains from it will no longer be called into question. *The Glass Bead Game*, which is the accomplishment of this mastery, creates a space in which he will finally be able to detach himself from himself, and in which the work will be able to stop being the stake of his personal difficulties.

2. The Game of Games

The Glass Bead Game was composed from 1931 to 1942 or even 1943, at a time when the world experienced the greatest travail and Germany its fatal hours. Hesse, as withdrawn as he is, feels the suffering and, he will tell us, the shame. It is in part like a dream of compensation that, under

the name Castalia, he will build the city of the intellect where, after the
great upheavals of the twentieth century, in a temporarily reconciled
world, the sciences and the arts flourish once again. This occurs around
the year 2400. The date matters little. It is not a question of a prophetic
novel, or even of a utopian narrative. What Hesse pursues is subtler and
more ambiguous. What he produces, with delicate nuances, is, at a certain
moment of time, the gathered existence of all times and, in the form of a
Game, in the spiritual space of the Game, the possibility of belonging to
all worlds, to all knowledges, and to all cultures. It is the *Universitas litterarum*, an ancient dream of humanity.

But it is also an ancient dream of Hesse's. From *Demian* forward, and in
almost all his books, there is always a *Bund*, a secret association, an esoteric community, all-powerful and without efficacy, present everywhere
and elusive, with which the central character seeks vainly to connect. We
can find here an idea of Goethe and an idea of Nietzsche, and even more
the memory of German Romanticism. But it is not only a borrowed
theme. Hesse's tormented aspiration expresses itself first toward unity and
the wish to be able, without violating solitude, to enter a community, to
reestablish, through ways of art and magic, ties with the little circle of
those who might be in possession of this unpossessable truth. Magic is the
temptation to which Hesse is always ready to succumb. It allows him
readily to reconcile his horror of modern times with his need to find at the
same time a world where he would no longer be alone. One year before
beginning *The Glass Bead Game*, he writes *The Pilgrimage to the East*. This
little narrative is a naïve—willfully naïve—representation of the great
community of minds, of enlightened and awakened beings, of all those
who seek the East, when the East "is not just a country, something geo-
graphical, but the native country of the soul in its youth, everywhere and
nowhere, the unification of all times."

We are here in the condition of romantic wonder. During this pilgrimage, H. H. sets side by side the characters of his preceding books with
those of Hoffmann or Novalis, all the characters of childhood faerie. The
aim is the same as the one Novalis assigned to *Märchen* [folktales], the re-
vitalization of the state of legend, the rebirth, by memory and premonition, of the vanished original realm. The travelers to the East constitute an
order and, like any order, it has a secret at its center, the sealed writing that
no one must divulge. Obviously, what Hesse wishes is to join enchantment and allegory, artless faith and problematic quest, the simplicity of

the tale and the initiation into knowledge—in other words, always to rec-oncile the two sides of his intellect and his talent. But just as the journey gets stuck in questionings and doubts, so in the narrative the naïve vapor-izes at contact with allegory, and allegory becomes naïve.

However, this little narrative certainly helped him write his great novel, which picks up its themes again. It freed him from the facility of his dreams: having expressed them in their immediate form, he gained the patience to ripen them and the strength to confront them at a higher level.

A NEW ART

Castalia is also an order, but a monastic rather than a magical one, a province called, in memory of Goethe, "the pedagogical Province," where, separated from the world, obeying a strict and ceremonious hierarchy, a certain number of men chosen at a very early age and trained in special schools devote themselves to pure studies and their instruction. Grammar, philology, music, mathematics, all the scientific disciplines, all the arts are practiced there in a spirit of rigorous purity. Is it, then, an order of culti-vated men, a sort of living encyclopedia, an enclosed space where the mind protects itself so as to be no longer liable to extinction in the event of universal upheavals? In one sense. But if Castalia were made up only of a reserve in which culture could be perpetuated apart from the ever-threatening world—which is also an old dream of human scholarship—we would lose interest in such a conventional enterprise. But Castalia has in its center a rarer presence around which it is gathered, celebrates itself, and plays itself in the form of a new art. That is the gift of Castalia, and that too is Hesse's present, which is not mediocre, for it is not every day that a creator, even in the framework of a novel, succeeds in bringing close to us the fiction of a great impossible game.

In writing *Doctor Faustus*, Thomas Mann too had the ambition of imagining a new art form, and he knew how, through a skillful, precise, and fascinating evocation, to give the rich and convincing feeling of works written by a great unknown composer. Proust had Vinteuil, and Balzac the "unknown masterpiece." But Hesse promises us more, not another musician, or even a form of music that seems to carry music a little be-yond what we have ever heard, but a new language, expressing itself ac-cording to a new discipline he actually invents. Not entirely, though, and that is how he acts as the tempter, awakening our expectation and almost our faith. This art is already in us, and the chronicler who sententiously tells us the story is not reluctant to point out all those who had some premonition of it, from Heraclitus and Pythagoras to Nicholas of Cusa and Leibniz, the great German Romantics, with a particular nod to the Chinese authors who were closest to it.

It is like an idea that has developed throughout the course of history. Sometimes it is the simple dream of a universal language grouped, in accordance with the time, around a particular science or a particular art, by which one seeks to express values and forms in signs perceptible to the senses. Sometimes—and this is already a higher degree—this great game in which the mind is at play wants to make itself master of the totality of knowledge, cultures, and achievements and, submitting them to a common measure, to translate them into a harmonious domain where new relationships will be born, while at the same time, like a song, the hidden rhythm, the final law, or simply the possibility of infinite exchanges will be asserted.

At this stage, the Game comes directly from the Pythagorean dream, but no less directly from the speculations of Novalis who, in the great intoxication of the final years of the eighteenth century, asserted that poetry is a science and that the perfected form of science must be poetic. At this same stage, when we see the players, by means of minute studies, take apart works, analyze systems, and extract from them the measures that allow a dialogue of Plato or a law of physics or a Bach chorale to resound together, we are indeed close to recognizing in this Game a virtuoso juggling act, destined to make us reflect on the excesses into which, in their quests, over-pure intellectuals fall.

But, above the Game, there is a higher Game; or more precisely, these labors of erudition, these studies of synthesis, these great efforts to gather into one common space the infinite variety of knowledge and human works, make up only one aspect of it. Meditation, also understood as a discipline and a technique, forms its other aspect. The game then becomes the Game of Games, the great cultural celebration, a collective ceremony in which, by the concerted, inspired, and skillful alliance of music, mathematics, and meditation, the art of universal relationships can be developed in the mind and heart of the participants, an art capable each time of awakening the premonition of the infinite or of producing the experience of unity. The Game stops being the animated and harmonious inventory of values and forms. It is no longer, for the players engrossed in the perceptible resonance of formulas, even a particularly delicate way of enjoying the mind: it is a severe cult, a religious celebration in the course of which one can approach an essential vision, a sacred language, a sublime alchemy, and perhaps also the bodying forth of a new man.

Naturally, Hesse did realize that he could not represent the idea of such a game in a clear and logical way, and we must admire with what art—a sure, refined, and ironic art, an art he usually lacked—without trying magically to fool us and also without fixing his image by dogmatic exposition, by skillfully combining the precise and the imprecise, by varying the points of view, by tracing circles around the same thought from different directions, he has succeeded in making us think realizable the art whose essential characteristic is to be incapable of realization.

AT THE END OF CASTALIA

His book does not just have Castalia at its center, the pedagogical Province, the village of players, its institutes, its cells, the evocation of which restores to us, in a lively and persuasive way borrowed from his memories of Maulbronn, the image of a closed intellectual community. At first Hesse seems to have dreamed about his work as a sort of opera without characters in which the themes, as they developed, would have represented the game of the eternal movement of powers and forms, but finally he decided to tell about the life of one of the Masters of the Game, an exceptional personality whom he called Josef Knecht—Joseph the Servant—less to contrast him with Wilhelm Meister than to make a successor to the great Master of the Travelers to the East, Leo the Servant, and above all to mark his rejection of all führers, even if they are of the spiritual variety. This biography could have served only the purposes of exposition: to illustrate and bring to life the domain of Castalia through the story of one of its privileged representatives. Perhaps Josef Knecht was at first only a proud Castalian, a man of spirit entrenched in his difference. In a poem composed at the time,[4] Hesse evokes the Game as an activity he could practice himself, one that consoles him and brings him peace; its secret was taught him by Josef Knecht: "And now begins in my heart a game of thoughts to which I have applied myself for many years, called the Glass Bead Game. A pretty invention that has music as support and meditation as principle. Josef Knecht is its master, to whom I owe what I know of this beautiful imagination."

Josef Knecht also became a very close companion to Hesse, a virtual man who no longer served just to make the essence of an impossible art pass onto the plane of existence, but also to explore the meaning and

perhaps the dangers of the strange experiment he had proposed for himself. The result was almost surprising. An exemplary interpreter of a
supreme art and a sacred language, the same impulse that links Knecht to
Castalia leads him, in the end, to reject Castalia, no longer able to content
himself with what still seems to him like an image of the absolute. This
step, to be sure, is accomplished in an equivocal way. On one hand we
have here a reasonable criticism of that proud province of the mind that
has isolated itself from the world, ignores history, and scorns its times,
while its chief role should be pedagogical, that of educating the earth, as
Novalis had already said about poets: "We are charged with a mission, we
are summoned to create the earth." Hesse pathetically rejects his own isolation and, accomplishing a decisive step toward the world, he means to
make unity no longer a secret relationship between the two poles of the
mind, God and self, but an affirmation that exists first of all through the
living community of men. This is the verdict on his solitary experience,
and it is fitting and positive as well. But for his book and for the fiction of
the book a certain awkwardness results. For as long as we willingly accept
the timeless time that the age of the Game evokes, we are surprised, looking at the world through the windows of Castalia, to see it resemble the
Germany of the eighteenth century rather than this future time, historically dated and situated, in which we are invited to enter. Doesn't Hesse
somewhat contradict here the impulse that he makes the issue of his
book? He wants to restore its rights to the reality of the ordinary world,
but in his narrative this world is no longer anything but a background of
scenes where obviously nothing will ever happen. We suspect that his return to the world is a pious vow he himself did not fulfill, which now has
only an allegorical sense. Which weakens our interest.

Fortunately, we have another suspicion. Knecht's end is simple but
strange. Supreme Master of the Game, he resigns from his functions, decides to reenter everyday life and to take up the profession of schoolmas-
ter, becoming the mentor of a young schoolboy, gifted and undisciplined,
a touching image of the young Hesse. Scarcely has he crossed the ideal
threshold of Castalia and rejoined his student than he vanishes, during a
morning swim, in the icy waters of a high mountain lake. His end seems
to involve only natural causes. But Knecht's biographer insistently reminds us that the disappearance is legendary and that, from the moment
Knecht left the Province, he entered a region where historic truth is not
enough. So we are invited to understand Knecht's final steps, his resigna-

tion, the joyous decision that frees him from the past like the realization of a will superior to his own, and the final cold defeat as the mystery that crowns everything. This ultimate scene speaks, in fact, for itself. Thomas Mann admired it and found in it, curiously, a great erotic meaning. Before the rising sun, Knecht's young student gives in to wild gesticulations, a sort of effervescent dance to which he abandons himself, to his own surprise and, finally, to his shame, as if he were yielding his secret to this strange teacher. To regain his composure, he wants to throw himself into the water of the lake and swim to the other shore, which has not yet been touched by the light of the sun. Knecht, tired by the altitude, feels uneasy but does not want to disappoint his student by seeming unsportsmanlike. He in turns throws himself into the biting cold of the water, which soon conquers him. The adolescent will hold himself obscurely responsible for this death, and more than any lesson, it will contribute to awakening in him the new being he must become to answer the call of future times.

We have, in this conclusion, an example of Hesse's art and of the simplicity with which he opens himself up to allegorical transparency. Each detail is there for itself and for an ideal meaning that it clearly evokes. Knecht's return to the world is symbolized by the climbing of the mountain, an ultimate surpassing by means of which he must go beyond his personal existence. The rising sun is like the appearance of the absolute, of which Castalia is only the temporary glorification, and which does not permit duration in any form, even the purest. Knecht ends in legend, transformed into an anonymous Demian, a victim offered in sacrifice to the absolute he serves and disappearing so that the human horizon can be broadened. (Hesse sought to express poetically and perhaps felicitously the enigmatic nature of his hero, his personality-impersonality, by adding to the narrative three imaginary biographies that the character Knecht is supposed to have written. These are school exercises, we are told. At the end of his studies, each Castalian selects a time and a culture, and imagines what he himself could have been in that time. Hesse thus raises his own method of experiment to a higher power. It is also a way of making his book a sort of Bead Game, to show the unity of a person through the mirroring of changing circumstances and the variety of disparate cultures. Finally, by a method of analysis that is no longer psychological, he tries to penetrate the profundity of a life by suggesting the fullness of possibilities that the trajectory of a linear narrative could never convey.)

Many other details are charged with significance. Even the lake suggests the attraction of obscure forces, the call of the maternal depths into which the one who returns to the world falls because of a higher passion. This kind of death haunted Hesse to such an extent that in some of his narratives there are no less than four or five deaths by drowning. Here, allegorical meaning gives way to magical provocation. In *The Glass Bead Game*, in which the protagonist represents the work rather than its author, Hesse did not fail to establish, between his fiction and his life, an entire network of relationships. Thus he describes himself ironically in the character of an almost maniacal hermit who lives on the borders of Castalia, consulting the oracles in the Chinese manner. The school where Knecht studies bears the name Hellas, in memory of the scholarly institute where long ago at Maulbronn a schoolboy was so unhappy. The first inventor of the Glass Bead Game is Bastian Perrot of Calw. But Perrot of Calw on the river Nagold is in fact the craftsman who accepted the young Hesse as apprentice when Hesse, having renounced classical studies, tried several professions in vain. Father Jacobus, who introduces Knecht to history, is Jacob Burckhardt. Thomas von der Trave, one of the Masters of the Game, is Thomas Mann. Do these names signify that the Bead Game might be yet another game, a roman à clef, and even a novel of contemporary criticism in which, making a faithful, friendly, and respectful portrayal of, for instance, Thomas Mann, Hesse might be critiquing his intellectual situation, that of an all-too-pure man of letters? We would be wrong to imagine it. These names, these allusions, these details, which are secret only for the reader not forewarned, have the role of a magical memorial in which the past beckons to the writer and amicably insinuates itself into the chill space of things and times that do not exist. And no doubt, in this final work, Hesse tries more seriously to grasp once again the obscure event on which his entire life has depended: Knecht leaves the closed community of Castalia, as the young Hesse ran away one day from the Maulbronn seminary. The mature man in the mastery of his vocation, as well as the adolescent in the distress of his sensibility, both free themselves and dangerously fulfill their destiny. Finally, it is toward his childhood that the writer, at the final limit of his experience, turns back one last time, and the heir he chooses, the successor he gives himself, is the young boy, difficult, tricky, who he once was and to whom he resolutely gives the keys to the future.

THE MIND GROWN OLD

The book has many outcomes, then, and could be read in various ways. But it is the image of the Game that remains the center around which everything gravitates, this superior dream of unknown times, which nonetheless awakens a memory in us. We have here a new answer to the questions that Malraux revealed a little later by giving a name to the experience of the Imaginary Museum. The Game is the Museum of Museums. In it, each time it is played, all the human works, all the arts, and all knowledge come to life and wake up, in their infinite variety, in their changing relationships, in their fugitive unity. It is indeed a supreme accomplishment. Might we, then, be at the end of history? At that moment of twilight when Minerva's (and Hegel's) bird, beginning its nocturnal flight, makes day into night, makes the active, creative, and unthinking day into the calm, silent transparency of night? The day must be finished to be able to tell about itself and speak. But day, having become its own narrative, is precisely night. Does such a perspective belong to Hesse's book? The narrator of it makes this remark: the new art of the Game could be born only by the heroic and ascetic decision to renounce the creation of all works of art. It is no longer the time to write more poems or to enrich music with new "pieces." The creative mind must flow back on itself, and the only work of art will henceforth be the infinite presence of all works. Art is the singing consciousness—knowledge, music, meditation—of the totality of the arts and, even more, of everything hidden in this everything, a half-aesthetic, half-religious celebration in which the whole is played and put into play as a sovereign entertainment.

The Game is the crowning of culture. An absolute demand is accomplished. That could be our fate, and it is obvious that Hesse loved this fate. But he was also frightened of it. *The Glass Bead Game*, in which, under this childlike name,[5] the true community he has always dreamed of is realized, is a late flourishing. With what is highest begins the decline. The mind of Castalia is the mind grown old. If it refrains from the creation of new works, it is because it has stopped being triumphant. The absolute is now nothing more than the tired isolation of a high spiritual form, foreign to living reality and, unaware of this, it thinks it is everything, while it is only the empty totality of ignorance.

Now we have fallen very low. The Game becomes a sterile dream and a deceiving consolation, at best the melancholy music of decline. Between these two interpretations, Hesse hesitates. From this uncertainty, his book takes on the deceptive light of an enigma, and this division sometimes enriches it, sometimes weakens it. That is because there is another, more serious hesitation. What is the Game? A supreme creation that consists of gathering together into a living unity the ensemble of all works of art and all creations of all times. But what counts here, what is first? Unity or the whole? Unity, which is God, or the whole, which is the affirmation of the perfected man? Some German commentators were prone to see in Hesse's book a Hegelian work. This is scarcely reasonable. The Game is perhaps the erudite and melodious consciousness of the whole, but it is precisely for that reason that decadence and exhaustion threaten it. On the contrary, to the extent that it is a stage toward unity, the provisional realization of unity, the Game, according to the author, carries great promise, for it signifies "a chosen, symbolic form of the search for the perfect, a sublime alchemy, the approach, beyond all images and diversities, to the mind that is one in the self, the approach to God."

In any case, the Game must be transcended. Knecht's death is the religious moment when the transcendence is accomplished. But does it have to be surpassed because it betrays history and its progress, or because it is the true way leading to the center and therefore stops when the center is reached, the unitary vision with the God who abides in us? Hesse's book says all this, but that is perhaps too much to say at once; it is more than he can say. As far as the coherence of the novel is concerned, we have to wonder if it isn't dangerous to take a great image, placed at the heart of the work and completely supporting it, and then to seem to degrade it to a superficial symbol, which then seems constructed expressly for the criticism we intend to make of it. In any work, the questioning of the work is perhaps its essential aspect, but this questioning must always be carried out through the sense and development of the image that is its center, and which is just beginning to appear when the end comes, at which time it disappears.

§ 19 Diary and Story

The diary—which seems so removed from rules, so responsive to life's impulses and capable of all liberties, since thoughts, dreams, fictions, commentaries on itself, important or insignificant events are all suitable for it, in whatever order or disorder one likes—is however subject to a seemingly negligible but formidable law: it must respect the calendar. That is the pact it signs. The calendar is its demon, inspirer, composer, provocateur, and guardian. To write one's diary is to place oneself temporarily under the protection of everyday time, to place writing under this protection; and it is also to protect oneself from writing by submitting it to this fortunate regularity that one undertakes not to threaten. Whoever writes about himself embeds himself, then, for good or for ill, in the day-to-day and in the perspective that dailiness delimits. The most distant, most aberrant thoughts are kept within the circle of daily life and must not wrong its truth. Thus sincerity represents, for the diary, the requirement it must attain but not surpass. No one has to be more sincere than the diarist, and sincerity is that transparency that allows him not to cast a shadow on the contained existence of each day to which he limits the task of writing. One has to be superficial to preserve sincerity, a great virtue that also requires courage. Profundity has its comforts. At least, profundity demands the resolution not to hold oneself to the oath that ties us to ourselves and to others by means of some truth.

THE PLACE OF MAGNETIZATION

It is not the fact that a story may recount extraordinary events that distinguishes it from the diary. The extraordinary also is an integral part of the ordinary. It is because story grapples with what cannot be proven, what cannot be the subject of a report or an account. A story is the place of magnetization that draws the actual figure to a point where it must be placed to respond to the fascination of its shadow. *Nadja* is a story. It opens with these words: "Who am I?" The answer is a living figure we might have been able to meet one day, on some street we know. This figure is not a symbol, or even a pale dream. She does not resemble the Dorothée who appeared from time to time to the young Jünger, or the Demian that Hesse had as companion at school: attractive image of the eternal genius. Nadja was just as she is represented in the surprising story: a life of chance, born from chance and met by chance; faithful to chance to the point of forcing anyone who wants to follow her to enter the most dangerous—and dirtiest—byways of a chanceful life. But why wouldn't the form of the diary, the account that is the diary, have suited such an event, placed, dated, caught in the network of daily actions? Because nothing is more foreign to the reality where we live, in the certainty of the ordinary world, than chance, this chance that has taken, for Breton, the form of a young woman, and nothing can be more different from the daily reckoning than the anxious progression, without roads and without boundaries, that the pursuit of what has taken place requires, but which, through the fact of having taken place, tears the fabric of events. For whoever encounters chance, like the one who "really" meets an image, the image, chance opens onto his life an unperceived gap where he must renounce habitual language and the calm light of day to keep himself under the fascination of another day and in relation to the measure of another language.

One tells about what one can report. One tells about what is too real in order not to ruin the conditions of the modest reality that is ours. *Adolphe* is not the purified history of Benjamin Constant: it is a sort of magnet to detach him from his shadow—which he does not know—and to bring it behind his feelings, into the burning space that they make for it but which the very fact of "living" them, as well as the progress of the life and doings of every day, constantly hid from him. In her diary, Mme de Staël is no less tempestuous, and Constant no less torn apart, than in narrative. But in *Adolphe* feelings turn toward their center of gravity, their true place, which they wholly occupy by banishing the movement of the hours, by dissipating the world and, with the world, the ability to live them: far from being attenuated one by one in an equilibrium that would make them bearable, they fall together toward the space of the narrative, a space that is also that of passion and night, where they cannot be reached or surpassed or betrayed or forgotten.

THE TRAP OF THE DIARY

The interest of the diary is its insignificance. That is its inclination, its law. To write every day, under the warranty of just this day, and to remind it of itself, is a convenient way of escaping both silence and the extravagance of speech. Each day tells us something. Each day noted down is a preserved day. Doubly advantageous operation. We live twice. We save ourselves both from forgetfulness and the despair of having nothing to say. "Let us pin down our treasures," Barrès abominably says, and Charles du Bos, with the simplicity unique to him: "The diary in the beginning represented for me the supreme recourse to escape total despair confronting the act of writing," and also: "The curious thing in my case is how little I have the feeling of living when my diary accumulates only its deposit."[1] But that a writer as pure as Virginia Woolf, that an artist as passionate to create a work that retains only transparency, the luminous aureole and light contours of things, felt obliged to come back to herself in a journal of chatter in which the "I" pours itself out and consoles itself, that is significant and troubling. Here, the diary seems very like a safeguard against the danger of writing. Down there, in *The Waves*, roars the risk of a work in which one has to disappear. Down there, in the space of the work, everything is lost and perhaps the work too is lost. The diary is the anchor that scrapes against the bottom of the day-to-day and clings to the roughness of vanity. In like manner, Van Gogh has his letters, and a brother to whom to write them.

There is, in any diary, the fortunate reciprocal compensation, one by the other, of a twofold nullity. Someone does nothing in his life but writes that he does nothing, and there, all of a sudden, something is done. One who lets himself be sidetracked from writing by the futilities of the day returns to these nothings to tell about them, bewail them, or take pleasure in them, and lo, there is a day fulfilled. It is "the meditation of zero on itself," of which Amiel courageously speaks.

The illusion of writing and sometimes of living that it gives, the little recourse against solitude that it assures (Maurice de Guérin tells his Notebook: "My sweet friend, . . . here I am, yours now, entirely yours," and Amiel, why would he get married? "The diary takes the place of a confidant, that is to say, of friend and wife"); the ambition to eternalize the good moments and even to make the whole of life a solid mass that one can hold close, firmly embraced; finally the hope, by uniting the insignificance of life with the nonexistence of the work, to raise null life up to the beautiful surprise of art, and formless art to the unique truth of life—the interlacing of all these various motives makes the diary an undertaking of redemption: one writes to save writing, to save one's life by writing, to save one's little self (the revenges one takes on others, the nastiness one distills) or to save one's great self by giving it scope, and then one writes in order not to be lost in the poverty of the days or, like Virginia Woolf, like Delacroix, in order not to be lost in this ordeal that is art, that is in the limitless demand of art.

What is peculiar about this hybrid form, seemingly so easy, so obliging and, sometimes, so displeasing because of the pleasant rumination on oneself that it involves (as if there were any interest in thinking about oneself, in turning to oneself), is that it is a trap. One writes to save the days, but one entrusts one's salvation to writing, which changes the day. One writes to save oneself from sterility, but one becomes Amiel who, returning to the fourteen thousand pages in which his life has been dissolved, recognizes in them what ruined him "artistically and scientifically" by "a busy laziness and a phantom of intellectual activity."[2] One writes to remember oneself, but, says Julien Green, "I figured that what I noted down would revive in me the memory of the rest, of all the rest . . . but today nothing more remains than a few hasty and insufficient sentences that give only an illusory reflection of my past life."[3] Finally, then, one has neither lived nor written, a double failure from which the diary wins its tension and its gravitas.

The diary is linked to the strange conviction that one can observe oneself and that one must know oneself. But Socrates did not write. The most Christian centuries ignore this examination, whose only intermediary is silence. We are told that Protestantism favors this confession without confessor, but why should the confessor be replaced by writing? We must rather return to a cumbersome jumble of Protestantism, Catholicism, and Romanticism so that writers, setting off in search of themselves in this false dialogue, can try to give form and language to what cannot speak in them. Those who realize this and little by little recognize that they cannot know themselves, but only transform themselves and destroy themselves, and who pursue this strange struggle in which they feel drawn outside of themselves to a place to which they nonetheless do not have access, have left us, according to their abilities, fragments, sometimes even impersonal ones, that we may actually prefer to any other works.

THE EDGES OF THE SECRET

It is tempting for the writer to try to keep a journal of the work he is writing. Is it possible? Is *Le journal des* Faux-Monnayeurs [The journal of *The Counterfeiters*] possible? To question oneself on one's projects, weigh them, verify them; as they develop, to comment on them for oneself—that does not seem difficult. Doesn't the critic who, as they say, is a second creator, have his word to say? Can't this word take the form of a ship's log, in which from day to day the fortunes and blunders of navigation can be inscribed? And yet such a book does not exist. It seems that the experience unique to the work, the vision by which it begins, "the sort of wandering" that it provokes, and the unusual relationships it establishes between the man we meet every day and who carefully keeps a journal of himself and the being we see rise up behind each great work, the relationship between the work and the act of writing it, as between Isidore Ducasse and Lautréamont,[4] must remain incommunicable.

We see why the writer can keep the diary only of the work that he does not write. We see, too, that this diary can be written only by becoming imaginary and by immersing itself, like the one who writes it, in the unreality of fiction. This fiction does not necessarily have to do with the work it prepares. Kafka's *Diary* is made not only of dated notes that relate to his life, descriptions of things he has seen, people he has met, but of a great number of drafts of stories, some of which are a few pages, most a few lines, all unfinished, though often already formed, and—what is most striking of all—almost none relates to another, none is the resumption of a theme already used, nor does it have a clear connection with the events of the day. But we have the strong feeling that these fragments "are structured," as Marthe Robert says, "between actions lived and art," between Kafka who lives and Kafka who writes. We also feel that these fragments constitute the anonymous, obscure traces of the book that is trying to be realized, but only insofar as they do not have a visible connection with the life from which they seem to come, nor with the work to which they form the approach. If, then, we have here a presentiment of what the diary of the creative experience could be,[5] we have at the same time the proof that this diary might also be as enclosed as, and more separated from, the completed work. For the edges of a secret are more secret than the secret itself.

The temptation to keep the log of the most obscure experience "up to date" [*à jour*] is undoubtedly naïve. But it persists. A sort of necessity always gives it its chances. It is in vain that the writer knows that he cannot turn beyond a certain point without masking, by his shadow, what he has come to contemplate; the attraction of his sources, the need to grasp head on what always turns away, finally the wish to link himself to a quest without concern for the results—all this is stronger than his doubts, and moreover the doubts themselves push us rather than hold us back. Don't the firmest and least dreamy poetic attempts of our time belong to this dream? Isn't there Francis Ponge? Yes, Ponge.

§ 20 Story and Scandal

It is possible that the most "beautiful" contemporary narrative was published in 1941 by an author whose name, Pierre Angélique, has remained unknown. Fifty copies came out then; fifty more in 1945; today a few more. The title of it is *Madame Edwarda*, but when, having finished reading it, one comes to the back cover, one finds, identical to the first, this other title: *Divinus Deus*.

I put the word *beautiful* in quotes. Not because its beauty is hidden: it is obviously beautiful. But that which is beautiful in it makes us responsible for our reading in a way that lets us reward it with such a judgment. What is at stake in these few pages?

"If you are afraid of everything, read this book, but first, listen to me: if you laugh, it is because you are afraid. A book, you think, is an inert thing. That is possible. And yet, what if, as sometimes happens, you do not know how to read? should you dread . . . ? Are you alone? are you cold? do you know to what point man is 'yourself'? stupid? and naked?"

I would like to quote the first sentence of the story: "On the corner of a street, anguish, a dirty and intoxicating anguish, overwhelmed me (perhaps because I had seen two furtive girls on the steps of the bathroom)," and finally the final paragraph: "I have finished. From the sleep that left us, for a short time, in the back of the taxi, I awoke first, ill. . . . The rest is irony, long wait for death."

Between these boundaries, is what is written scandalous? Definitely. But it is the truth of this story to offend us with an obvious scandal that we do not quite know where to locate. We would like to be able to incriminate the words—but never were they stricter; or the circumstances, the fact that Madame Edwarda is a whore in a brothel, but on the contrary, that very fact could be reassuring; and certain details, which we have to call obscene, are obscene with a necessity that ennobles them, making them inevitable not by art alone, but by a perhaps moral, perhaps fundamental constraint. Contradiction certainly has a great scandalous power; and if base things, actions of which it is not proper to speak, suddenly impose themselves on us as charged with the highest value, this assertion, the instant it reaches us, with an upsetting, unarguable, and intolerable force, touches us scandalously, however liberal we may be regarding what seems degraded or exalted.

The efforts we make theoretically to isolate the point where scandal touches us (calling, for instance, on what we know of the sacred, object of desire and horror), are like the work of blood cells to restore the wounded part. The body returns to normal, but the experience of the wound remains. One cures the wound, one cannot cure the essence of a wound.

"I babbled softly: 'Why are you doing that?' 'You see,' she said, 'I am GOD...' ' 'I am mad...' ' 'No, you have to look: look!'" Such a dialogue, in the circumstances in which it takes place, can appear absurd, can also seem one of the easiest things to write. If we do not subscribe to it—and in a certain way, the author does not seek our conviction; similarly, his own has a meaning that hides from him: that is how scandal is, its nature is such that it escapes us, while we do not escape it—even if we answer it only with laughter, irony, uneasiness, or indifference, there is, in the situation the story sets before us, such a simple certainty, although entirely uncertain, linked to such an exclusive and extensive truth that we feel that our attitude, whatever it may be, is already part of it and confirms it. There is no way to react to this story that is not implicated and included within it, immediately testifying to its necessity. That is how the book holds us, since it could not leave us intact, a properly scandalous book, if it is the property of scandal that we cannot protect ourselves from it and that we expose ourselves to it the more we try to defend ourselves against it.

In that, the author is no different from any reader. We can't say that just because he's been affected by the event whose narrative alone touches us, he might thus be closer to the center of the story. However things actually happened, it is from the instant he tells about them that everything becomes serious for him, just as for Phaedra everything begins when she agrees to disclose her secret because of Oenone, becoming guilty not on account of her monstrous, innocent passion, but guilty of making it guilty by making it something possible, by letting it change from the pure impossibility of silence to the scandalous truth of being realized in the world. There is in every tragic writer this necessity of the encounter between Phaedra and Oenone, this movement toward revelation of what cannot be illumined, the excess that becomes overweening and scandal... only in words.

That the most incongruous book, as Georges Bataille qualifies it in his preface, is finally the most beautiful book, and perhaps the most tender—that is utterly scandalous.

PART IV

Where Is Literature Going?

§ 21 The Disappearance of Literature

One sometimes hears strange questions asked, like: "What are the tendencies of today's literature?" or: "Where is literature going?" Surprising questions, but the most surprising thing is that if there is an answer, it is easy: literature is going toward itself, toward its essence, which is disappearance.

Those who need such general assertions can turn to what is called history. It will teach them what is signified by Hegel's famous saying: "Art is and remains for us . . . a thing of the past," a phrase uttered boldly in front of Goethe, when Romanticism was becoming popular and when music, the plastic arts, and poetry were preparing considerable works. Hegel, who introduces his course on aesthetics with this weighty statement, knows that. He knows that art will not lack new works, he admires the works of his contemporaries and sometimes he prefers them (he also misunderstands them), and yet art "for us is a thing of the past." Art is no longer capable of supporting the need for the absolute. What counts absolutely is henceforth accomplishment in the world, the seriousness of action, and the task of actual freedom. Art is close to the absolute only in the past, and it is in the Museum alone that it still has worth and power. Or, an even graver disgrace, it falls to the point of becoming a simple aesthetic pleasure for us, or an auxiliary of culture.

That is well known. It is a future already present. In the world of technique, we can continue to praise writers and make painters rich, we can honor books and expand libraries; we can reserve a place for art because it is useful or because it is useless, constrain it, reduce it, or let it be free. Its fate, in this favorable case, is perhaps the most unfavorable. Apparently, art is nothing if it is not sovereign. Thence the artist's embarrassment at still being something in a world in which he nonetheless sees himself as unjustified.

AN OBSCURE, TORMENTED SEARCH

That is roughly how history speaks. But if one turns to literature or to the arts themselves, what they seem to say is quite different. Everything happens as if artistic creation, as times exclude its importance by following impulses foreign to art, came closer to itself through a more demanding and profound view. Not prouder: it is the *Sturm und Drang* that thinks it exalts poetry by the myths of Prometheus and Muhammad; what is glorified then is not art but the creative artist, the powerful individual, and each time the artist is preferred to the work, this preference, this exaltation of genius, signifies a degradation of art, a falling off confronting his own power, the search for compensatory dreams. These disordered but admirable ambitions, as mysteriously expressed by Novalis—"Klingsor, eternal poet, does not die, remains in the world," or Eichendorff—"The poet is the heart of the world," are quite unlike those that come after 1850 (to choose a date after which the modern world most decisively goes toward its fate) and are heralded by Mallarmé or Cézanne, names that all modern art upholds with its movement.

Neither Mallarmé nor Cézanne makes us dream of the artist as an individual more important or more visible than others. They do not look for fame, that burning and shining void with which an artist's head had always, since the Renaissance, wished to wreathe itself. They are both modest, turned not toward themselves but toward an obscure quest, toward an essential concern whose importance is not linked to the affirmation of their person or to the improvement of modern man, but is incomprehensible to almost everyone, and yet they cling to it with a stubbornness and a methodical force of which their modesty is only the hidden expression.

Cézanne does not exalt the painter, or even (except through his work) painting, and Van Gogh said: "I am not an artist—how coarse it is even to think that of oneself," and he adds: "I say that to show how stupid I think it is to speak of gifted or ungifted artists." In the poem, Mallarmé foretells a work that does not reflect the one who made it, foretells a decision that does not depend on the initiative of some privileged individual. And, unlike the ancient idea according to which the poet said, "It is not I who speak, it is the god who speaks in me," this independence of the poem does not designate the proud transcendence that would make literary creation the equivalent of the creation of a world by some demiurge; it does not even signify eternity or the immutability of the poetic sphere; on the contrary it reverses the ordinary values that we attach to the word "to make" [*faire*] and to the word "to be" [*être*].

This surprising transformation of modern art, which occurs at the moment when history offers humanity tasks and aims that are entirely different, could seem like a reaction against these tasks and these aims, an empty effort of affirmation and justification. That is not so, or it is true only superficially. Writers and artists sometimes answer the summons of community with a frivolous withdrawal, answer the powerful work of their century with a naïve glorification of their idle secrets or with a despair that makes them recognize themselves, like Flaubert, in the condition they reject. Or rather they think they can save art by enclosing it in themselves: art might be a state of the soul; "poetic" should mean "subjective."

But precisely, with Mallarmé and with Cézanne (to use these two names symbolically), art does not seek out these paltry refuges. What counts for Cézanne is *realization*—not the states of the soul of Cézanne. Art strives powerfully for the work, and the work of art, the work that has its origin in art, shows itself as an affirmation entirely different from works that have their measure in labor, values, and exchanges—different, but not opposite: art does not negate the modern world, or the world of technique, or the effort toward liberation and transformation that relies on this technique, but it expresses and perhaps achieves connections that *precede* any objective, technical accomplishment.

Obscure, difficult, and tormented quest. It is an essentially risky experiment in which art, the work, truth, and the essence of language are called back into question and enter into risk. That is why, at the same time, literature is devalued, is stretched out on the wheel of Ixion, and the poet becomes the bitter enemy of the figure of the Poet. Outwardly, this crisis and this critique only remind the artist of the uncertainty of his condition in the powerful civilization in which he plays so small a role. Crisis and criticism seem to come from the world, from political and social reality, and seem to submit literature to a judgment that humiliates it in the name of history: it is history that criticizes literature and that pushes the poet aside, replacing the poet with the publicist, whose task is at the service of current events. That is true, but by a remarkable coincidence, this external criticism answers to the actual experiment that literature and art conduct on their own behalf and that exposes them to a radical questioning. The skeptical genius of Valéry and the firmness of his opinions cooperate with this questioning, as do the violent assertions of surrealism. Similarly, it seems that there is almost nothing in common between Valéry, Hofmannsthal, and Rilke. Yet Valéry writes: "My verse has had no other interest for me than suggesting reflections on the poet to me," and Hofmannsthal: "The innermost core of the poet's essence is nothing other than the fact that he knows he is a poet." As for Rilke, we do not betray him if we say that his poetry is the lyrical theory of the poetic act. In all three cases, the poem is profundity opened onto the experience that makes it possible, the strange impulse that goes from the work toward the origin of the work, the work itself having become the anxious and boundless search for its own source.

We must add that if historical circumstances exert their pressure on such movements until they seem to direct them (thus it is said that the writer, taking as the object of his activity the ambiguous essence of this activity, is content to reflect the uncertain situation that his becomes socially), events do not themselves possess the ability to explain the meaning of this search. We have just cited three names who are more or less contemporary, and contemporaries of great social transformations. We have chosen the date 1850, because the revolution of 1848 is the moment when Europe begins to open itself up to the maturity of the forces that form it. But all that has been said of Valéry, Hofmannsthal, and Rilke could have been said, and at a much deeper level, of Hölderlin, who nonetheless precedes them by a century and in whom the poem is essentially poem of the poem (to paraphrase Heidegger). Poet of the poet, poet in whom the possibility, or impossibility, of singing is made song—such is Hölderlin and such, to cite a new name, younger by a century and a half, is René Char, who answers him and by this answer makes rise up before us a form of experienced time [*durée*] very different from the time that simple historical analysis grasps. That does not mean that art, works of art, let alone artists, ignoring time, achieve a reality withdrawn from time. Even "the absence of time" toward which the literary experience leads us is hardly the region of the timeless, and if by the work of art we are reminded of the weakening of an actual initiative (a new and unstable appearance of the fact of existing), this beginning speaks to us in the intimacy of history, in a way that perhaps gives a chance to the initial historical possibilities. All these problems are obscure. To present them as clear and even susceptible to being clearly formulated could lead us only to acrobatics of writing, and deprive us of the help they do lend us, which is to resist us strongly.

What we can sense is that the surprising question "Where is literature going?" undoubtedly expects its answer from history, an answer that in some way is already given to it, but at the same time, by a ruse in which the resources of our ignorance are involved, it appears that by this question literature, profiting from the history it anticipates, questions itself and indicates, not an answer certainly, but the deeper, more essential meaning of the actual question it possesses.

LITERATURE, WORK OF ART, EXPERIMENT

We are speaking of literature, work [*oeuvre*], and experiment; what do these words mean? It seems false to see in the art of today a simple occasion of subjective experiences or a dependence on aesthetics, and yet we never stop, when on the subject of art, talking about experiment. It seems right to see in the concerns that animate artists and writers not an interest in themselves, but a concern that demands expression in work. The works, then, should play the greatest role. But is that how it is? Hardly. What attracts the writer, what moves the artist, is not directly the work; it is the search, the impulse that leads to it, the approach of what makes the work possible: art, literature, and what these two words conceal. Thus the painter prefers the various states of a painting to a painting. And the writer often wishes not to finish anything entirely, leaving as fragments a hundred stories that led him to a certain point and that he must abandon to try to go beyond that point. Thus, by another surprising coincidence, Valéry and Kafka, separated by almost everything, close only in their concern to write rigorously, meet each other to affirm: "My entire work is only an exercise."

Similarly, we are irritated at seeing literary works replaced by an always greater mass of texts that, under the name of documents or reports, terms that are almost coarse, seem to ignore any literary intention. They seem to say: we have nothing to do with creating things of art; they also seem to say: accounts of a false realism. What do we know of them? What do we know of this approach, even failed, toward a region that escapes the grasp of ordinary culture? This anonymous, authorless language, which does not take the form of books, which soon disappears and wants to disappear, couldn't it be alerting us to something important, about which what we call literature also wants to speak? And isn't it remarkable, but enigmatic, remarkable in the manner of an enigma, that this very word "literature," a late word, a word without honor, which is helpful mostly just to reference books, which accompanies the ever more pervasive progress of prose writers, and designates not literature but its mistakes and excesses (as if those were essential to it), and becomes, the moment that questioning becomes most earnest, when genres scatter and forms are lost, when on one hand the world no longer needs literature and on the other hand each book seems foreign to all the other books and indifferent to the reality of genres, the instant when what seems to express itself in art works is not eternal truths, types, and characters, but a demand that is opposed to the order of essences, literature, thus questioned as valid activity, as unity of genres, as a world where the ideal and the essential are sheltered, becomes the preoccupation, ever more present, although hidden, of those who write and, in this preoccupation, gives itself to them as what must be revealed in its "essence."

It is a preoccupation in which, it is true, what is called into question is perhaps literature, but not as a definite, certain reality, an ensemble of forms, or even a mode of perceptible activity: rather as what is not discovered, is not verified, and cannot be directly justified, to which we come close only by turning away from it, which we grasp only when we go beyond it, through a quest that must not be preoccupied with literature, with what "essentially" is, but which on the contrary is preoccupied with reducing it, neutralizing it, or more precisely, with descending, through a movement that finally escapes it and neglects it, to a point where only impersonal neutrality seems to speak.

NON-LITERATURE

These are necessary contradictions. Only the work matters, the affirmation that is in the work, the poem in its compressed singularity, the painting in its own space. Only the work matters, but finally the work is there only to lead to the quest for the work; the work is the impulse that carries us toward the pure point of inspiration from which it comes and which it seems it can reach only by disappearing.

Only the book matters, such as it is, far from genres, outside of categories—prose, poetry, novel, testimony—under which it refuses to be classed, and to which it denies the ability to assign its place and determine its form. A book no longer belongs to a genre; every book belongs to literature alone, as if literature possessed beforehand, in their generality, the secrets and formulae that alone allow what is written to assume the reality of a book. It seems as if genres have vanished, and literature alone asserted itself, gleamed solitary in the mysterious clarity that it propagates, and which each literary creation reflects by multiplying it—as if there were, in short, an "essence" of literature.

But the essence of literature is precisely to escape any essential determination, any assertion that stabilizes it or even realizes it: it is never already there, it always has to be rediscovered or reinvented. It is not even certain that the word *literature* or the word *art* corresponds to anything real, anything possible or anything important. It has been said that to be an artist is not to know that art already exists, or that the world already is there. Undoubtedly, the painter goes to the museum and there gleans a certain awareness of the reality of painting: he knows painting, but his painting does not know it; his painting knows that painting is impossible, unreal, unrealizable. Whoever asserts literature in itself asserts nothing. Whoever looks for it looks for only what is concealed; whoever finds it finds only what is on this side of literature or, what is worse, beyond it. That is why, finally, it is non-literature that each book pursues as the essence of what it loves and wants passionately to discover.

We need not say that every book forms part of literature—in fact every single book determines absolutely what literature is. We need not say that every work draws its reality and its value from its ability to conform to the essence of literature, or even from its right to reveal or affirm this essence. For a work can never take as its subject the question that sustains it. Never could a painting even begin if it set out to make painting visible. It is possible that every writer feels called to answer alone, through his own ignorance, for literature, for its future, which is not only a historical question but, through history, the movement by which, while necessarily "going" outside of itself, literature nonetheless tries to "come" to itself, to what it essentially is. It is possible that being a writer is the vocation of answering this question, one that the writer must uphold with passion, truth, and technical mastery, and which nevertheless he can never outwit, even less so when he undertakes to answer it, to which he can at the very most, through his work, give an indirect answer—this work of which he is never master, never certain, which does not want to answer to anything but itself and which makes art present only there where it hides itself and disappears. And why is that?

§ 22 The Search for Point Zero

That books, writings, language are destined for metamorphoses to which, without our knowing it, our habits are already opening, but which our traditions still deny; that libraries impress us by their other-world appearance, as if there, with curiosity, surprise, and respect, we might suddenly discover, after a cosmic voyage, the vestiges of another, older planet, fixed in the eternity of silence—we would have to be quite out of touch not to perceive this. To read, to write—we don't doubt that these words are summoned to play in our mind quite a different role from the one they still played at the beginning of this century: that is obvious, no matter what radio set, no matter what screen alerts us to it, and even more obvious is this rumor surrounding us, this anonymous and continuous murmuring in us, this wonderful, unheard, agile, tireless language, which endows us each moment with an instantaneous, universal knowledge and turns us into the pure passage of a movement in which each one is always, already, in advance, exchanged for everyone else.

These expectations are understandable. But this is more striking: well before the inventions of technology, the use of radio waves, and the transmission of images, it would have been enough to listen to the words of Hölderlin or Mallarmé to discover the direction and extent of these changes, which we accept today without surprise. Poetry, art, in order to come to themselves, have, through an impulse to which the times are not foreign, but through unique requirements that have given form to that impulse, shown and affirmed much more considerable upheavals than those whose impressive forms we now see, on another level, in daily use. Reading, writing, speaking—these words, understood with reference to the experience by which they are carried out, make us feel, says Mallarmé, that, in the world, we do not speak, we do not write, and we do not read. That speaking, writing, and the requirements implicit in these words must stop suiting modes of comprehension demanded by the effectiveness of the work and of specialized knowledge, that speech can stop being indispensable for understanding—all this does not speak of the destitution of this world without language; it speaks of the choice it made and the vigor of this choice.

DISPERSION

With singular brutality, Mallarmé separated the domains. On one side, useful speech, instrument and means, language of action, of work, of logic and knowledge, language that immediately conveys and which, like any good tool, disappears in the familiarity of use. On the other side, the language of the poem and of literature, in which speaking is no longer a transitory, subordinate, and common means, but seeks to accomplish itself as an actual experience. This brutal division, this distribution of empires that tries rigorously to determine the spheres, should at least have helped literature to gather itself together, to make it more visible by giving it a language that distinguishes and unifies it. But it is the opposite phenomenon that we have witnessed. Until the nineteenth century, the art of writing formed a stable horizon that those who practiced it did not dream of violating or surpassing. To write in verse was the essential point of literary activity, and there was nothing more obvious than verse, if in this rigid framework poetry remained nonetheless elusive. One is tempted to say that in France at least, and no doubt in any classical period of writing, poetry was charged with the mission of concentrating in itself the risks of art, and of thus saving language from the dangers that literature makes it run: one protects common understanding against poetry by making poetry very visible, very particular, a domain closed by high walls—and, at the same time, one protects poetry against itself by making it firmly fixed, by giving it rules so determined that the poetic indeterminate finds itself disarmed by it. Perhaps Voltaire still wrote in verse in order to be in his prose the purest and most effective prose writer. Chateaubriand, who could be a poet only in prose, began to transform prose into art. His language becomes a speech from beyond the grave.

Literature is a domain of coherence and a common realm only as long as it does not exist, only as long as it does not exist for itself and hides itself. As soon as it appears in a distant premonition of what it seems to be, it is shattered, it enters the way of dispersion where it refuses to be recognized by precise and determinable signs. Since at the same time tradition still remains powerful, humanism continues to seek the aid of art, and prose still wants to fight for the world, a confusion results in which at first sight it is unreasonable to insist on deciding what is at stake. In general, we find limited causes and secondary explanations for this shattering. We blame individualism: each person writes according to his own self, which wants to stand out from all the others.[1] We blame the loss of shared values, the profound division of the world, the dissolution of the ideal and of reason.[2] Or, in order to reestablish a little clarity, we restore the distinctions of prose and poetry: we abandon poetry to the disorder of the unforeseeable, but we note that the novel dominates literature today, that literature, in the form of the novel, remains faithful to the habitual, social intentions of language, remains, in the boundaries of a circumscribed genre, capable of channeling it and making it specific. The novel is often called monstrous, but with a few exceptions, it is a well-educated and extremely domesticated monster. The novel announces itself by clear signs that do not lend themselves to misunderstanding. The predominance of the novel, with its apparent freedoms, its audacious moves that do not put the genre in danger, the discreet certainty of its conventions, the richness of its humanistic content, is, like the predominance of regular verse before it, the expression of this need we have to protect ourselves against what makes literature dangerous: as if, along with the poison, literature was quick to secrete for our use the antidote that alone allows for its calm, lasting consumption. But perhaps it dies from what makes it inoffensive.

We must, to this search for subordinate causes, respond that the shattering of literature is essential, and that the dispersion into which it enters also marks the moment at which it approaches itself. It is not the individuality of writers that explains why writing places itself beyond a stable horizon, in a fundamentally divided region. More profound than the diversity of temperaments, humors, and even lives is the tension of a search that calls everything into question. More decisive than the rending of worlds is the demand that rejects the very horizon of a world. The word "experiment" must not make us believe that, if literature seems to us today to be in a state of dispersion unknown to previous eras, it is due to this license that makes it the arena for ever-renewed attempts. Undoubtedly, the feeling of a limitless freedom seems today to animate the hand that sets to write: one thinks one can say everything and say it every way; nothing holds us back, everything is available to us. Everything—isn't that a lot? But everything is finally very little, and the one who begins to write, in the insouciance that makes him master of the infinite, perceives, in the end, that he has at best devoted all his strength to searching for only one single point.

Literature is not more varied than before; it is perhaps more monotonous, the way one can say that night is more monotonous than day. It is not disunited because it is more given over to the arbitrariness of those who write or because, beyond genres, rules, and traditions, it becomes an open field for manifold and disordered attempts. It is not the diversity, fantasy, and anarchy of the attempts that make literature a dispersed world. I must express it another way and say: the experience of literature is the very test of dispersion, it is the approach of what escapes unity, the experience of what is without understanding, without agreement, without law—it is error and the outside, elusive, irregular.

LANGUAGE, STYLE, WRITING

In a recent essay, one of the rare books in which the future of literature is inscribed, Roland Barthes distinguished between language, style, and writing.[3] Language is the state of common speech as it is given to each of us together, at a certain moment of time and according to our belonging to certain places in the world; writers and nonwriters share it alike: experience it uneasily, welcome it constantly, or refuse it deliberately, it doesn't matter, language is there, it testifies to a historic state into which we are thrown, it surrounds us and surpasses us, it is for all of us the immediate, although historically elaborate and far from any beginning. As for style, it is the obscure part, linked to the mysteries of blood, of instinct, violent profundity, density of images, language of solitude in which the preferences of our body, of our desire, of our time—secret and closed to ourselves—blindly speak. No more than he chooses his language does the writer choose his style, that necessity of temperament, that anger in him, that tempest or state of tension, the slowness or rapidity that come to him from an intimacy with himself, of which he knows almost nothing, and that give his language as singular an accent as that which makes his face recognizable. All that is not yet what can be called literature.

Literature begins with writing. Writing is the totality of rites, the overt or subtle ceremony by which, independently of what one wants to express and of the way in which one expresses it, this event is announced: that what is written belongs to literature, that the one who reads it is reading literature. This is not rhetoric, or rather it is a particular kind of rhetoric, destined to make us understand that we have entered this closed, separate, and sacred space that is literary space. For instance, as is shown in a chapter rich with reflections on the novel, the grammatical historic past tense [*passé simple*], foreign to the spoken language, serves to announce the art of the narrative; it indicates in advance that the author has accepted the linear and logical time that is narration; clarifying the field of chance, it imposes the security of a well-delimited story which, having had a beginning, goes with certainty toward the happiness of an end, even if it's an unhappy one. The historic past tense, or the privileged use of the third person, tells us: this is a novel, just as the canvas, colors and, previously, perspective told us: that is painting.

Roland Barthes wants to arrive at this statement: there was a time when writing, being the same for everyone, was welcomed by an innocent consent. All writers then had only one wish: to write well, to carry ordinary language to a higher degree of perfection or consonance with what they were trying to say; for all of them there was a unity of intention, an identical morality. It is no longer like that today. Writers who distinguish themselves by their instinctive language are even more opposed, by their attitude, to the literary ceremony: to write is to enter a templum that imposes on us, independently of the language that is ours by right of birth and by physical destiny, a certain number of uses, an implicit religion, a rumor that changes beforehand all that we can say, that charges it with intentions that are all the more effective since they are not avowed; to write is first of all to want to destroy the temple before building it; it is at least, before passing over its threshold, to question the constraints of such a place, the original sin that formed the decision to enclose ourselves in it. To write is finally to refuse to pass over the threshold, to refuse to "write."

Thus we explain, and better discern, the loss of unity from which literature today suffers, or on which it prides itself. Each writer makes writing his problem and this problem the object of a decision that he can alter. It is not only by their vision of the world, the characteristics of their language, the chance of talent, or their particular experiences that writers are divided; as soon as literature makes itself seen as an environment in which everything is transformed (and embellished), as soon as one sees that this air is not the void, that this clarity does not just illumine but distorts by giving objects a conventional daylight, as soon as one feels that literary writing—genres, signs, the use of the past-historic and the third person— is not a simple transparent form, but a world apart in which idols reign, in which prejudices slumber, and in which live, invisible, the powers that change everything; for each person has to try to extricate himself from the world, and it is a temptation for everyone to destroy it in order to recon-struct it pure of any previous use or, even better, to leave the place empty. To write without "writing," to bring literature to that point of absence where it disappears, where we no longer have to dread its secrets, which are lies, that is "the degree zero of writing," the neutrality that every writer seeks, deliberately or without realizing it, and which leads some of them to silence.

A TOTAL EXPERIENCE

This way of seeing[4] should help us better grasp the extent and gravity of the problem before us. It seems first, if we strictly follow the analysis, that, freed from writing, from this ritual language that has its uses, its im-ages, its symbols, its tested formulae (of which other civilizations— Chinese, for instance—seem to offer much more accomplished exam-ples), the writer might come back to immediate language, or to that solitary language that speaks instinctively in him. But what would this "re-turn" signify? Immediate language is not immediate, it is charged with history and even literature, and above all—this is the essential point—as soon as a writer tries to grasp it, it changes its nature in his hand. Here we recognize the "leap" that is literature. We use ordinary language and it makes reality available, it says things, it gives them to us by distancing them, and the language itself disappears in this use, always neutral and unnoticed. But having become the language of "fiction," it becomes, apart from usage, uncommon, and no doubt we think we still get what it des-ignates as we do in ordinary life, and even more easily since it is enough to write the word *bread* or the word *angel* to make immediately available to our imagination the beauty of the angel and the taste of bread—yes, but on what conditions? That the world, where we have only things to use, first of all collapsed, that things have become infinitely distanced from themselves, have recovered the inalienable distance of the image—that is why I am no longer myself and can no longer say "I." A formidable trans-formation. What I possess through fiction, I possess only on condition of

being it, and the being by which I approach it is what divests me of myself and of any being, just as it makes language no longer what speaks but
what is; language becomes the idle profundity of being, the domain where
the word becomes being but does not signify and does not reveal.

It is a formidable transformation, and elusive, imperceptible at first,
endlessly evading. The "leap" is immediate, but the immediate escapes all
verification. We know that we write only when the leap is accomplished,
but in order to accomplish it we must first write, write without end, write
straight from the infinite. To want to return to the innocence or the natural essence of spoken language (as Raymond Queneau invites us to do,
not without irony) is to claim that this metamorphosis can be calculated
like an index of refraction, as if it were a matter of a phenomenon immo-
bilized in the world of things, whereas it is the very emptiness of this
world, a call that one hears only if one is oneself changed, a decision that
compels whoever makes it to indecision. And what Roland Barthes calls
style, visceral, instinctive language, language that stems from our secret inwardness—what is closest to us, then—is also what is the least accessible
to us, if it is true that in order to get hold of it again we must not only set
aside literary language but meet again and silence the empty profundity
of incessant speech, what Éluard perhaps had in mind when he said "uninterrupted poetry."

Proust at first speaks the language of La Bruyère, of Flaubert: that is the
alienation of writing, from which he little by little frees himself by writing incessantly, especially letters. It is through writing, it seems, "so many
letters" to "so many people" that he slips toward the gesture of writing
that will become his own. It is a form that we admire today as wonderfully
Proustian, and that naïve scholars link to its organic structure. But who is
speaking here? Is it Proust, the Proust who belongs to the world, who has
the vainest social ambitions, an academic vocation, who admires Anatole
France, who is the society columnist for the *Figaro*? Is it the Proust who
has vices, who leads an abnormal life, who finds his pleasure in torturing
rats in a cage? Is it the Proust already dead, immobile and buried, whom
his friends no longer recognize, foreign to himself, nothing but a hand
that writes, who "writes every day at any hour, all the time" and as if outside of time, a hand that no longer belongs to anyone? We say Proust, but
we sense that it is the entirely other who writes, not only someone else but
the very demand of writing, a demand that uses the name Proust but does

not express Proust, that expresses him only by disappropriating him, by making him Other.

The experience that is literature is a total experience, a question that does not allow limits, does not accept being stabilized or reduced, for instance, to a question of language (unless into this single point of view everything is collapsed). It is the very passion of its own question, and it forces anyone it attracts to enter wholly into this question. And it is not enough for it to make us suspicious of the literary ceremonial, the consecrated forms, the ritual images, the fine language, and the conventions of rhyme, number, and narrative. When one encounters a novel written using all the conventions of the historic past tense and the third person, one has, of course, in no way encountered "literature," but neither has one encountered what might keep it away or thwart it; one has in fact encountered nothing that prevents or assures its approach. Hundreds of novels, as they are today—masterfully or negligently written, or with a fine style, or passionate, or boring—are all equally foreign to literature, due no more to mastery than to negligence, no more to slack language than to intense language.

By directing us, through serious thought, toward what he called the zero degree of writing, Roland Barthes perhaps also designated the moment when literature might be grasped. But the fact is that at that point it would be not only a bland, absent, and neutral writing, it would be the very experience of "neutrality," which one never hears, for when neutrality speaks, only one who imposes silence on it prepares the conditions for its hearing, and yet what there is to hear is this neutral speech; what has always been said cannot stop being said and cannot be heard, a torment we get a presentiment of in the pages of Samuel Beckett.

§ 23 "Where now? Who now?"

Who is speaking in the books of Samuel Beckett? What is this tireless "I" that seemingly always says the same thing? Where does it hope to come? What does the author, who must be somewhere, hope for? What do we hope for, when we read? Or perhaps he has entered a circle where he turns obscurely, led on by a wandering speech, one that is not deprived of meaning, but deprived of center, that does not begin, does not end, yet is greedy, demanding, will never stop, one couldn't stand it if it stopped, for that is when one would have to make the terrible discovery that, when it does not speak, it is still speaking, when it ceases, it perseveres, not silently, for in it silence speaks eternally.

It is an experiment without outcome, although from book to book it is pursued in an ever purer way, rejecting the weak resources that would allow it to pursue itself.

It is this movement that strikes one first. Here, no one is writing for the honorable pleasure of making a beautiful book, or writing out of that fine constraint that we think we can call inspiration: in order to say important things that he needs to tell us, or because that is his task, or because he hopes, by writing, to venture into the unknown. To have done with it, then? Because he is trying to escape the impulse that compels him, by giving himself the impression that he is still master, and that, from the instant he speaks, he could stop speaking? But is it he who speaks? What is the void that becomes speech in the open intimacy of the one who disappears into it? Where has he fallen? "Where now? When now? Who now?"

IN THE REGION OF ERROR

He struggles, that is obvious. He struggles sometimes secretly and as if starting from a secret he hides from us, and hides also from himself. He struggles at first not without stratagem, then with that more profound stratagem that is to divulge his game. The former ruse is to interpose masks and figures between himself and speech. *Molloy* is another book in which what is expressed tries to take the reassuring form of a story, and indeed it is not a happy story, not only because of what it says, which is infinitely miserable, but because it does not succeed in saying it. This wanderer who already lacks the means of wandering (but he still has legs, he even has a bicycle), who revolves eternally around an aim that is obscure, hidden, avowed, hidden again, an aim that has something to do with his dead mother, but she is still dying, something that precisely because he reaches it as soon as the book begins ("I am in my mother's room. It is I who live there now") condemns him to wandering around it ceaselessly, in the strangeness of what is hidden and does not want to be revealed— we feel that this vagabond is held by a more profound error, and that this jerky movement is accomplished in a region that is one of impersonal obsession. But, as irregular as the view we are given of him is, Molloy remains an identifiable character, a definite name who protects us from a yet more troubling menace. There is nonetheless in the narrative a movement of unsettling disintegration: it is the movement that, unable to be satisfied with the vagabond's instability, demands more of him so that in the end he is redoubled, becomes another, becomes the policeman Moran, who pursues him without reaching him and in this pursuit in turn enters the way of error without end. Molloy without knowing it becomes Moran, that is to say, an other, that is to say, yet another character; it is a metamorphosis that does not undermine the element of certainty of the story, while still introducing into it an allegorical, perhaps deceptive, meaning, for we do not feel the scope of the profundity hidden there.

Malone Dies apparently goes further. Here, the vagabond has become a dying man, and the space where he must wander no longer offers the resources of a city with a hundred streets or the free horizon of forest and sea that *Molloy* still offered us. There is only the bedroom, the bed, the stick with which the dying man pulls things toward him or pushes them away, thus enlarging the circle of his immobility and above all the pencil that enlarges it even more by making his space the infinite space of words and telling. Malone, like Molloy, is a name and a figure, and it is also a series of narratives, but these stories no longer rest on themselves; far from being told so that the reader believes in them, they are immediately unmasked in their artifice as invented stories: "This time, I know where I'm going. . . . It is a game now, I am going to play. . . . I think that I could tell myself four stories, each one on a different theme." Why these vain stories? To fill the void into which Malone feels he is falling; out of the anguish of this empty time, which will become the infinite time of death; in order not to let this empty time speak, and the only way of silencing it is to force it to say something whatever the cost, to tell a story. Thus the book is no longer just a means of openly lying; thence the scathing compromise that unbalances it, this clash of artifices where experience is lost, for the stories remain stories; their brilliance, their sarcastic cleverness, all that gives them form and interest also detaches them from Malone, the one who is dying, detaches them from the time of his death in order to reattach them to the ordinary time of this story, in which we do not believe and which does not matter to us here, for we are waiting for something much more important.

THE UNNAMABLE

In *The Unnamable*, stories do try to remain stable. The dying man had a bed, a room; Mahood is a wretch enclosed in a jar that serves to decorate the entrance to a restaurant. There is also Worm, the one who was not born and whose only existence is his oppressive inability to exist; at the same time the old figures reappear, phantoms without substance, empty images revolving mechanically around an empty center that the nameless "I" occupies. But now everything has changed, and the experience enters its true profundity. It is no longer a question of characters under the reassuring protection of their personal name; it is no longer a question of a story, even conducted in the present tense without the form of interior monologue. What had been narrative has become struggle, what had assumed form, even if only as creatures in rags and in pieces, is now shapeless. Who is speaking here? What is this I, condemned to speak without rest, the one who says: "I am forced to speak. I will never be quiet. Never"? By a comfortable convention, we answer: it is Samuel Beckett. That way, we seem able to welcome the weightiness there is in a situation, not fictional, that evokes the actual torment of a real existence. The word *experience* alludes to what is actually felt. But that way too we try to find again the security of a name and to situate the "contents" of the book on this personal level at which everything that happens happens under the warrant of a conscience, in a world that spares us the worst unhappiness, the unhappiness of having lost the ability to say I. But *The Unnamable* is precisely experience lived under threat of the impersonal, the approach of a neutral speech that speaks itself alone, that goes through the one who hears it, that is without intimacy, excludes any intimacy, one that cannot be silenced, for it is the incessant, the interminable.

Who is speaking here, then? Is it "the author"? But what can this title designate, if in any case the one writing is already no longer Beckett but the demand that led him outside of himself, dispossessed him and let go of him, gave him over to the outside, making him a nameless being, the Unnamable, a being without being who can neither live nor die, cannot cease or begin, the empty place in which the listlessness of an empty speech speaks, one that with great difficulty regains a porous and agonizing I.

It is this metamorphosis that is taking shape here. It is in the intimacy of this metamorphosis that an eloquent survivor wanders, an obscure remnant that will not give way and fights in motionless vagrancy, with a perseverance that does not indicate any power but rather the curse of what can never stop talking.

We ought perhaps to admire a book deliberately deprived of all resources, one that accepts beginning at that point where no continuation is possible, obstinately clings to it, without trickery, without subterfuge, and conveys the same discontinuous movement, the progress of what never goes forward. But that is still the point of view of the detached reader, who calmly considers what seems to him an amazing feat. There is nothing admirable in an ordeal from which one cannot extricate oneself, nothing that deserves admiration in the fact of being trapped and turning in circles in a space that one can't leave, even by death, since to be in this space in the first place, one had precisely to have fallen outside of life. Aesthetic feelings are no longer appropriate here. We may be in the presence not of a book but rather something much more than a book: the pure approach of the impulse from which all books come, of that original point where the work is lost, which always ruins the work, which restores the endless pointlessness in it, but with which it must also maintain a relationship that is always beginning again, under the risk of being nothing. The Unnamable is condemned to exhaust infinity: "I have nothing to do, that is to say nothing in particular. I have to speak, that's vague. I have to speak, having nothing to say, nothing but the words of others. Not knowing how to speak, not wanting to speak, I have to speak. No one forces me to, there is no one, it is an accident, it is a fact. Nothing could ever relieve me of it, there is nothing, nothing to discover, nothing that diminishes what remains to be said, I have the sea to drink, so there is a sea."

GENET

How did this happen? Sartre has shown how literature, expressing the profound "illness" [*mal*] whose constraint Genet had to undergo, little by little gave Genet mastery and power, making him rise from passivity to action, from the formless to form, and even from indecisive poetry to a sumptuous, distinctive prose. "*Notre-Dame des Fleurs* [Our Lady of the Flowers] is, without the author suspecting it, the diary of a detoxification, a conversion: Genet detoxifies himself in it and turns toward the other; this book realizes detoxification itself: born from a nightmare, organic product, condensation of dreams, epic of masturbation, it proceeds line by line, from death to life, from dream to waking, from madness to health, a passage punctuated by falls." "By infecting us with his illness, he cured himself of it; each of his books is a crisis of cathartic possession, a psychodrama: each one seems only to reproduce the preceding one, but, step by step, this possessed man makes himself a little more master of the demon that possesses him."

This is a form of experience that can be called classical, whose traditional interpretation was expressed by Goethe's saying, "Poetry is deliverance." *Les chants de Maldoror* [The songs of Maldoror] also is an illustration of it, since in it we see, by the force of metamorphoses, the passion of images, and the return of ever more obsessive themes, a new being rise up little by little from the depths of night and by the very means of night, a being who wants to find in the radiance of day the reality of his countenance: thus Lautréamont is born. But it would be unwise to suppose that, when literature seems to lead us to the light, it leads to the peaceful enjoyment of reasonable clarity. The passion of the ordinary day, which in Lautréamont already rises up against the menacing exaltation of banality, and the passion of ordinary language, which is destroyed by becoming a sarcastic assertion of the commonplace and of pastiche, also cause it to be lost in the limitlessness of the light where it fades away. For Genet likewise, Sartre saw perfectly that if literature seems to open up to man a way out and help the accomplishment of his mastery, when everything has gone well, literature suddenly discovers the absence of outcome that is unique to it, or else it discovers the absolute failure of this success and itself dissolves in the insignificance of an academic career. "At the time of *Notre-Dame*, the poem was the way out. But today: awakened, rationalized, without anguish about the next day, without horror, why should one write? To become a man of letters? That is exactly what he does not want. . . . One imagines that an author whose work results from such a profound need, whose style is a weapon forged for such a precise intention, for whom each image, each argument, so obviously summarizes all of life, cannot begin suddenly to speak of something else. . . . Whoever loses wins: winning the title of writer, he at the same time loses the need, the desire, the occasion and the means to write."

It remains to be said that there is, in fact, a classical way of describing the literary experience, in which one sees the writer happily deliver himself from the dark part of himself by a work in which that part becomes, as if by a miracle, the happiness and clarity stemming from the work itself, in which the writer finds a refuge and, even better, the flourishing of his lonely self in a free communication with the other. That is what Freud asserted when he insisted on the virtues of sublimation, and by that moving confidence he maintained in the powers of consciousness and articulation. But things are not always so simple, and it must be said that there is another level of experience, where we see Michelangelo become ever more tormented and Goya ever more demon-ridden; we see the lucid, gay Nerval end up hanging himself, and we see Hölderlin die to himself, to the rational possession of himself, all for having entered the overpowering movement of poetic becoming.

APPROACH OF A NEUTRAL LANGUAGE

How does this happen? We can only suggest two fields of reflection here: the former, that for the man who sets out to write, the work is in no way a shelter in which he lives, in his peaceful and protected self, shielded from the difficulties of life. Perhaps he in fact thinks he is protected from the world, but he is exposed to a danger much greater and more menacing because it finds him powerless: the very danger that comes to him from outside, from the fact that he remains outside. And against this threat he must not defend himself; on the contrary, he must give in to it. The work demands that, demands that the man who writes it sacrifice himself for the work, become other—not other than the living man he was, the writer with his duties, his satisfactions, and his interests, but he must become no one, the empty and animated space where the call of the work resounds.

But why does the work demand this transformation? We might answer: because it cannot find its starting point in the familiar, and because it is looking for what has never yet been thought, or heard, or seen; yet this answer seems to leave the essential thing aside. We might also answer: because it deprives the writer, a living man, living in the community where he has a grasp of the useful, where he depends on the consistency of things done and to be done, and where he participates, whether he wants to or not, in the truth of a common aim, because it deprives this living man of the world by giving him the space of the imaginary to live in; and that is in part, in fact, the malaise of a man fallen outside of the world and, through this separation, floating eternally between being and nothingness, incapable henceforth of dying and incapable of being born, shot through with ghosts, his creatures, in which he does not believe and which tell him nothing, and which are evoked for us in *The Unnamable*. But that is still not the right answer. We find it rather in the impulse that, as the work strives to be accomplished, leads it toward that point where it is put to the test of impossibility. There, language does not speak, it is; in it nothing begins, nothing is said, but it is always new and always begins again.

It is this approach of origin that always makes the experience of the work more threatening, threatening for the one who has it, threatening for the work. But it is also this approach that alone makes art an essential search, and it is because it made it obvious in the most decisive way that *The Unnamable* has much more importance for literature than most of the "successful" works that literature offers. Let us try to hear "that voice that speaks, knowing it is lying, indifferent to what it says, too old perhaps and too humiliated ever finally to be able to say the words that will make it stop." And let us try to go down into that neutral region where someone has sunk, given over to words, someone who, in order to write, has fallen into the absence of time, there where he must die from an endless death: "Words are everywhere, in me, outside of me, there, just now I had no density, I hear them, no need to hear them, no need of a head, impossible to stop them, I am in words, I am made of words, of the words of others, what others, the place too, the air too, the walls, the floor, the ceiling, words, the whole universe is here, with me, I am the air, the walls, the immured, everything gives way, opens up, flows out, flows back, flecks, I am all those flecks, crossing, joining, separating, wherever I go I find myself, abandon myself, go toward myself, come from myself, never anything but myself, but a fragment of myself, taken up, lost, missed, words, I am all these words, all these foreigners, this word dust, bottomless where to place oneself, skyless where to dissolve, meeting oneself to say, fleeing from oneself to say, that I am all of them, those who unite with each other, those who leave each other, those who ignore each other, and nothing else, yes, everything else, that I am everything else, a silent thing, in a hard, empty, closed, dry, clean, black place, where nothing moves, nothing speaks, and that I am listening, and that I hear, and that I am searching, like an animal born in a cage of animals born in a cage of animals born in a cage of animals born in a cage . . . "

§ 24 Death of the Last Writer

We can dream about the last writer, with whom would disappear, without anyone noticing it, the little mystery of writing. To give a touch of the fantastic to the situation, we can imagine that Rimbaud, even more mythical than the real one, hears that speech fall silent in him, and it dies with him. Finally we can suppose that, throughout the world circle of civilizations, this final end would be noted. What would be the result? Apparently a great silence. That is what it is polite to say when some writer disappears: a voice has fallen silent, a way of thinking has disappeared. What a silence, then, if no one else spoke in that exalted way that is the language of texts that come accompanied by the rumor of their reputation.

Let us daydream about that. Such eras have existed, will exist, such fictions are reality at certain times in each of our lives. To the surprise of common sense, the day this light goes out, the era without language will arrive not because of silence but because of the recoil of silence, the rending of the silent density and, through this rending, the approach of a new sound. Nothing serious, nothing loud; scarcely a murmur, which will add nothing to the great tumult of cities from which we think we suffer. Its only characteristic: it is incessant. Once heard, it cannot stop being heard, and since one never truly hears it, since it escapes all understanding, it also escapes all distraction, it is all the more present when we turn away from it: the echo, in advance, of what has not been said and will never be said.

THE SECRET LANGUAGE WITHOUT A SECRET

It is not a noise, although at its approach everything becomes noise around us (and we must remember that we do not know today what such a noise might be). Rather it is a language: it speaks, it doesn't stop speaking, it is like the void that speaks, a light murmuring, insistent, indifferent, that is probably the same for everyone, that is without secret and yet isolates each person, separates him from the others, from the world and from himself, leading him through mocking labyrinths, drawing him always farther away, by a fascinating repulsion, below the ordinary world of daily speech.

The strangeness of this language is that it seems to say something, while it might be saying nothing. Further, it seems that profundity speaks in it, and the unprecedented makes itself heard. To each person, although it is surprisingly cold, without intimacy and without felicity, it seems to say what would be closest to him if only he could fix it in place for an instant. It is not deceptive, for it promises and says nothing, always speaking for one person alone, but impersonal, speaking entirely inwardly, but it is the outside itself, present in the single place where, by hearing it, we could hear everything, but it is nowhere, everywhere; and silent, for it is silence that is speaking, that has become this false speech that we do not hear, this secret speech without a secret.

How to silence it? How to hear it, how not to hear it? It transforms the days into night, it makes sleepless nights into an empty, piercing dream. It is beneath everything we say, behind each familiar thought, submerging, engulfing, although imperceptible, all the honest words of man; it is the third part of each dialogue, the echo confronting each monologue. And its monotony might make us think that it rules by patience, that it crushes by lightness, that it dissipates and dissolves all things like fog, turning men away from the ability to love each other by the objectless fascination that it substitutes for each passion. What is it, then? A human speech? Or divine? A language that has not been uttered and that demands to be? Is it a dead language, a sort of phantom, sweet, innocent, and tormenting, as specters are? Is it the very absence of all speaking language? No one dares to discuss it, or even to allude to it. And each person, in hidden solitude, seeks the right way to render it futile, this language that asks only to be futile and ever more futile: that is the form of its domination.

A writer is one who imposes silence on this speech, and a literary work is, for one who knows how to penetrate it, a rich resting place of silence, a firm defense and a high wall against this eloquent immensity that addresses us by turning us away from ourselves. If, in this imaginary Tibet, where the sacred signs could no longer be discovered in anyone, all literature stopped speaking, what would be lacking is silence, and it is this lack of silence that would perhaps reveal the disappearance of literary language.

Before any great work of plastic art, the evidence of a particular silence reaches us like a surprise that is not always a repose: a perceptible silence, sometimes masterly, sometimes proudly indifferent, sometimes agitated, animated and joyful. And the true book is always something of a statue. It arises and organizes itself like a silent power that gives form and firmness to silence and through silence.

We might object that, in this world where suddenly the silence of art will be lacking and where the obscure nakedness of an unknown and meaningless language will assert itself, capable of destroying all the others, even if there are no new artists or writers, there will still be the treasure of old works, the refuge of Museums and Libraries where each person can secretly come to seek a little calm, a little silent atmosphere. But we have to imagine that, on the day when this wandering language imposes itself, we will witness a distinctive disturbance of all the books: a reconquest, by this wandering language, of the works that had for an instant mastered it and that are always more or less its accomplices, for it is their secret. There is, in every well-made Library, a Hell where live the books that must not be read. But there is, in each great book, another hell, a center of unreadability where the entrenched force of this language that is not a language, fresh breath of eternal rehashing, watches and waits.

So that the masters of this time, it is not too bold to imagine, will think not of taking shelter in Alexandria but of dedicating its Library to the fire. Surely, a great disgust for books will overwhelm each person: a wrath against them, a vehement distress, and that wretched violence we observe in all the periods of weakness that call for dictatorship.

THE DICTATOR

The dictator—the word makes us reflect. He is the man of *dictare*, of imperious repetition, the one who, each time the danger of an unknown language appears, tries to struggle against it by the rigor of a commandment without rejoinder and without content. And in fact, he seems to be his own avowed enemy. To mere boundless murmuring, he opposes the cleanness of the word of command; to the insinuation of the unheard, the shouted order; for the wandering cry of the ghost in *Hamlet*, who, under the earth, old mole, wanders here and there without power and without destiny, he substitutes the fixed language of regal reason, which commands and never doubts. But this perfect adversary, the providential man, called into being to obliterate the fog of the ambiguity of phantom language with his commands and his iron decisions—isn't he, in reality, called into being by that ambiguity? Isn't he its parody, its mask even emptier than it, isn't he its lying reply, when, with the prayer of weary, unhappy men, in order to flee the terrible rumor of absence (terrible but deceptive) we turn toward the presence of the categorical idol who requires only our docility and promises the great repose of inner deafness?

Thus dictators come naturally to take the place of writers, artists, and men of thought. But whereas the empty language of command is the frightened, mendacious prolongation of what we would prefer to hear shouted in public squares, rather than having to welcome it and appease it in ourselves through a great personal effort of attention, the writer's task is an entirely different one, and also an entirely different responsibility: that of entering, more than anyone else, into a relationship of intimacy with the initial rumor. It is at that price alone that he can silence it, and hear it in this silence, then express it, after having transformed it.

There is no writer without such an approach, and who does not firmly experience its ordeal. This unspeaking speech very much resembles inspiration, but it is not confused with it; it leads only to that place unique to each person, the hell into which Orpheus descends, place of dispersion and conflict, where he must all of a sudden face up to things and find, in himself, in it and in the experience of all art, what transforms powerlessness into power, turns error into a path and unspeaking speech into a silence from which it can truly speak and allow the origin to speak in it, without destroying humanity.

MODERN LITERATURE

These are not simple things. The temptation, which literature is experiencing today, always to come closer to the lonely murmur is linked to many causes, unique to our time, to history, to the very development of art, and its effect is to make us almost hear, in all the great modern works, what we would be exposed to hearing if suddenly there were no more art or literature. That is why these works are unique, and also why they seem dangerous to us, for they are born directly from danger and scarcely enchant it.

There are, of course, many ways (as many as there are styles and works of art) to master the language of the desert. Rhetoric is one of these methods of defense, efficaciously conceived and even diabolically planned to ward off peril, but also to make it necessary and urgent at the very points where relationships with it can become easy and profitable. But rhetoric is so perfect a protection that it forgets what it had in mind when it was formed: not only to reject but to attract eloquent immensity by rerouting it; to be a rampart in the midst of the shifting sands, and not just a pretty folly that Sunday strollers come to visit.

We will also note that certain "great" writers have something peremptory in their voice, on the verge of trembling and tension, which evokes, in the domain of art, the domination of *dictare*. It is as if they were gathering into themselves, taking strength from some belief, from their sturdy but closed and limited awareness, in order to take the place of the enemy who is inside them and whom they muffle only by the magnificence of their language, the brilliance of their voice, and the bias of their faith, or of their lack of faith.

Other writers have a neutral tone, the self-effacement and barely rippled transparency by which they seem to offer solitary speech a mastered image of what it is, like a chill mirror that tempts an image to reflect itself—but often the mirror stays empty.

Admirable Michaux! He is the writer who, so close to himself, united with the foreign voice; he suspects that he was caught in a trap and that what is expressing itself here, with caprioles of humor, is no longer his voice but a voice that imitates his own. To surprise it and take hold of it again, he has the resources of redoubled humor, a calculated innocence, detours of stratagem, retreats, relinquishments—and, the instant he succumbs, the sudden, scathing point of an image that pierces the veil of rumor. Extreme combat, wonderful but unnoticed victory.

There is also chatter and what has been called interior monologue, which does not in the least, as we well know, reproduce what a man says to himself, for man does not speak to himself, and the deepest part of man is not silent but most often mute, reduced to a few scattered signs. Interior monologue is a coarse imitation, and one that imitates only the apparent traits of the uninterrupted and incessant flow of unspeaking speech. Let us recall that the strength of this speech is in its weakness; it is not heard, which is why we don't stop hearing it; it is as close as possible to silence, which is why it destroys silence completely. Finally, interior monologue has a center, the "I" that brings everything back to itself, while that other speech has no center; it is essentially wandering and always outside.

We must impose silence on it. We must lead it back to the silence that is within it. This language must for a moment be forgotten, so as to be born by a triple metamorphosis as a true speech: that of the Book, as Mallarmé will say.

§ 25 The Book to Come

1. Ecce Liber: Behold the Book

The Book: what did Mallarmé mean by this word? From 1866 on, he always thought and said the same thing. But the same is not the same as the same. One of our tasks might be to show why and how this repetition constitutes the movement that slowly opens up a path for him. All that he has to say seems fixed from the beginning, yet at the same time the similarities are only so on the surface.

NUMEROUS BOOK

Similarities: the book, which from the beginning is indeed the Book, the essential point of literature, is also "quite simply" a book. This single book is made of several volumes: five volumes, he says in 1866, many tomes, he asserts in 1855.[1] Why this plurality? It is surprising in an infrequent writer, especially one who in 1885 was a confirmed opponent of lengthy discourse. As a young man, he seems to need a book with many faces, one of which would have looked toward what he calls Nothingness [*le Néant*], the other toward Beauty, as Music and Letters, he will later say, "are the two faces of one solitary phenomenon: one stretching out into obscurity, the other sparkling with certainty." We see it, when this plurality of the unique comes from the necessity of staggering, level by level, the creative space, and if he speaks at the time so boldly of the plan of the Work, as if it were an already completed task, it is because he is meditating on its structure, which exists in his mind before its contents.[2]

For there is another invariable similarity: he first sees the necessary order of this book, a book that is "architectural and premeditated, and not a collection of chance inspirations, even marvelous"; these assertions come late (1885), but from 1868 on, he says his work is "so well prepared and organized" (and also, "perfectly delimited") that the author can take nothing away from it, cannot even withdraw some "impression," some thought or intentional arrangement. From which arises this remarkable conclusion: if he hereafter wants to write outside the Work, he can write only a "meaningless sonnet." Strangely the future is announced, for this demand to hold back the Book—which will never be anything but its own holding back—seems to have destined him to write nothing but meaningless poems, that is to say, to give force and existence only to what *is* outside of everything (and outside of the book, which is this everything), but thereby to discover the very center of the Book.

...WITHOUT CHANCE

What do the words "premeditated, architectural, defined, organized" mean? They all imply a calculated intention, the implementation of a force of extreme reflection, capable of inevitably organizing the whole of the work. First of all, it is a matter of simple care: to write according to the rules of strict composition; then of a more complex demand: to write in a rigorously premeditated way in harmony with the control of the mind and to assure its full development. But there is still another intention, represented by the word *chance* and the decision to suppress chance. In principle, it is always the same will toward a regulated and regulating form. In 1866, he writes to Coppée: "Chance does not enter into a line, that is the great thing." But he adds: "We have, many of us, attained that, and I think that, with lines so perfectly delimited, what we must aim for above all else, in the poem, is for words (which are already enough in themselves to reject any impression from outside) to reflect each other, until they seem no longer to have their own colors, but to be only the transitions of a scale." Here we have a number of assertions that later texts will develop. A decision to exclude chance, but in conformity with the decision to exclude real things and to refuse perceptible reality the right to poetic designation. Poetry does not answer the call of things. It is not destined to preserve them by naming them. On the contrary, poetic language is "the wonder of transposing a fact of nature into its vibratory near-disappearance." Chance will be held in check by the book, if language, going to the end of its ability, attacking the concrete substance of particular realities, lets nothing more appear but "the collection of relationships existing in everything." Poetry then becomes what music would be were it reduced to its silent essence: an entrainment, a deployment of pure relations, that is, pure mobility.

The struggle against chance signifies sometimes Mallarmé's work to complete the transformative work of language through the technique peculiar to verse and considerations of structure, sometimes an experience of a mystical or philosophical nature, that of the story that *Igitur* implemented with an enigmatic and partially realized richness.

But by using certain reference points here, I only want to recall that Mallarmé's relationships with chance are given in a twofold approach: on the one hand, it is the search for a necessary work that directs him toward a poetry of absence and negation in which nothing anecdotal, or actual, or fortuitous, can find a place. But on the other hand, we know he is directly experiencing these negative forces, which are also at work in language; he seems to use them, erasing the actual, only in order to arrive at a rigorous language; this experience is of essential importance and could be called immediate, if the immediate were not exactly "immediately" denied in this experience. We mustn't forget the statement in 1867 to Lefébure: "I created my work only by *elimination,* and every acquired truth was born only from the loss of an impression that, having sparkled, was consumed, and allowed me, thanks to its liberated shadows, to advance more deeply into the sensation of the Absolute Shadows. Destruction was my Beatrice."

...IMPERSONIFIED

The book that is the Book is one book among others. It is a numerous book, multiplied in itself by a movement unique to it, in which diversity, in accordance with the various depths and space where it develops, is necessarily perfected. The necessary book is subtracted from chance. Escaping chance by its structure and its delimitation, it accomplishes the essence of language, which uses things by transforming them into their absence and by opening this absence to the rhythmic becoming that is the pure movement of relationships. The book without chance is a book without author: impersonal. This assertion, one of Mallarmé's most important, steadily places us on two levels: one corresponds to questions of technique and language (the Valéry side, so to speak, of Mallarmé); the other responds to an experience, the one that the 1867 letters explained. One does not occur without the other, but their relationships have not been elucidated.

A detailed study would be needed to clarify all the levels at which Mallarmé makes his assertion. Sometimes, he wants only to say that the book must remain anonymous: the author will restrict himself to not signing it ("allow the volume to bear no signature"). There are no direct relationships, and even less ownership, between the poem and the poet. The poet cannot attribute what he writes to himself. And what he writes, even if it is under his name, remains essentially nameless.

Why this anonymity? We can see an answer when Mallarmé speaks of the book as if it already existed, innate in us and inscribed in nature. "I believe all that is written in nature so that only those interested in seeing nothing are allowed to close their eyes. This work exists, everyone has attempted it without knowing it; there is no genius or buffoon who has not discovered one of its characteristics without knowing it." These remarks were in response to a questioner, and perhaps say no more than what is accessible to external curiosity. Writing to Verlaine, he scarcely expresses himself differently. He writes at another time: "An ordering of the book of verse dawns innate or everywhere, eliminates chance; still the author must be left out." But here the meaning is already different. Mallarmé experienced the temptation of the occult. Occultism offered a solution to the problems that literary demands pose. This solution consists of separating art from some of its powers, of trying to realize them apart by transforming them into powers that are immediately usable for practical ends. It is a solution that Mallarmé does not accept. We quote his declarations of sympathy, but we neglect the reservations with which he always accompanies them: "No, you are not content, like them [the poor Cabalists] with inattention and misunderstanding, to separate from an Art operations that are integral and fundamental to it in order to accomplish them wrongly, separately, that is a clumsy veneration. You erase its initial sacred meaning."[3]

For Mallarmé, there could be no other magic than literature, which is accomplished only by confronting itself in a way that excludes magic. He notes that, if there are only two ways open to mental investigation, the aesthetic and the economic, "it is to this latter aim, mainly, that alchemy was the glorious, hasty, and troubled precursor." The word *hasty* is remarkable. Impatience characterizes magic, ambitious to control nature right away. It is patience, on the contrary, that is at work in poetic affirmation.[4] Alchemy tries to create and to make. Poetry decrees and institutes the reign of what is not and cannot be, ascribing to man as his supreme calling something that cannot be set out in terms of ability (here we must note that we are opposing Valéry).

Mallarmé, who in any case had only society contacts with occult doctrines, was sensitive to exterior analogies. He borrows words, a certain color, from them, and welcomes their nostalgia. The book written in nature evokes the Tradition transmitted since the beginning and confided to the safekeeping of initiates: hidden and venerable book that shines in fragments scattered here and there. The German Romantics expressed the same thought of the single, absolute book. To write a Bible, said Novalis—that is the madness that every knower must welcome in order to be complete. He calls the Bible the ideal of every book, and Friedrich Schlegel evokes "the thought of an infinite book, the book absolutely, the absolute book," while Novalis again means to make the poetic form of *Märchen*, the folktale, serve the aim of continuing the Bible. (But here we are straying far from Mallarmé. His severe criticism of Wagner: "If the imaginative and abstract, therefore poetic, French mind shows brilliance, it will not be that way: [the French mind] is in harmony with the integrity of art, which is invention, and therefore averse to Legend.")

There is no doubt a level at which Mallarmé, expressing himself in the manner of the occultists, of the German Romantics, and of *Naturphilosophie*, is ready to see in the book the written equivalent, the very text, of universal nature. "Chimera, the thought of it proves . . . that, more or less, all the books contain a blend of a few oft-repeated statements; and even that there is only one bible—a law for the world—though nations make their own."[5] That is one of his penchants, we cannot deny it (just as he dreams of a language that would be "materially the truth").

But there is another level at which the affirmation of the book without author takes on quite a different meaning and, in my opinion, a much more important one. "The work implies the elocutory disappearance of the poet, who cedes the initiative to words, set in motion by the clash of their inequality." "The elocutory disappearance of the poet" is an expression that is very close to the one we find in the famous sentence: "What is the use of the miracle of transposing a fact of nature into its almost vibratory disappearance, according to the game of language however; if it is not. . . . " The poet disappears beneath the pressure of the work, by the same impulse that causes natural reality to disappear. More precisely: it is not enough to say that things dissipate and the poet is effaced; you still have to say that both of them, while not experiencing any actual destruction, assert themselves in this disappearance itself and in the development of this disappearance—one vibratory, the other elocutory. Nature is transposed by language into the rhythmic movement that makes it disappear, endlessly and indefinitely; and the poet, by the fact that he speaks poetically, disappears into this language and becomes the very disappearance that is accomplished in language, the only initiator and principle: the source. "Poetry, ritual." The "omission of self," "death of the individual," which is linked to the poetic rite, thus makes poetry into an actual sacrifice, but not in view of vague magic exaltations—for an almost technical reason: because the one who speaks poetically exposes himself to the kind of death necessarily at work in actual speech.

"MADE, BEING"

The book is without author because it is written from the eloquent disappearance of the author. It needs the writer, insofar as the writer is absence and place of absence. The book is book when it does not refer back to someone who made it, as unstained by his name and free of his existence as it is of the actual intention of the one who reads it. The man of chance—the particular one—if he has no place in the book as author, how, as reader, could he be important in it? "Impersonified, the book, as long as one separates oneself from it as author, does not demand the approach of a reader. As such, know, among human accessories, it takes place all alone: something made, being [*fait, étant*]."

This last assertion is one of Mallarmé's most glorious. It expresses, in a form that bears the mark of decision, the essential demand of the work. Its solitude, its accomplishment starting from itself as if from a place, the double assertion juxtaposed in it, separated by a logical and temporal hiatus, of what *makes* it and of the *being* in which it belongs, indifferent to "making"—its simultaneity, then, of instantaneous presence and of the process of its realization: as soon as it is done, finished with being made, and saying no more than this, that it is.

Here we are as far as possible from the Book of the Romantic and esoteric traditions. The book in esoteric tradition is a substantial book, which exists by virtue of the eternal truth of which it is the hidden, although accessible, disclosure: a disclosure that puts the one who grasps it in possession of the divine secret and divine being. Mallarmé rejects the idea of substance, as well as the idea of permanent, real truth. When he names the essential—whether it be the ideal or dream—it always relates to something that has for foundation only the acknowledged and affirmed unreality of fiction. Hence his major problem is: Does something like Literature exist? In what way does it exist? What relationship is there between literature and the assertion of being? We also know that Mallarmé denies all reality to the present. "There is no present, no—a present does not exist." "Badly informed is the one who proclaims himself his own contemporary." And for the same reason he does not allow continuity in the historic process; everything is break and rupture, "everything is interrupted, real, in the story, not much transition." His work is sometimes fixed in a white, immobile virtuality; sometimes—and this is more significant— animated by an extreme temporal discontinuity, given over to changes of tempo and accelerations, decelerations, "fragmentary pauses," sign of an entirely new essence of mobility, in which it is as if another time makes itself known, foreign both to eternal permanence and to everyday time: "Here anticipating, there recollecting, in the future, in the past, under *a false appearance of the present.*"

Beneath these two forms, time expressed by the work, contained by it, within it, is a time without present. Similarly, the Book must never be regarded as being truly there. We cannot hold it in our hand. However, if it is true that there is no present, if the present is necessarily nonpresent and in some way false and fictive, it will be above all the time of the unreal work, not the time that the work expresses (that is always past or future, a leap and a jump over the abyss of the present), but the time in which the work asserts plainly what is unique to it, when by the coincidence of its own unreality and of the unreality of the present, it causes one to exist by the other in a bolt of lightning that illumines, flashing from the obscurity of which it is only the dazzling focus. Mallarmé, denying the present, reserves it for the work, while still making this present that of an affirmation without presence, in which what exists shines at the same time as it fades away ("the instant they shine there and die in a rapid flower, on some transparency like ether"). The appearance of the book, its manifest brilliance, are thus such that we must say of it that it is, that it is present, since without it nothing would ever be present, but that nonetheless it is always lacking in relation to the conditions of actual existence: being, but impossible.

Jacques Scherer says that the posthumous manuscript[6] shows that the Book, contrary to the mocking remarks of the critics, was not a fable, and that Mallarmé gave serious thought to its effective realization. His remark is perhaps naïve. Almost all the theoretical writings of Mallarmé allude to this project of the Work; it is their constant preoccupation, they give ever more profound views into it, so that the unrealized Work is asserted for us in a nonetheless essential way. Those who are indifferent to this kind of guarantee and who continue to see in Mallarmé someone who, for thirty years, tricked the world by talking loftily of the nonexistent Work and circulating insignificant little papers with a mysterious air will not be convinced by these new proofs. On the contrary, in these details where, around a nonexistent book, are meticulously set forth the material and financial questions of its publication, they will find only the symptoms of a well-known and thoroughly documented morbid state.

We must say more: if the book existed, I would like to know how Scherer would undertake to tell us, *Ecce liber* [Behold the book], and how he would make us recognize it, if the very essence of this book is to make even its own recognition unreal, and if it is in fact the infinite conflict of its obvious presence and its forever problematic reality.

"MEMORABLE CRISIS"

What we can discover, though, from these practical (Balzacian) conditions—financing, printing, figures—in which the manuscript seeks to project the work's realization, is that they confirm the extreme attention that Mallarmé always paid to the possibilities of historic action and to the literary process itself. For some time we have begun to be aware that Mallarmé was not always enclosed in his room on the Rue de Rome. He wondered about history. He wondered about the relationships between general action—grounded in society—and action that is determined by the work ("limited action"). "The epoch" is perhaps always a "tunnel" for the writer, he states, a time of interval like a between-time. He expressed the idea that, rather than basing extreme judgments about art ventured within the integrity of the book on external circumstances that could never be other than incompletely favorable, it is better to play them against all the chances of history, doing nothing to adjust them to the time, but on the contrary, revealing the conflict, the gaps in time, in order to elicit their clarity. The work must then be the consciousness of the conflict between "the moment" and the game of literary time, and this discord is part of the game, is the game itself.[7]

Mallarmé was no less attentive to the major crisis that pervades literature in his time. We have finally stopped seeing a symbolist poet in him, just as we no longer think of enrolling Hölderlin as a Romantic. It is not a question of symbolist peripeteia, when, in *La Musique et les Lettres*, he formulates in the clearest way the crisis that was his own thirty years before, while still rightly making it a historic crisis, belonging to the recent generation: "In the turbulence, all due to the recent generation, the act of writing was scrutinized right to its origin. Much progress, at least, in terms of the point I raise: to know if there is a place for writing." And a little later: "Does something like Literature exist . . . ? Very few have taken stock of this darkening enigma as I am doing now, late in life, struck by a sudden doubt about that which I want to speak of with enthusiasm." "Extraordinary summons," to which we know that he answers: "Yes, Literature does exist and, if you like, exists by itself alone, apart from everything."

The aim and the accomplishment of the Book are obviously linked to this radical calling into question. Literature could be conceived in its essential integrity only beginning with the experience that withdraws it from the ordinary conditions of possibility. It was thus for Mallarmé, since, if he conceives of the Work, it is at the very moment when, having "felt worrisome symptoms caused by the mere act of writing," he continues to write, because writing stops presenting itself to him as a possible activity. "Storm, lustral." However, this storm in the course of which all literary conventions are washed away, which forces literature to seek its foundation where two abysses meet, has another upheaval as consequence. Mallarmé bears witness to it with loud surprise: "I bring news, in fact. . . . Something never seen before. They have been experimenting with the [poetic] line." "Governments change; prosody remains intact." That is the sort of event that, in his eyes, essentially defines history. History revolves because there is a total change of literature, which forms its ground only by radically questioning itself and by investigating "its very coming into being." This change starts by calling traditional meter into question.

This is a serious attack for Mallarmé. Why? That is not so clear. He always asserted—it is one of his most persistent statements—that wherever there is rhythm there is verse, and that only the discovery and mastery of pure rhythmical patterns of being are of consequence. He recognized that for everything to achieve speech, breaking the great literary rhythms was indispensable. But, at the same time, speaking of this now-to-be neglected prosody, he speaks of a pause of poetry, of the interval it crosses, granting itself a time of rest, as if the failure of traditional verse marked the rupture of poetry itself. All this makes us feel the great upheaval that the attack on the "guardian" rhyme represents for him. But his final work is a "poem." An essential poem (and not a prose poem), but one that, for the first and only time, breaks with tradition: not only consents to rupture but intentionally inaugurates a new art, an art still to come, the future as art. It was a major decision, and a work that was itself decisive.

2. A New Understanding of Literary Space

If (a little hastily) we accept that Mallarmé always recognized in traditional verse the means to conquer chance "word by word," we will see that there is in *Un coup de dés* [A throw of the dice] a strict correspondence between the authority of its central sentence, declaring chance to be invincible, and the renunciation of that least chanceful form, traditional verse. The phrase *A throw of the dice will never abolish chance* only produces the meaning of the new form whose disposition it conveys. But exactly by doing that, from the moment there is a precise correlation between the form of the poem and the assertion that pervades it and underlies it, necessity is reestablished. Chance is not liberated by the breaking of regular verse: on the contrary, to be precise, it is subject to the exact law of the form that responds to it and to which it must respond. If chance is not conquered by that, it is at least drawn into the rigor of language and raised to the firm image of a form in which it is enclosed. The result once again is a contradiction that sets necessity free.

GATHERED THROUGH DISPERSION

No less firmly indicated, in *Un coup de dés*, is the very work it constitutes; it does not make the poem a present or future reality but, under the doubly negative dimension of an unfinished past and an impossible future, refers it to the extreme distance of an exceptional perhaps. If we try to follow certainties that alone determine the actual production of things, everything is arranged so that the poem cannot take place. *Un coup de dés*, whose definite presence is affirmed by our hands, our eyes, and our attention, not only is unreal and indefinite, but could not exist unless the general rule, which gives chance the status of law, is broken in some region of being, where the necessary and the fortuitous are both put in check by the force of disaster. A work that is not there, then, but present in the single coinciding with what is always beyond. *Un coup de dés* exists only insofar as it expresses the extreme and exquisite improbability of itself, of that Constellation that, thanks to an exceptional perhaps (with no other justification than the emptiness of the sky and the dissolution of the abyss), is projected "onto some vacant and superior surface": birth of a still unknown space, the very space of the work.

This is very close to the Book, for only the Book is identified with the announcement and expectation of the work it is, without any other content than the presence of its infinitely problematic future, always existing before it can exist and never ceasing to be separated and divided in order to become, in the end, its very division and separation. "Keeping vigil doubting rolling shining and meditating."[8] We should pause here on these words by which the work is presented in the invisibility of becoming that is unique to it. These words free of any magical provocation and which, in the undefined tension in which a new time seems to develop, the pure time of expectation and attention, appeal to thought alone so that it can keep watch over the brilliance of the poetic impulse.

Naturally, I will not assert that *Un coup de dés* is the Book, an assertion that the Book's specifications would deprive of all meaning. But much more than those notes that Jacques Scherer revives, *Un coup de dés* gives the Book support and reality; it is its reserve and its forever hidden presence, the risk of its venture, the measure of its limitless challenge. It has the essential quality of the Book: present with this lightning-stroke that divides it and gathers it back together, and yet it is extremely problematic, so much so that even today for us, so familiar (we think) with all that is not familiar, it continues to be the most unlikely work. It could be said that we have assimilated Mallarmé's work more or less readily, but not *Un coup de dés*. *Un coup de dés* implies a completely different book from the book that we have: it makes us feel that what we call "book" according to the traditional Western usages, in which the gaze identifies the act of comprehension with the repetition of linear back-and-forth motions, is justified to facilitate analytic comprehension. In fact, we must realize this: we have the poorest books that can be conceived, and after a few millennia we continue to read as if we were still only beginning to learn to read.

Un coup de dés orients the future of the book both in the direction of the greatest dispersion and in the direction of a tension capable of *gathering* infinite diversity, by the discovery of more complex structures. The mind, says Mallarmé, following Hegel, is "volatile dispersion." The book that collects the mind thus collects an extreme capacity for rupture, a limitless anxiety, one that the book cannot contain, one that excludes all content from it, all limited, defined, and complete sense. It is a movement of diaspora that must never be repressed but instead preserved and welcomed as such into the space that is projected from it and to which this movement does nothing but answer, an answer to an indefinitely multiplied void, where dispersion takes on the form and appearance of unity. Such a book, always in movement, always on the verge of scattering, will also always be gathered in all directions, through dispersion itself and according to the division essential to it, which it makes not disappear but appear, maintaining this dispersion so the book can accomplish itself there.

Un coup de dés was born from a new understanding of literary space: by new links of movement, new relationships of comprehension can be engendered in it. Mallarmé was always aware of the fact, misunderstood before him and still perhaps after him, that language is a system of infinitely complex spatial relationships, whose originality neither ordinary geometric space nor the space of practical life permits us to grasp. We create nothing and we speak in a creative way only by a preliminary approach to the place of extreme vacancy where, before becoming determined and denotative words, language is the silent movement of relationships, that is to say, "the rhythmic scansion of being." Words are always there only to designate the extent of their connections: the space where they are projected and which, scarcely designated, is folded and bent, not actually existing anywhere it is.[9] Poetic space, both the source and "result" of language, is never the same as a thing; but always, "it spaces itself out and disseminates itself." Thus Mallarmé's interest in all that leads him to the unique essence of the actual place—theater and dance—mindful as he is of the fact that the essential quality of thoughts and human feelings is also to produce an "environment." "Every emotion that comes from you enlarges a place; or founds it on you and incorporates it." Poetic emotion is thus not an inner sentiment, a subjective modification, but a strange outside into which we are thrown in us outside of us. Dance, he adds, is like that. "Thus this multiple emanation around a nakedness, great with contradictory flights in which this orders it, tempestuous, gliding, magnifies it there to the point of dissolving it: central."

This new language that we claim that Mallarmé created for himself through some desire for esotericism—and that Scherer has studied carefully—is a strict language, destined to elaborate, following new ways, the space unique to language, which we others, in daily prose as well as in literary usage, reduce to a simple surface crossed by a uniform and irreversible movement. To this space, Mallarmé restores profundity. A sentence is not content with unfolding in a linear way; it opens up. This opening allows to be arranged, extricated, spaced, and compressed, at depths on different levels, other movements of phrases, other rhythms of words, which are related to each other according to firm considerations of structure, though foreign to ordinary logic—the logic of subordination—which destroys the space and makes the movement uniform. Mallarmé is the only writer who can be called profound. He is not profound in a metaphorical way or because of the intellectually deep meaning of what he says. It is because what he says supposes a space with many dimensions and cannot be understood except according to this spatial profundity, which must be apprehended simultaneously on different levels. (Furthermore, what does the phrase we use so often mean, "that is profound"? Profundity of meaning consists of the step backwards—in retreat—that meaning makes us take in relation to it.)

Un coup de dés is the actual affirmation of this new space. It is this space become poem. The fiction that is at work in it seems to have no other aim (by the ordeal of the wreck from which figures more and more subtly allusive to ever more distant spaces are born and exhaust themselves) than arriving at the dissolution of all actual expanse, at "the neutrality identical with the chasm," with which, to the uttermost point of dispersion, only the place is asserted: nothingness, like the place where nothing took place. Is this, then, the eternal nothingness that *Igitur* sought to attain? A pure and definitive vacancy? No, but an indefinite stirring of absence, "lower lapping of waves," the "vacant billows into which all reality dissolves"—without this dissolution ever being able to dissolve the movement of this dissolution, to become incessantly becoming in the depth of place.

For it is the place, "gaping profundity" of the abyss, that, reversing to the altitude of exception,[10] founds the other abyss, of empty sky, to take the form of Constellation: infinite dispersion gathering itself in the delimited multiplicity of stars, a poem in which, the words enduring only as their space, this space shines in pure stellar brilliance.

POETIC SPACE AND COSMIC SPACE

It is obvious that if Mallarmé's poetic thought is formulated in a privileged way in terms of the universe, it is due not merely to the influence of Poe ("Eureka," "The Power of Words"), but rather to the demand of creative space—creative insofar as it is infinitely empty and of an infinitely moving emptiness. The dialogue of *Toast funèbre* [A toast at a funeral] gives us a presentiment of what, according to Mallarmé, accurately qualifies man: he is a being of the horizon; he is the demand of this distance that is in his speech, enlarging, even by his death, the space with which he is confused as soon as he speaks:

> Nothingness to this abolished Man of the past:
> "Memory of horizons, O thou, what is the Earth?"
> Shouts this dream; and, voice whose clarity falters,
> Space as a joke has this cry: "I do not know!"

Between Pascal's terror faced with the eternal silence of space and Joubert's delight before the starry sky of the voids, Mallarmé endowed man with a new experience: space as the approach of an *other* space, creative origin and adventure of the poetic impulse. If anguish, the wish for the impossible, the awareness of nothingness, and that time of distress that is his time, "time of the interval and the interregnum," belong to the poet, it would be incorrect to place the stoic mask on Mallarmé's face, as we tend to do, and to see in him nothing but the combatant of lucid despair. If we had to choose between the terms of vague philosophy, it would not be pessimism that best reflects his thought, for it is always on the side of joy, of exultant affirmation, that poetry declares itself, each time Mallarmé feels constrained to situate it. The famous phrase, in *La Musique et les Lettres* [Music and Literature], tells of this felicity; it says that the "edennic civilized one"[11] who has taken care to preserve piety in the twenty-four letters, along with the meaning of their connections, possesses "above any other goodness, the element of joy, a doctrine that is at the same time a country." The word *country* [*contrée*] sends us back to the word *stay* [*séjour*]. Poetry, says Mallarmé, answering a correspondent with some impatience, "thus endows our stay with authenticity."[12] We stay authentically only where poetry takes place and gives place. This is close to the phrase attributed to Hölderlin (in a late and contested text): "Poetically man dwells." And there is also this other line by Hölderlin: "But what remains, poets build it." We think about all that, but perhaps in a way that does not accord with the interpretation adduced in Heidegger's commentaries. For Mallarmé, what the poets build, space—abyss and foundation of language—is what does not remain, and the authentic dwelling is not the shelter where man is preserved, but has to do with a pitfall, with perdition and the chasm, and with that "memorable crisis" that alone allows one to reach the moving void, place where the creative task begins.

When Mallarmé gives this as duty to the poet, and as task for the Book: "orphic explanation of the Earth," "explanation of mankind," what does he mean by this repeated word, *explanation*? Precisely what this word entails: the unfolding of the Earth and of man in the space of song. Not the knowledge of what both naturally are but the development—outside of their given reality and within the mysterious, unclear quality they have, because of the scattering force of space and the collecting power of the rhythmic process—of mankind and of the world. Because there is poetry not only is something changed in the universe, but there is an essential change of the universe, whose meaning the realization of the Book only discovers or builds. Poetry always inaugurates *something else*. In relation to the real, one can call it unreal ("this country did not exist"); in relation to the time of our world, "the interregnum" or "the eternal"; in relation to the action that modifies nature, "restrained action." But these ways of speaking do nothing but encourage the understanding of this *something else* to settle back into analytic comprehension.

A remark is necessary here. *Toast funèbre*, the sonnet *Quand l'ombre commença* [When the shadow began], and *Un coup de dés* form three works in which, over a twenty-five year gap, poetic space and cosmic space are placed equally in relation to one another. Of the many differences between these poems, one is striking. In the sonnet, there is nothing more certain than the poetic work lighting up in the sky like "a star in celebration": it is of exalted dignity and reality, sun of suns, around which the "vile lights" of actual stars turn only to testify to its brilliance. "Yes, I know. . . . " But in *Un coup de dés*, the confidence has disappeared: as distant as it is improbable, hidden by the height to which exception raises it, not present but only and always in reserve in the future where it might be formed, the Constellation of the work is forgotten before it exists, rather than proclaiming itself. Should we conclude that, conquered by doubt, Mallarmé scarcely believes any longer in the creation of the work or in its stellar equivalence? Should we see him approaching death in a state of poetic disbelief? This would be logical enough. But we see here precisely how deceptive logic is when it tries to legislate for *something else* (and undertakes to create another world beyond the earth, or another spiritual reality). On the contrary, *Un coup de dés* expresses, much more firmly than the sonnet and in a way that involves us in a more essential future, the decision unique to creative language. And Mallarmé himself, by ceasing to give the work the sort of certainty that is suitable only to things and by evoking it beneath the single perspective from which its presence can reach us, like the expectation of what is most distant and least certain, is in a much more confident relationship with the affirmation of the work. We could convey this by saying (imprecisely): doubt belongs to poetic certainty, just as the impossibility of affirming the work brings us close to its own affirmation, one whose care the words "keeping vigil doubting rolling shining and meditating" bring back to our minds.

THE WORK AND THE SECRET OF BECOMING

The presence of poetry is still to come: it comes from beyond the future and does not stop coming when it is here. A temporal dimension different from the one of which the time of the world has made us masters is at play in language when language lays bare, by the rhythmic scansion of being, the space of its unfolding. Nothing certain seems to appear. Whoever clings to certainty or even to the lower form of probability is not on the way to "the horizon," any more than is the traveling companion of the musical thought whose five ways of being played are played in the intimacy of chance.

The work is the expectation of the work. Into this expectation alone is gathered the impersonal attention that has the unique space of language as road and residence. *Un coup de dés* is the book to come. Mallarmé clearly asserts his aim, especially in the preface: to express the connections of space and the movement of time in a way that changes them. Space, which does not exist but "is scanned," "is intimated," space dissipates and remains according to the various expressive forms of the written work, space excludes ordinary time. In this space—the actual space of the book—instant never follows instant according to the linear progression of an irreversible future. In this space one does not recount something that happened, even fictively. Story is replaced by hypothesis: "If it were. . . . " The event the poem uses as point of departure is not given as a historic, actual fact, fictively real: it has value only relative to all the turns of thought and language that can result from it and whose perceptible role "with retreats, prolongings, flights" is like another language instituting a new game of space and time.

That is, of course, ambiguous. On one hand, we have the attempt to exclude narrative time by substituting for it relations of proportion and reciprocity, the investigation of which Mallarmé always pursued: "if this is that, that is this," we read in the notes of the posthumous manuscript, or: "two alternatives of one single subject—either this or that—(and not treated in succession, historically—but always intellectually)." Just as he regretted that the seventeenth century in France, instead of finding tragedy in memories of Greece and Rome, didn't look for it in the work of Descartes (Descartes joined with Racine: Valéry will try a little superficially to remember this dream), so Mallarmé seeks to imitate the procedures of geometric rigor to liberate language from naïve successiveness and make it the master of its own relationships. But this is just an imitation. Mallarmé is not Spinoza. He does not geometrize language. *If it were* is enough for him. From then on "everything happens by a shortcut, hypothetically; we avoid narrative." Why do we avoid the story? Not only because the time of narrative is eliminated, but because instead of telling, we show. That, we know, is the innovation in which Mallarmé takes pride. For the first time, the inner space of thought and language is represented in a perceptible way. The "distance . . . that mentally separates groups of words, or words from each other" is visible typographically, as are the importance of such terms, their power of assertion, the acceleration of their connections, their concentration, their scattering, and finally the reproduction, by the pace of words and by their rhythm, of the object they designate.

The effect is of great expressive power: truly astonishing. But the surprise is also in the fact that here Mallarmé contradicts himself. Now he gives language—whose unreal force of absence he had pondered—all the existence and all the material reality that this very language had been commanded to dispel. The "tacit flight of abstraction" is transformed into a visible landscape of words. I no longer say "a flower"; I draw it with syllables. This contradiction is at once in language and in Mallarmé's double attitude to language: it has been frequently pointed out and studied. What else does *Un coup de dés* teach us? The literary work is suspended there between its visible presence and its readable presence: musical score or painting that must be read and poem that must be seen. Thanks to this oscillating alternation, it tries to enrich analytic reading by global and simultaneous vision, and also to enrich static vision by the dynamism of the play of optical movements. Finally, it contrives to place itself at the point of intersection where hearing is seeing and reading, but places itself also at that point where, no junction made, the poem occupies only the central void that represents the future of exception.

Mallarmé wants to stay at this previous point—the song previous to concept[13]—where all art is language, and where language is undecided between the being it expresses by making it disappear and the appearance of being it gathers into itself so that the invisibility of meaning acquires form and eloquent mobility. This moving indecision is the very reality of the space unique to language. Only the poem—the future book—is capable of asserting the diversity of tempos and tenses that constitute it as meaning while still reserving it as source of all meaning. The book is thus centered on the understanding formed by the almost simultaneous alternation of reading as vision and vision as readable transparency. But it is also constantly decentered in relation to itself, not only because the work is at once entirely presence and entirely in movement, but because the very *becoming* that deploys it is elaborated in it and depends on it.

The time of the work is not borrowed from our own. Formed by the work, the time at work in it is of the least imaginable immobility. And to say "the" time, as if there were only one way of enduring here, is to misunderstand the essential enigma of this book and its inexhaustible attractive force. Even without entering into detailed study, it is obvious that, "under a false appearance of the present," different temporal possibilities keep superimposing themselves on one another, not in a confused mixture but because such a collection (represented most often by the two-page spread), to which such time is suited, belongs also to other times insofar as the *group* of collections in which it occurs causes another temporal structure to predominate—while, "at the same time," like a powerful median beam, throughout the entire work the firm central voice resounds in which the future speaks, but an eternally negative future—"will never abolish"—which nonetheless is doubly prolonged: by a past future perfect, annulling the act until the appearance of its noncompletion—"will not have taken place"—and by a completely new possibility toward which, beyond all the negations and gaining support from them, the work dashes forward again: the time of exception to the height of a perhaps.

READING, THE "OPERATION"

We wonder if Mallarmé entrusts reading with the task of making present this work in which the times that make it inaccessible are at play. He did not suppress this problem by suppressing the reader. On the contrary, reader aside, the question of reading is only more essential. Mallarmé thought a great deal about it. "Desperate practice," he says. It is about the communication of the book—the work communicating with itself in the *becoming* that is unique to it—that the posthumous manuscript brings us fresh clarifications. How could the authorless, readerless book, which is not definitively closed but always in movement, assert itself according to the rhythm that constitutes it if it does not in some way go out from itself and find, to correspond with the inner mobility that is its structure, that outwardness where it will be in contact with its own distance? There must be a mediator. That is reading. This reading is not that of any reader whatsoever, who would tend always to bring the work closer to his own fortuitous individuality. Mallarmé will be the voice of this essential reading. Vanished and suppressed as author, he is, by this very disappearance, related to the appearing and disappearing essence of the Book, and to its incessant oscillation—which is its communication.

We can compare this role of intermediary to that of the conductor of an orchestra or to that of the priest during Mass. But, if the posthumous manuscript tends to give reading the quality of a sacred ceremony that borders on stage magic, the theater, and Catholic liturgy, we must above all remember that Mallarmé, not being an ordinary reader, is aware of not being a simple privileged interpreter either, capable of commenting on the text, of making it pass from one meaning to the other or keeping it in movement between all its possible senses. He is not really a reader. He is the reading [*la lecture*]: the movement of communication by which the book communicates with itself—first according to the various physical interactions that the mobility of the pages makes possible and necessary;[14] then according to the new movement of the understanding that the language develops by integrating various genres and various arts; finally by the exceptional future from which the book comes toward itself and comes toward us by exposing us to the supreme game of space and time.

Mallarmé calls the reader "the operator." Reading, like poetry, is "the operation." But he always uses this word in the sense it derives from the word "work" [*oeuvre*][15] and the almost surgical meaning it ironically acquires from its technical aspect: operation is suppression; in some way it is the Hegelian *Aufhebung*. Reading is operation, it is the work that is accomplished by being suppressed, that proves itself by confronting itself and suspends itself while still asserting itself. In the posthumous manuscript, Mallarmé insists on the danger and daring that reading implies. The danger is seeming to assume a right of authorship over the book that would make it once again an ordinary book. A danger that stems from communication itself: from this movement of adventure and ordeal that does not allow even the reader Mallarmé to know beforehand what the book is, or if it is, or if the future to which the book responds while still constituting it by its infinite suppression will have from now on a meaning for us, or will ever have a meaning. "Keeping vigil doubting rolling shining and meditating," this collapse of times, tenses, in which is expressed the undetermined exchange by which the work is made, will it in the end clash with the moment at which everything must be finished, the ultimate time that, fleeing before the book, immobilizes it in advance by placing before it the "last point that crowns it"? The moment at which all moments stop in the final accomplishment, the end of what is without end. Is that the end? Is it in this point of immobility that we should, from now on, regard any work with this future gaze of universal death, which is always, somehow, the gaze of the reader?

ON HIGH PERHAPS

But through this pause and beyond this beyond, *Un coup de dés* teaches us that there is still something to say, an affirmation whose firmness is like the summary and "result" of the entire book, a resolute speech in which the work is resolved by being revealed: "All Thought emits a Throw of Dice." This maxim is difficult to place, isolated as it is almost harshly on a line by itself, as if, by it, the isolation of language were achieved once and for all. The line has a force of closure that prohibits us from speaking further, but it is itself already as if outside the Poem, its boundary, which does not belong to it. Setting thought in communication with chance, the rejection of fate with the summons of fate, thought that plays and play as thought, the maxim tries to contain in one short sentence the whole of what is possible. "All Thought emits a Throw of Dice." That is the closure and the opening, the invisible passage where movement in the form of a sphere is end and beginning without end. Everything is finished and everything begins again. The Book is thus, subtly, affirmed in the *becoming* that is perhaps its meaning, a meaning that might be the very becoming of the circle.[16] The end of the work is its origin, its new and old beginning: it is its possibility opened one more time, so that the dice thrown once again can be the very throw of the masterful words that, preventing the Work from existing—*Un Coup De Dés Jamais* [A Throw of the Dice Never]—lets the final wreck return in which, in the profundity of place, everything has already disappeared: chance, the work, thought, EXCEPT *on high* PERHAPS . . . [EXCEPTÉ à l'altitude PEUT-ÊTRE—from *Un coup de dés*—Trans.].

§ 26 The Power and the Glory

I would like to summarize some simple assertions that can help to situate literature and the writer.

There was once a time when the writer, like the artist, had to do with glory. Glorification was his work, glory was the gift he gave and received. Glory, in the ancient sense, is the shining forth of presence (sacred or sovereign). To glorify, Rilke says, does not mean to make known; glory is the manifestation of being that goes forward in its magnificence of being, freed from what hides it, established in the truth of its revealed presence.

Glory is followed by renown. Renown is linked more closely to name. The power of naming, the strength of what denominates, the dangerous confidence of the name (there is danger in being named)—all these become the privilege of the man able to name and make what he names heard. Understanding is subject to impact. Language that is eternalized in written work promises some immortality. The writer joins forces with what triumphs over death; he ignores the temporary; he is the friend of the soul, man of the spirit, guarantee of the eternal. Many critics, even today, seem sincerely to believe that the vocation of art and literature is to eternalize the individual.

Fame is followed by reputation, as opinion follows truth. The act of publishing—publication—becomes the essential thing. We can take this in an obvious sense: the writer is known by the public, he is reputable, he seeks to be valued, because he needs what value is, money. But what awakens the public, what generates value? Publicity. Publicity itself becomes an art, it is the art of all arts, it is what is most important, since it determines the power that determines all the rest.

Here, we enter an order of consideration that we should not simplify by polemic skill. The public writer. To publish is to make public; but to make public is not only to make something pass from the private state to the public state, as from a place—deep within, the closed room—to another place—outside, the street—by a simple displacement. Nor is it to reveal to a particular person a piece of news, or a secret. The "public" is not made up of a great or small number of readers, each one reading for himself. The writer likes to say that he writes his book for the special friend. Mistaken wish. In the public, the friend has no place. There is no place for any chosen individual, nor is there one for chosen social structures—family, group, class, nation. No one is part of it, and the whole world belongs to it, not just the human world but all worlds, all things, and nothing: the others. Hence, however rigorous the censors are and however faithfully the laws are obeyed, there is always, for authority, something suspicious and badly timed in the very act of publishing. That is because this act makes the public exist, which, always undetermined, escapes the sternest political determinations.

To publish is not to cause oneself to be read, or to offer anything at all to be read. What is public does not exactly need to be read; it is already known beforehand, with a knowledge that knows everything and wants to know nothing. Public interest, always awake, insatiable yet always satisfied, which finds everything interesting while still not being interested, is a tendency that we have been quite wrong to describe with denigrating bias. We see there, although in a relaxed and stable form, the same impersonal power that, as obstacle and resource, is at the origin of literary work. It is against an indefinite and incessant language—without beginning and without end, against it but also with its help—that the author expresses himself. It is against public interest, against inattentive, vague, universal, and omniscient curiosity, that the reader comes to read, emerging with difficulty from this first reading, a reader who before reading has already read: reading against it but still through it. The reader and author participate, one in a neutral understanding, the other in a neutral language, which they want to suspend for an instant so it may give way to an expression that is better understood.

Let us recall the institution of literary prizes. Easy enough to explain it by the structure of modern publishing and the social and economic organization of intellectual life. But if we think of the satisfaction that, with a few exceptions, a writer does not fail to feel when receiving a prize that often represents nothing, we can explain it, not as the satisfaction of vanity, but by the strong need for this communication before communication that is the nature of public understanding, by the appeal to profound, superficial rumor, in which everything is reflected, appearing, disappearing, in a vague presence, a sort of River Styx that flows in full daylight through our streets and irresistibly attracts the living, as if they were already shades, greedy to become memorable in order to be better forgotten.

Nor is it a question of influence. It is not even a question of the pleasure of being seen by the blind crowd or of being known by the unknown, a pleasure that supposes the transformation of undetermined presence into *an* already defined public, that is to say, the degradation of the elusive movement into a perfectly manageable and accessible reality. A little lower down, and we will have all the political frivolities of public spectacle. But the writer, in this final game, will always be ill served. The most famous writer is less well known than the daily radio announcer. And, if he is greedy for intellectual power, he knows that he wastes it in this insignificant notoriety. I think the writer desires nothing, either for himself or for his work. But the need to be published—that is to say, to attain outer existence, this opening onto the outside, this divulging-dissolving for which our great cities are the venue—belongs to the work, like a memory of the impulse from which it comes, which it must endlessly prolong, yet which it wants radically to surmount and which in fact it stops, in effect, for an instant, each time it is the work.

This reign of the "public," understood in the sense of the "outside" (the magnetic force of a presence always there, not close, not distant, not familiar, not strange, deprived of center, a sort of space that assimilates everything and keeps nothing) has changed the purpose of the writer. Just as he has become a stranger to glory, just as he prefers an anonymous quest to renown, just as he has lost all desire for immortality, so—and this at first sight might seem less certain—he little by little abandons the ambition for power, of which Barrès on one hand, Monsieur Teste on the other have embodied, two strongly characteristic types—either exercising an influence or refusing to exercise it. Some will say: "But people who write have never before been so engaged in politics. Look at the petitions they sign, the attitudes they evince, the quickness with which they think they are authorized to judge everything just because they write." It is true: when two writers meet, they never talk about literature (fortunately), but their first words are always about politics. I will suggest that, for the most part entirely lacking any wish to play a role, or wield power, or occupy a public office, but on the contrary of a surprising modesty in their very fame and quite remote from the cult of the individual (it is in fact by this very trait that one can always distinguish, between two contemporaries, the writer of today and the writer of the past), they are all the more under the attraction of politics because they keep themselves more in the thrill of the margin, on the edge of public anxiety and in search of this communication before communication whose call they feel constantly induced to respect.

That can give rise to the worst. It produces "these know-it-all *interferers*, these know-it-all *loudmouths*, these know-it-all *pedants*, informed about everything and judging everything immediately, quick to decide absolutely about what has scarcely happened, so that soon it will be impossible for us to learn anything: we already know everything," of whom Dionys Mascolo speaks in his essay "On the Intellectual Poverty of France."[1] Mascolo adds: "People here are informed, intelligent, and curious. They understand everything. They understand everything so quickly that they don't take the time to think about anything. They don't understand anything. . . . Go try to make those who have already understood everything admit that something *new* has taken place!" We can find in this description exactly the same characteristics, only a little more accentuated and focused, and even more debased, of public existence—neutral comprehension, boundless opening, sensing and guessing, a sort of comprehension in which everybody is always in the know about what's going on and has already decided about everything, meanwhile destroying anything worthwhile. That evidently makes for the worst. But that also makes for a new situation in which the writer, in some way losing his own existence and his personal certainty, testing a still undetermined communication as powerful as it is powerless, as complete as it is nonexistent, sees himself, as Mascolo notes, "reduced to powerlessness, . . . but also reduced to simplicity."

When the writer today becomes involved in politics, with an energy that displeases the experts, he is not yet involved with politics but only with this new, difficult-to-see relationship that literature and language want to awaken in contact with public presence. That is why, speaking of politics, it is always of something else that the writer speaks: of ethics; speaking of ethics, it is ontology; of ontology, poetry; speaking finally of literature, "his single passion," it is to return to politics, "his single passion." This mobility is deceptive and can, once again, engender the worst: those vain discussions that practical men always characterize as byzantine or intellectual (adjectives that naturally are themselves part of empty chatter, when they are not used to conceal the stressed weakness of men in authority). Of such a mobility—whose difficulties and simplicities, demands and risks, Surrealism, which Mascolo correctly designates and defines,[2] has shown us—we can only say that it is never mobile enough, never faithful enough to the anguishing and extenuating instability that, endlessly increasing, develops in every language the refusal to stop at any definitive assertion.

It should be added, if because of this mobility the writer is kept from being a specialist, can't even be a specialist in literature, let alone a particular literary genre, even so he does not aim for the universality that the gentleman-scholar of the seventeenth century, and then the Goethean man, and finally the man of classless society, not to speak of the ultimately remote man of Teilhard de Chardin, offer us as illusion and goal. Just as public understanding always has all its understanding beforehand but makes all real comprehension fail, just as public rumor is the absence and emptiness of all clear and decisive language, always saying something other than what is said (hence perpetual and formidable misunderstandings, at which Ionesco lets us laugh), just as the public is the indeterminacy that ruins every group and every class, so the writer, when he succumbs to the fascination of what is at stake by the fact that he "publishes," seeking the reader in the public, as Orpheus sought Eurydice in the underworld, turns toward a language that will be no one's and that no one will understand, for it is always addressed to someone else, awakening in the one who receives it always an other and always the expectation of something else. Nothing universal, nothing that makes literature a promethean or divine power, having right over everything, but the movement of a dispossessed and uprooted language, which prefers to say nothing with the claim of saying everything and, each time it says something, only designates the level below which one must still descend if one wants to begin to speak. In our "intellectual poverty," there is also, then, the riches of thought, there is the indigence that makes us feel that thinking is always learning to think less than we think, to think about the lack that thought also is—and, speaking, how to preserve this lack by bringing it to speech, even, as happens today, if it is by the excess of hackneyed prolixity.

However, when the writer comes, through such a process, to a concern for the anonymous and neutral existence that is public existence, when he seems not to have any other interests or any other horizon, isn't he becoming preoccupied with what should never concern him, or should concern him only indirectly? When Orpheus goes down to the underworld in search of the work, he confronts an entirely different Styx: that of nocturnal separation, which he must enchant with a gaze that does not turn it to stone. It is the essential experience, the only one in which he must become wholly involved. Having returned to daylight, his role with regard to external authorities is limited to disappearing, soon to be torn to pieces by their delegates, the Maenads, while the daytime Styx, the river of public rumor in which his body was scattered, carries his lyric work, and not only carries it, but wants to make itself the song in it, to maintain in it its own fluid reality, its infinitely murmuring becoming, foreign to any shore.

If today the writer, thinking of going down to the underworld, is content with going out into the street, that is because the two rivers, the two great movements of elementary communication, passing through each other, tend to be confused. That is because the profound original rumor—where something is said but without speech, where something is silent but without silence—is not unlike the unspeaking speech, the badly understood and always listening understanding that is "the public mind" and the public "way." Often the work wants to be published before it exists, seeking realization not in the space that belongs to it but in outer activities, the life that seems rich but, when one wants to appropriate it, turns dangerously flimsy.

Such a confusion does not happen by chance. The extraordinary turmoil that causes the writer to publish before writing, that causes the public to form and transmit what it does not understand, the critic to judge and define what he does not read, and the reader, finally, to have to read what is not yet written—this movement that confuses, by anticipating them each time, all the various moments of the work's formation, also gathers them together in the search for a new unity. Thus the richness and poverty, the pride and humility, the extreme disclosure and the extreme solitude of our literary work, which has at least the merit of desiring neither power, nor glory.

A little modified, these texts belong to a series of little essays published start-ing in 1953, in *La Nouvelle Revue Française*, under the title "Investigations." An-other selection will follow, perhaps. What is at issue in this series of "Investiga-tions," what may have shown through here and there, or, failing that, the very necessity of keeping the investigation open in this place of discovery, is to show traces, not to invent proofs. Here, I quote René Char, a name that ought to have been evoked from time to time throughout these pages, were it not for the fear of obscuring it or restricting it to one thought. At the end of this volume, I in-scribe these three phrases, though: "In the explosion of the universe that we are experiencing, a miracle! The pieces that are coming down are *alive*." "Everything in us should be nothing but a joyous celebration when something we have not foreseen, which we do not shed light on, which will speak to our heart, by its means alone, is accomplished." "To look at the night beaten to death; to let it be enough for us."

Notes

The Experience of Proust

1. Here it is a question, naturally, for Proust and in the language of Proust, of a psychological event, a sensation, as he calls it.

2. *Le Balzac de M. de Guermantes*, in which Proust contrasts his own aesthetic ideal to Balzac's.

"There could be no question of ending well"

1. André Breton: *La clé des champs* [The key to the fields].

2. Kafka.

3. Presumably Friederike Brion, whom Goethe deserted in 1771. —Trans.

4. Paul Valéry, *Une soirée avec Monsieur Teste* (An evening with Monsieur Teste). —Trans.

Artaud

1. "And I have told you: no works, no language, no speech, no mind, nothing. Nothing, except a subtle Nerve-Scale [*Pèse-nerfs*]."

Rousseau

1. Jean Starobinski, *Jean-Jacques Rousseau: La transparence et l'obstacle*.

2. "Nothing tires me so much as writing, except thinking."

3. Starobinski notes that the very form of these obsessive stanzas gives "concretely the impression of a lack of support, of the absence of a positive grasp of things."

4. "It would be necessary, for what I have to say, to invent a language as new as my intention."

5. "It is up to him [the reader] to assemble these elements and to determine the being that they compose: the result must be his work."

6. Pierre Burgelin, *La philosophie de l'existence de J.-J. Rousseau.*

Joubert and Space

1. "One must resemble art without resembling any work of art."

2. Georges Poulet, *La distance intérieure* [Inner distance]. Georges Poulet certainly emphasizes the discrepancies as well.

3. These observations are carried out only in August. This genius, so sensitive to the cold, is not going to ponder in winter, against his nature.

4. "1st August (*insomni nocte*). I want thoughts to succeed each other in a book like stars in the sky, with order, with harmony, but with ease and at intervals, without touching each other, without being confused with each other."

5. *Carnets*, February 7, 1805.

6. "Newton. He was gifted with the ability of knowing the 'how much' in all things." "Newton invented only the how-much."

7. "All that is beautiful is indeterminate." "It is always that which ends or limits a thing that makes its character, its precision, its cleanness, its perfection."

8. One that symbolism would be wrong to apply is music. "Thoughts must follow each other and be tied together like sounds in music, by their sole relationship—harmony—and not like the links of a chain." Joubert regrets, in a moving but naïve way, the unknown thoughts whose expression, by painting or music, might have given him a presentiment: "Ah! if I could express myself through music, through dance, through painting, as I express myself through speech, how many ideas I might have that I do not have, and how many feelings that will always be unknown to me."

9. "Tormented by the wretched ambition of always putting an entire book into a page, an entire page into a sentence, and that sentence into a word. That is me."

10. "Repose is not a mere nothing to it [the soul]. It represents a state in which it [the soul] is uniquely given over to its own movement without foreign impulses."

11. *La pointe du jour*, like the English phrase "the top of the morning." — Trans.

Claudel and the Infinite

1. The fact escaped Claudel that Baudelaire, in this line, famous as it is, had said: *At the bottom of the Unknown* [*Au fond de l'Inconnu*]. His misunderstand-

ing suggests that, in the unknown from which he turns away, it is still the infinite that he refuses. The word "infinite" certainly belongs to the language unique to Baudelaire.

2. "Novembre," "Ardeur," "La descente," "Le sédentaire," "Heures du jardin" speak of his approach to light.

3. "I had contrived so well to withdraw, to leave the realm of humankind, it was done!"

4. And we know that Claudel, caring little for literary beauty alone, wanted to suppress this text, which he judged unbearable. Mesa sometimes has terrible lines, by which he tells Ysé that her husband is dead—the husband he himself hypocritically sent to his death—so they can now love each other without sin. "But now I'm telling you that Ciz is dead and I can take you as wife. And we can love each other without secret and without remorse."

5. To a certain extent, *Partage de Midi* was an act of revenge against the young woman who had freed him by a sin. Later, Claudel will try to give her her due by making her live again in Dona Prouhèze. How can we not be struck, though, by the (almost sadistic) violence he exercises against all these young women whom he torments, not without pleasure, in order to save them: the Princess in *Tête d'or*, Violaine, Sygne, Prouhèze. "Many times he whipped and tortured me," says Prouhèze of Don Camille, who is her husband and who is perfectly cruel: one of the most indispensable—and most present—figures of *Le soulier de satin*, and (one has the strong feeling) in no way foreign to the author. There is in Claudel a cruelty of thought that is perhaps responsible for his dramatic genius and to which one regrets that he did not give freer rein. (Cf. the penetrating remarks of Stanislas Fumet on the "intellectual cruelty" of Claudel.)

6. The state of emptiness in which, after Ligugé, his failed decision leaves him, when he feels rejected both by the world that he himself refused and by the other world, which has just refused him, is precisely the proof of powerlessness, the approach of impossibility without which poetry remains remote from its essence. It is "the time of distress" of which Hölderlin was the pure expression and of which Mallarmé also had a presentiment, a presentiment whose meaning Claudel, the theorist in him, did not always consent to recognize. But the poet in Claudel knew how to signify, through inspired words, that powerlessness—impossibility—is the measure of poetic power:

> And in fact I looked and saw myself all alone all of a sudden,
> Detached, refused, abandoned,
> Without duty, without task, outside in the middle of the world,
> Without law, without cause, without strength, without admittance.

Each of these words corresponds to the poetic situation, the very one he reproached Mallarmé with having tried to sustain.

7. "La Maison Fermée" is the last of the *Cinq grandes odes*. The "great

foursquare Muses" are the four Cardinal Virtues: Prudence, Fortitude, Temperance, and Justice.—Trans.

Prophetic Speech

1. Max Weber and Martin Buber have compared Greek prophecy and Biblical prophecy. With the Greeks, as Plato precisely noted in *Timaeus*, the being in trance, wildly affected by inspired divination, reveals, through a babble that is not even speech, the secret that prophets, priests or poets, poet-priests, will be charged with interpreting, that is to say, with elevating to human language. In the Biblical world, says Max Weber, the Pythian and the interpreter are not separate; the prophet of Israel unites both in one single being. That is because Greek divination is not yet a language; it is an original sound that only someone not possessed by it, someone capable of understanding and moderation, can form into speech and rhythm. In the Biblical world, the one whom the spirit touches immediately speaks a language that is already actual to begin with but complete, rhythmically rigorous, even if it is carried away by the violence of the instant.

2. André Neher, *L'essence du prophétisme*.

3. "The breath of God rises from the desert" (Hosea).

4. *L'essence du prophétisme*, p. 239. This "nonetheless" is also a "similarly": *but now and for the same reason*. "Just as I brought onto this people this entire immense misfortune, so I will bring them all the goodness that I promise them." When Kafka places all his hope in the word *nonetheless, despite everything, trotzdem*, it is prophetic hope that speaks in him.

5. Jérôme Lindon, *Jonah*, translation and commentary.

6. When, after Adam has eaten from the tree, God calls out: "Where are you?" this questioning is anxious. God no longer knows where man is. Essential disorientation. God has truly lost man, notes Neher. That is because evil is breaking the Throne. "Where are you?" It is a question which, later, in Jeremiah, the other question echoes: "Where is God?"

7. Ezekiel, on the river's edge, hearing uninterrupted speech, knows that a voice is speaking, but does not yet know that it is speaking to him, and the voice must address him and say to him: "Pay attention, I am going to speak to you."

8. *L'essence du prophétisme*, p. 240.

9. Alain was a French philosopher, 1868–1951. —Trans.

10. In *Jonah*, Jérôme Lindon says: "The Hebrew proceeds neither by symbol nor by allegory, it expresses reality in its pure state."

11. *Figure* can mean either "symbol" or "face." —Trans.

12. Buber says: It is living existence; it is a sacred action of terrible seriousness, a veritable sacramental drama. The *nabi* lives in the form of a sign. It is not what he says that is a sign, but, by saying it, he himself is a sign. And what is a "sign" in the language of the Bible? To ask for a sign is not to ask for a proof, it is to ask

that the message take a concrete and corporeal shape; it is thus to wish that the spirit express itself more perfectly, more authentically than through a word: that it incarnate speaking.

13. Jeremiah, without saying so, wants to stop the insistence of the disastrous Word. He keeps it in him, seeking to quiet it while, "enclosed in his bones," it becomes a devouring fire. "I told myself: 'Let's not think of it anymore, let's proclaim nothing.' But it was in my heart like a devouring fire that I exhausted myself in vain to contain." (French translation by Jean Grosjean.)

14. Jean Grosjean, *Les prophètes*. Let us read, for instance, the honest, useful and often courageous *Bible of Jerusalem*: "The roads of Zion are in mourning, no one comes any more to its festivals. All its gates are deserted, its priests moan, its virgins despair. It is in bitterness!"

> No more festival in Zion: roads in mourning,
> Gates abandoned, priests in tears,
> Virgins in despair, tragedy without bounds.

It seems to me that the translations of Amos, of Hosea, sometimes of Isaiah, are the most beautiful ones, the ones most capable, by intonation, of evoking a language absent till now from our language.

The Secret of the Golem

1. One could say that the symbol grasps again, but retroactively, the creative adventure. It thus makes the reading participate in the profundity of this adventurous movement, but perhaps all the more so since the writer was less tempted intentionally to prepare the way for the symbol.

Literary Infinity: The Aleph

1. *Erreur* is related to *errer*, "to wander." —Trans.

The Failure of the Demon: The Vocation

1. *Journal d'un écrivain* [Journal of a writer], translated [into French] by Germaine Beaumont. Cf. the moving commentary by Dominique Aury in no. 67 of *La Nouvelle Revue Française*.

2. Writers whose forum was the *Nouvelle Revue Française*, the dominant French literary journal of the 1930s and 1940s. —Trans.

3. Beginning a new novel, Julien Green notes in his journal (*Le bel aujourd'hui* [The beautiful today]): "Experience does nothing for it, brings nothing, gives no ease. . . . Wanting to write and being unable to, as I was this morning,

is for me a sort of tragedy. The strength is there, but it is not free, for reasons I do not know."

4. *The Diary of Virginia Woolf*, vol. 3: 1925–30, New York: Harcourt Brace Jovanovich, 1980, p. 235.

5. In English in the original. —Trans.

6. Monique Nathan, *Virginia Woolf par elle-même* [Virginia Woolf in her own words].

7. *The Diary of Virginia Woolf*, vol. 3, p. 209.

8. *A Writer's Diary* (New York: Harcourt Brace Jovanovich, 1981), pp. 129–30.

9. *A Writer's Diary*, p. 130.

10. In the essay entitled *Letter to a German*, reproduced in French in the collection *Le spectateur tenté* [The tempted spectator].

11. Quoted by Georges Cattaüli in his study, *T. S. Eliot*. [From an essay on Yeats in *On Poetry and Poets*, New York: Farrar, Straus and Cudahy, 1957, p. 297. —Trans.]

12. *The Diary of Virginia Woolf*, vol. 3, p. 235.

13. This is Rhoda speaking, in *The Waves* (London: The Hogarth Press, 1933), pp. 60–61.

At Every Extreme

1. "Mallarmé's error is to have wanted to isolate the poetic essence and to present it in its pure state, by juxtaposing, without a profound soldering, verbal combinations of unsurpassable beauty." (*Les abeilles d'Aristée* [The bees of Aristaeus].)

2. Nathalie Sarraute, *L'ère du soupçon* [The era of suspicion].

Broch

1. Virgil grants Octavius what he had refused Augustus. When Augustus says to him, "You hate me," he cannot bear this suspicion. It is thus to friendship that he finally yields his work.

2. This double reality is emphasized by the work of metamorphosis of translation. *The Death of Virgil*, a difficult work, had the good luck to be translated well—into English first by Jean Starr Untermeyer, a talented writer who worked for many years with Broch—and recently into French by Albert Kohn. These two versions are both remarkable. But the characteristic nature of the two languages had the effect of sometimes highlighting the intellectual aspect of the work, sometimes its expressive magic. The French version is of a logical fidelity that continues into the least nuances and maintains the clarity and exactitude in a thought that never loses its rigor. The English version sings more; it makes more obvious

the great flux of interior monologue, that liquid unity or even more that iridescence, that rainbow light that sometimes shines, sometimes shines brighter while fading away, with which dying thought seems to be accompanied and which prolongs it beyond itself. The English version is almost more poetic than the original work, and the French version, almost clearer, more well-wrought. One sees, once again, on this occasion, how much what we call interior monologue has difficulty acclimating itself to the French language. The double intellectual origin of Samuel Beckett was necessary to open our language to the truth of this form.

3. This is not the place to try to find out why so many artists are ready to welcome Nietzsche's thinking on the eternal return. "Und das Ende war der Anfang" [And the end was the beginning—Trans.], says Broch. "In my beginning is my end, in my end is my beginning," says T. S. Eliot, in *East Coker*. And, for Joyce's entire oeuvre, especially, it seems, for *Finnegans Wake*, Joyce's saying is true: "The vico road goes round to meet where terms begin."

4. This is in fact the mysterious thinking of [Virgil's] Fourth Eclogue: *Magnus ab integro saeclorum nascitur ordo* ["The great order of the ages is born all over again" —Trans.].

The Turn of the Screw

1. It is tempting to think that that is his way of constantly alluding to the accident of which he was a victim when he was about ten and about which he has spoken only rarely and obscurely: as if something had happened to him that brought him as close as possible to a mysterious and exalting impossibility. It has naturally been suggested that this dorsal wound had made him incapable of a normal life (no definite affair can be ascribed to this bachelor, although he took infinite pleasure in the world of relationships with women). It has also been thought that he had more or less voluntarily provoked this accident (which occurred while he was helping to put out a fire in Newport), in order to avoid fighting in the Civil War. If we speak of "psychic self-wounding," then we're sure we've said everything, without meaning anything.

2. James speaks elsewhere of the nervous fear of letting himself go, which always paralyzed him.

3. Thus speaks, in a proud and pathetic avowal, the old writer of *The Final Years*, when he discovers both that he is dying, having done nothing, and that he has wonderfully accomplished everything he could do.

Musil

1. Ca. 1956–57. —Trans.

2. Musil's term, formed from the K. u. K. monogram used by the imperial

Austrian government—*kaiserlich und königlich,* or "imperial and royal," i.e., the Empire of Austria and Kingdom of Hungary—suggests "kaka" (English "caca"). Blanchot, alluding to the endless gossip (*cancan*) so studied in Musil's book, suggests *Cancanie* as a better term. —Trans.

3. Irony is the interchange between coldness and feeling.

4. In an interesting study that he devotes to it, Martin Flinker quotes this letter that Musil addressed to him in 1934: "Of problems in my work, I can unfortunately talk only briefly. Are there today still problems? Sometimes one has the opposite feeling. The only reason that could make me think that I am not entirely wandering astray is the long duration of my investigations; since the beginnings, which go back to before 1914, my problems have been so often worked over that they have acquired the density of a certain permanence" (*Almanach* 1958).

5. However, Agathe says (although in a later fragment): "We were the last romantics of love." "An attempt at anarchy in love," says Musil in another later fragment, to describe the couple's attempt.

6. According to the scholars who have studied the manuscripts, it is on this very episode that Musil was still working when he died, and precisely on those pages of a mystical nature entitled *Breezes of a Summer's Day.*

7. A little girl with long, silky blond hair whom he loved when he was a little boy, and whose image passed into his book, had the same name as this unknown sister, Elsa. He notes this similarity in his autobiographical essay, and it does not seem mere chance to him. In 1923, Musil published a poem called "Isis and Osiris," which contains, he says, his novel *in nucleo.*

8. From this view of nascent modern society, whose profound forces Musil proposes to reveal to us, the revolutionary class struggle is almost absent. Only a secondary episode is devoted to it (which might perhaps have been intended for development, as certain drafts indicate). Musil has explained why, though not a conservative, he had a horror, not of the revolution, but of the forms it takes to manifest itself. But the man without particularities—is he not essentially the proletarian, if the proletariat, characterized by not-having, is directed only toward the suppression of any individual mode of being? It is strange and significant that Musil, ready to set himself all questions on the subject of his theme, avoids precisely this one, which is close at hand. On the other hand, his book already shows certain forces at work to which National Socialism owed its rise.

9. More precisely, "Catacombs" is the name of the category under which he ranges the ideas that come to him on the subject of his novel, at a time when the novel's title was still uncertain (1918–20). Musil had in mind at the time several projects that all ended up being absorbed into one single book.

10. In reality, Musil often inclines toward an intermediary language between

the impersonality of objective truth and the subjectivity of his person. He says, for instance, in an essay: "If the coherence of ideas between them is not sufficiently firm, and if one scorns the coherence that could give them the person of the author, a progression will remain that, without being subjective or objective, will be able to be both at once: a *possible* image of the world, a *possible* person, that is what I seek."

The Pain of Dialogue

1. Intelligence, and no longer reason: whatever the tendency of criticism to simplify may be, it must be discreetly noted that this word, inserted in place of the other, distances us considerably from Socrates. Intelligence is interested in everything: worlds, arts, civilizations, the debris of civilizations, rough attempts and accomplishments, everything matters to it and everything belongs to it. It is the universal interest that understands everything passionately, everything in relation to everything.

The Clarity of the Novel

1. In [Robbe-Grillet's] *La jalousie* [Jealousy], a powerful absence is at the center of the plot and of the narration. According to the critics, we are to understand that what is speaking in this absence is the very character of the jealous one, the husband who watches over his wife. I think this misunderstands the authentic reality of this narrative as the reader is invited to approach it. The reader indeed feels that something is missing; he has the premonition that it is this lack that allows everything to be said and everything to be seen—but how could this lack be identified with someone? How could there still be a name and an identity there? It is nameless, faceless; it is pure anonymous presence.

H. H.

1. Hölderlin also studied at Maulbronn, and we know from his letters that he suffered much there. Hugo Ball thinks that in eighteenth- and nineteenth-century Swabia there was a sort of "neurosis of religious boarding schools," *eine Stiftlerneurose*: this would be true for Hölderlin, Waiblinger, and Möricke.

2. In a story from this period, *Under the Wheel*, Hesse no doubt evokes his time in seminary, and Hermann Heilner's escape is his own escape. But in approaching this event he tries anxiously to keep his distance from it as much as he can.

3. To this symbolic drunkenness, which does not convince us, I will contrast the fate of solitude, misery, and damnation that Malcolm Lowry could represent,

describing the drunkenness of the "Consul," Geoffrey Firmin. *Under the Volcano* is one of the great dark works of this era. A few are familiar with it.

4. When Hesse is working on a novel, he often tries out its themes by giving them a poetic expression. It should be pointed out that Hesse copiously illustrated several of his books with watercolors. At certain moments of his life, he painted hundreds of paintings. The plastic art, art of mastery, is for him a salutary discipline, a way of getting hold of himself, unlike music. Paul Klee is one of the characters in *Journey to the East*.

5. With this name, Hesse undoubtedly wanted to make us reflect on the relationship of the highest culture with childlike awakening. But in his final book, *Beschwörungen* [Conjurations], he tells us that as a child he played a game with a deck of cards representing authors and artists, enumerating their works. And he adds: "This pantheon of colored images can well have given the first hint to the notion of representing, under the name Castalia and the Glass Bead Game, the *Universitas litterarum et artium* [University of human letters and the arts] embracing all times and all cultures."

Diary and Story

1. Some of these quotations are taken from Michèle Leleu's book, *Les journaux intimes* [Diaries].

2. Similarly, Jules Renard: "I think I have touched the bottom of the well. . . . And this Diary that distracts me, amuses me and sterilizes me."

3. Who, more than Proust, wants to remember himself? That is why there is no writer more foreign to the day-to-day recording of his life. Whoever wants to remember himself must entrust himself to forgetfulness, to the risk that absolute forgetfulness is, and to the beautiful chance that memory then becomes.

4. But for Lautréamont, this book exists, perhaps: it is *Les chants de Maldoror* [The songs of Maldoror]. For Proust, the work of Proust.

5. There are others: Rilke's *The Notebooks of Malte Laurids Brigge*, for instance; *The Adventurous Heart* by Ernst Jünger; Joubert's *Notebooks*; perhaps *L'expérience intérieure* [Inner experience] and *Le coupable* [The guilty one] by Georges Bataille. One of the secret laws of these works is that the deeper the movement goes, the more it tends to approach the impersonality of abstraction. Similarly, Kafka substitutes little by little for dated entries about himself considerations that become all the more general as they get more intimate. And if we bring to mind the narratives of mystical experience, so concrete, of Saint Theresa of Avila, and compare them to Meister Eckhart's sermons or treatises or to the commentaries of Saint John of the Cross, we will see that, here again, it is the abstract work that is closer to ardent experience, of which it speaks only impersonally and indirectly.

The Search for Point Zero

1. But we still complain of the monotony of talents and of the uniformity, the impersonality of works of art.

2. But from the literary point of view, there is almost nothing that distinguishes Catholic novelist from Communist novelist, and the Nobel Prize and the Stalin Prize reward the same uses, the same literary signs.

3. Roland Barthes, *Le degré zéro de l'écriture* [Writing degree zero].

4. Or (this is the important point) pursuing the same effort with regard to literature as Marx did with regard to society. Literature is alienated, in part because the society with which it is in relation rests on the alienation of mankind; it is so also because of the demands that it betrays, but today it betrays them in the two senses of the word: it acknowledges them and deceives them, thinking it denounces itself.

The Book to Come

1. In 1867, he "confines" the development of the Work to three poems in verse and four prose poems. In 1871 (but here the idea is a little different), he announces a volume of stories, a volume of poetry, a volume of criticism. In the posthumous manuscript, published by Jacques Scherer, he foresees four books, which can be spread over twenty volumes.

2. Later on, he will express the connection that, from the one volume to the many, continues and enlarges the manifold relationships present in each volume and ready to be singled out and put into play: "Some symmetry, at the same time, which from the location of lines in the poem is linked to the authenticity of the poem in the volume, leaps, outside the volume, to many [volumes], inscribing, on the spiritual space, the enlarged signature of the anonymous genius, perfect existence as art" (*Oeuvres complètes* [Complete works], Pléiade, p. 367).

3. Mallarmé here contrasts journalists with the poor Cabalists accused of having killed the Abbé Boullan by bewitching him. But from the point of view of Art, the former are much guiltier than the latter, although the latter are wrong "to detach from an Art operations that are integral to it." (Magic must not be separated from art.)

4. *Prose pour des Esseintes* [Prose for Des Esseintes].

5. But if we compare this text with the one in which he proposes to bring all theater back to one unique and manifold play "expanding in parallel with a renewed cycle of years," we see that he is here probably far from Romantic and occultist aims: what we write is necessarily the same, and the future of what is the same is, in its renewal, of an infinite richness (*Oeuvres complètes*, p. 313).

6. The manuscript relayed by Henri Mondor to Jacques Scherer, carefully organized by the latter and published under the title *Le "Livre" de Mallarmé: Premières recherches sur des documents inédits* [The "Book" of Mallarmé: Preliminary investigations into some unpublished documents]. Does this manuscript enlighten us about the central project? Perhaps, but only on condition that we don't think we are confronted with the material manuscript of the Book. Of what is this "Book" composed? Not of a sustained text like *Igitur*, or long fragments gathered together, but of tiny notes, isolated words, and indecipherable letters jotted down on scraps of paper. Do all these sheets and notes relate to a common labor? We do not know. Does the order in which they are published today have anything to do with the order in which they were found after Mallarmé's death, and could it then have been only a chance arrangement or the accidental order of some earlier working? We do not know. We do not know— and this is more serious—what these notes saved by some unknowable decision represent with regard to all the others, most of which were destroyed, according to Mondor. Consequently, we do not know the place that Mallarmé assigned them in the whole of his project: perhaps they signified only things that had become a little remote from him, not what he selected but what he would not have chosen; or perhaps they were idle thoughts that had been written down in a daydream, for amusement. Finally, since he recognized meaning and reality only in what was expressed in the unique structure and formal firmness of his language, these unformed notes had no value for him, and he prohibited anyone from distinguishing anything in them: they were the indistinct itself. There is uncertainty about the date or dates of these notes, their background, their outer coherence, their orientation, and even their reality. In such a way we find presented, as the most chanceful publication, composed of fortuitous words, dispersed in an unpredictable way on pieces of paper collected by accident, the only essential book written as if by itself to subdue chance. It is a failure that does not even have the interest of being Mallarmé's own, since it is the naïve work of posthumous publishers, much like travelers who, from time to time, bring back pieces of Noah's Ark to us, or fragments of stone representing the Tablets of the Law smashed by Moses. Such at least is one's first thought before these documents presented as a draft of the Book. But our second thought is different; that the publication of these almost empty pages, more sketched with words than written, which makes us touch the point where necessity meets with the image of pure dispersion, would perhaps not have displeased Mallarmé.

I will recall, however—not to be indignant about it, but to evoke the interesting moral rupture to which even the most upright men consent, each time they come to the question of posthumous publications—that this manuscript is published against the formal wish of the writer. If Kafka's case is ambiguous, Mallarmé's is clear. Mallarmé dies unexpectedly. Between the first crisis—from which he nonetheless recovers, and which is still just an uncertain threat—and the second, which gets the better of him in a few moments, very little time passes. Mallarmé takes advantage of the respite to write the "recommendation as to my papers." He wants everything to be destroyed. "Burn, then: there is no literary inheritance there, my poor children." Even more, he refuses all interference by others, and any prying investigation: what must be destroyed must be withdrawn beforehand from everyone's view. "Do not yield to anyone's appreciation: refuse any curious or friendly interference. Tell them that they will make nothing of it, which is true, in any case." This is a firm resolve, and also a disregarded one, and made in vain. The dead are indeed weak. A few days later, Valéry is already allowed to look at the papers and, for fifty years now, with a constant and surprising regularity, important and indubitable, previously unpublished manuscripts keep coming to light, as if Mallarmé had never written more than since his death.

I know the rule formulated by Apollinaire: "Publish everything." It makes a lot of sense. It attests to the profound tendency of what is hidden to lean toward the light, of the secret toward the revelation beyond secret, of all that is silent toward public affirmation. This is not a rule or a principle. It is the power under the sway of which whoever sets out to write falls, and falls all the harder if he opposes it and contests it. The same power confirms the impersonal nature of works of art. The writer has no right over them, and he is nothing in the face of them, always already dead and always suppressed. Let his will not be done, then. Logically, if we judge it suitable to misunderstand the intention of the author after his death, we should also accept that it is not to be respected during his life. Yet while he is alive, what happens is apparently the opposite. The writer wants to publish and the publisher does not want to. But that is only surface appearance. Think of all the forces—secret, personal, ideological, unexpected—that are exercised over our will to force us to write and publish what we do not want to. Visible or invisible, the power is always there, it pays no attention to us and, to our surprise, hides our papers from us in our very hands. The living are indeed weak.

What is this power? It is neither the reader, nor society, nor the State, nor culture. To give it a name and realize it, in its very unreality, was also Mallarmé's problem. He called it the Book.

7. *Oeuvres complètes*, p. 373.

8. English versions of *Un coup de dés* used in this chapter are from Henry Weinfield, *Collected Poems of Stéphane Mallarmé* (Berkeley: University of California Press, 1994). —Trans.

9. Here we ought to remark that the attention brought to language by Heidegger, which is of an extremely probing nature, is attention to words considered apart, concentrated in themselves, to such words thought of as fundamental and tormented to the point that, in the history of their formation, the

history of being is made to be understood—but never to the connections of words, and even less to the anterior space that these connections suppose, and whose original movement alone makes possible language as unfolding. For Mallarmé, language is not made of even pure words: it is what words have always already disappeared into, the oscillating movement of appearance and disappearance.

10. The phrase "à l'altitude de l'exception" is from *Un coup de dés*. —Trans.

11. "Edennic [*édennique*]": Mallarmé writes it that way, contrary to normal usage.

12. "Poetry is the expression, by human language brought back to its essential rhythm, of the mysterious sense of aspects of existence; it thus endows our stay with authenticity and constitutes the sole spiritual task." And, in the "reverie of a French poet" on Richard Wagner: "Man, and his authentic earthly stay, exchange a reciprocity of proofs."

13. "The song gushes forth from an innate spring: previous to concept."

14. The Book, according to the manuscript, is made up of movable pages. "Thus one can," Scherer writes, "change their place and read them, not of course in any order whatsoever, but according to several distinct orders determined by the laws of permutation." The book is always other, it changes and is exchanged by comparing the diversity of its parts, and thus we avoid the linear movement—the one-way direction—of reading. Moreover, the book, unfolded and refolded, scattering and being gathered back together, shows that it has no substantial reality: it is never there, endlessly to be unmade while it is made.

15. *Operation, operator*, and *oeuvre* are all conneced with the Latin *opus*, work. —Trans.

16. The conditional verb form here indicates that it is not a question of the last word of *Un coup de dés* on the meaning of poetic becoming that is at issue here. Confronting this poem, we feel how poorly our notions of book, work, and art respond to all the possibilities to come that are hidden in them. Painting often makes us feel today that what it seeks to create, its "productions," can no longer be works, but want to answer to something for which we do not yet have a name. It is the same for literature. What we are going toward is perhaps not at all what the actual future will give us. But what we are going toward is poor and rich with a future that we should not set in the tradition of our old structures.

The Power and the Glory

1. Dionys Mascolo, *Lettre polonaise sur la misère intellectuelle en France* [Polish letter on the intellectual poverty of France].

2. "We must insist on the extreme importance of the only movement of

thought that France has known in this first half of the twentieth century: Surrealism. . . . It alone, between the two wars, could articulate, with a rigor that has not been surpassed, demands that are at once those of pure thought and those of the immediate role of man. It alone, with an untiring tenacity, could never forget that *revolution and poetry are one.*"

Ernst Bloch, *The Spirit of Utopia*

Giorgio Agamben, *Potentialities: Collected Essays in Philosophy*

Ellen S. Burt, *Poetry's Appeal: French Nineteenth-Century Lyric and the Political Space*

Jacques Derrida, *Adieu to Emmanuel Levinas*

Werner Hamacher, *Premises: Essays on Philosophy and Literature from Kant to Celan*

Aris Fioretos, *The Gray Book*

Deborah Esch, *In the Event: Reading Journalism, Reading Theory*

Winfried Menninghaus, *In Praise of Nonsense: Kant and Bluebeard*

Giorgio Agamben, *The Man Without Content*

Giorgio Agamben, *The End of the Poem: Studies in Poetics*

Theodor W. Adorno, *Sound Figures*

Louis Marin, *Sublime Poussin*

Philippe Lacoue-Labarthe, *Poetry as Experience*

Ernst Bloch, *Literary Essays*

Jacques Derrida, *Resistances of Psychoanalysis*

Marc Froment-Meurice, *That Is to Say: Heidegger's Poetics*

Francis Ponge, *Soap*

Philippe Lacoue-Labarthe, *Typography: Mimesis, Philosophy, Politics*

Giorgio Agamben, *Homo Sacer: Sovereign Power and Bare Life*

Emmanuel Levinas, *Of God Who Comes to Mind*

Bernard Stiegler, *Technics and Time, 1: The Fault of Epimetheus*

Werner Hamacher, *pleroma—Reading in Hegel*

Serge Leclaire, *Psychoanalyzing: On the Order of the Unconscious and the Practice of the Letter*